D1474058

The Welfare State and Canadian Federalism
Second Edition

Like all advanced countries, Canada has developed a complex welfare state. But, unlike many, it has done so within a federal system with strong governments in Ottawa and the provinces. How federalism has affected the development and operation of Canadian social security policies is the subject of this compelling book.

The Welfare State and Canadian Federalism documents the role of the federal and provincial governments in providing the basic building blocks of the modern welfare state, paying particular attention to income security. Keith Banting examines the origin, operation, and consequences of programs designed to raise the living standards of lower-income citizens and to protect Canadians against losses in earning power, whether from illness, accident, unemployment, family responsibilities, or old age.

In addition to providing a lucid description of the character and scope of Canadian income security policies, Banting presents an impressive analysis of the impact of our political institutions on this important sector of public policy. In doing so, he compares Canada's performance with that of other industrialized countries and discusses such complex issues as the effect of economic forces, cultural traditions, and political dynamics on the scope and content of social policy, and the implications of federalism for income redistribution in Canada.

The first edition of *The Welfare State and Canadian Federalism* focused on the impact of federalism on social policy during a period of economic growth and expanding social expenditures. The revised edition extends the analysis by asking how the federal system has shaped the social policy response to neo-conservatism, recession, and restraint during the 1980s. Banting analyses policy trends in detail, examines the implications of constitutional changes such as the Charter of Rights and the Meech Lake Accord, and highlights the ways in which the federal system has constrained the influence of economic crisis and ideological change on social security in Canada.

Keith G. Banting is a member of the School of Public Administration, Queen's University.

Keith G. Banting

The Welfare State and Canadian Federalism

Second Edition

McGill-Queen's University Press
Kingston and Montreal

354.71
B21w2

© McGill-Queen's University Press 1987
Second edition

ISBN 0-7735-0630-6 (cloth)
ISBN 0-7735-0631-4 (paper)

Legal deposit 4th quarter 1987
Bibliothèque nationale du Québec

First edition, 1982, published in conjunction with the Institute of
Intergovernmental Relations, Queen's University.

Canadian Cataloguing in Publication Data

Banting, Keith G., 1947-
   The welfare state and Canadian federalism

2nd ed. Includes index. Bibliography; p.
ISBN 0-7735-0630-6 (bound)
ISBN 0-7735-0631-4 (pbk.)

1. Income maintenance programs — Canada.
2. Social security — Canada. 3. Federal-provincial relations —
Canada. 4. Canada — Social policy. I. Title.

HC120.I5B36 1987   354.710082′56   C87-090196-6

For my parents

Contents

Tables

Figures

Preface

The 1980s represent a new era in the politics of social policy. Economic crisis, social and demographic changes, and ideological challenges to the postwar consensus have intensified the pressures on the contemporary welfare state. Nowhere are these pressures more visible than in the income security field. On one side, the number of Canadians depending primarily on social programs for their basic livelihood has risen dramatically; on the other, income security programs themselves are under challenge, and proposals for their radical restructuring abound.

Canadian experience in this respect parallels that of other western industrial nations. In this country, however, the impact of these pressures on social programs is also conditioned by the complexities of the federal system of government, which is also changing in important ways. The Constitution Act of 1982 introduced significant reforms, and the Meech Lake Accord reached by the Prime Minister and the provincial premiers in April 1987 proposes to extend those changes in ways that may prove critical to the future of social policy.

Understanding contemporary social policy thus requires an examination of the subtle relationships between the changing balance of political pressures and the evolving institutional framework within which struggles over public policy are conducted. The first edition of this book traced these linkages from the interwar period of limited social programs to the expansionist phase of the postwar era. This new edition extends the analysis into the 1980s.

Chapter 11 surveys the record of recent years. It analyses the growing pressures on contemporary social policy, examines the changes made in income security programs, and highlights the critical role of the transfer system in buffering the distribution of income from the worst economic crisis since World War II. The chapter then explores the relationship between federalism and income security in the 1980s, assessing the implications of constitutional change for social programs and examining the extent to which the federal structure has muted the impact of economic trends and neoconservative politics on the network of social programs built up over the preceding decades.

Revising this book has extended the already lengthy list of people in whose debt I stand. My colleagues at Queen's University, especially Peter Leslie, Richard Simeon, Bill Lederman and John Whyte, have influenced my thinking on the new constitutional provisions, and Patti Peppin has guided me through the implications of the Charter of Rights and Freedoms. As always, my debts to Ken Battle of the National Council of Welfare are enormous, and I despair of ever being able to repay them fully. In addition, Patti Candido worked her magic with the wordprocessing and Joan Harcourt provided able editorial assistance.

Finally, as in the first edition, my deepest gratitude goes to Marilyn, Alan, and James, who have borne the true social costs of this book.

Keith G. Banting

1 Introduction

More than ever before, the state shapes the contours of modern life. The political landscape of the twentieth century has been transformed by the steady expansion of government, until today few if any economic and social relationships remain completely immune from political decisions. Government expenditures now equal almost half of the gross national product in most western nations, and government regulations multiply steadily. Canadian experience faithfully parallels that of other western countries in this regard, and for better or worse, the future of the Canadian communities depends increasingly on the decisions of governments. Understanding the forces that shape the role of the modern state, in Canada and elsewhere, is one of the most fascinating challenges confronting students of contemporary society.

This book addresses one small part of this task, by asking what influence the structure of political institutions has on public policy in Canada. To what extent is the role of the Canadian state moulded by the structures through which it operates? To what extent are the decisions taken each day by political leaders shaped by the institutions within which they work: our federal system, our particular version of parliamentary government, our electoral system? This study seeks to answer these questions in one area of public policy that is vital to millions of individual Canadians, income security.

From the vantage point of the individual citizen, the most visible part of the expansion of government over the last century has been the emergence of the welfare state. Industrial nations have created a vast complex of social programs dealing with the health, education, and income needs of their citizenry, and have levied unprecedented levels of taxation to finance them. By the mid-1970s expenditures on such programs equalled, on average, about a fifth of the gross domestic product (GDP) of the nations that comprise the

Table 1   *Public Welfare Expenditures in OECD Nations: percent of GDP in current prices, 1974 or near year*

	Education	Income maintenance expenditure	Health	Total "welfare"
Australia	3.8	4.0	5.0	12.8
Austria	4.0	15.3	3.7	23.0
Belgium	4.9	14.1	4.2	23.2
Canada	6.5	7.3	5.1	18.9
Denmark	7.0	9.9	6.5	23.4
Finland	5.6	9.9	5.5	21.0
France	3.2	12.4	5.3	20.9
Germany	3.0	12.4	5.2	20.6
Greece	2.3	7.1	2.3	11.7
Ireland	4.9	6.4	5.4	16.7
Italy	4.0	10.4	5.2	19.6
Japan	2.6	2.8	3.5	8.9
Netherlands	5.9	19.1	5.1	29.1
New Zealand	4.4	6.5	4.2	15.1
Norway	4.9	9.8	5.3	20.0
Sweden	5.9	9.3	6.7	21.9
United Kingdom	4.4	7.7	4.6	16.7
United States	5.3	7.4	3.0	15.7
OECD average (unweighted)	4.9	9.5	4.9	18.8

Source: OECD, *Public Expenditure Trends.*

Organization for Economic Co-operation and Development (OECD), and their management consumed an even larger share of the time and effort of public leaders. The largest pillar in the modern welfare state is income security. In virtually every industrial nation, expenditure on cash transfer programs is greater than those on health or education, often dramatically so, as Table 1 indicates. While the particular form of income security varies from nation to nation, it tends to cover a similar range of social needs, compensating for the loss of earnings resulting from retirement, disability, sickness, and unemployment, supplementing the incomes of families with children, and in some jurisdictions also augmenting the incomes of low-wage earners. These programs represent one of the most important functions of government, one with consequences for the well-being of millions of citizens, for the stability of social relations, and for the legitimacy of the process of government itself.

The question addressed here, then, is: to what extent have Canadian efforts in this major dimension of public policy been shaped by the institutions within which we conduct our collective political life?

The book is organized in four parts and ten chapters. Part One sets out the basic framework of the study. Chapter two describes the Canadian income security system, examining its public and private sides, its rate of growth in recent decades, and its critical role in the lives of Canadians. Chapter three then develops the theoretical core of the book. A phenomenon as complex as the modern welfare state is inevitably influenced by a broad range of factors—economic, demographic, cultural, as well as political—and it is impossible to assess the relative importance of any one of these factors by focusing on it alone. The chapter therefore surveys the findings of comparative studies of the determinants of income security in industrial nations, in order to pinpoint those aspects of welfare policy that seem to be influenced most by the particular structures of the state. In effect, chapter three sets the agenda for the subsequent analysis of the impact of federal institutions on income security in Canada.

Part Two is the empirical heart of the book. Chapter four examines the constitutional division of responsibility for income security in Canada, tracing the dramatic centralization of power which has transformed institutional relationships in this field during the last half century. The following chapters then examine the impact of this change on three dimensions of income security identified by comparative studies as sensitive to institutional differences. Chapter five examines the impact of federal institutions on the *scope* of income security, asking whether federal institutions are a conservative force in welfare politics, as some have argued, or whether modern federalism actually stimulates the expansion of public programs, as others have recently countered. Chapter six examines the impact of institutions on the *redistributive processes* of the Canadian state, concluding—contrary to much of the literature on the subject—that Canadian institutions have not altered the redistributive goals of government, but that the shifting balance between federal and provincial governments has altered the actual redistributive impact of income security. Chapter seven then investigates the extent to which Canadian political institutions influence the *balance of interests* that shape policy, testing propositions that our institutions insulate welfare policy from public pressures, and examining the ways in which the broader economic and political interests of governments can intensify conflict in this field.

Part Three moves to a more speculative level. Another way to explore the relationship between the structures of the state and income security is to ask what would happen to income security programs if existing political institutions were suddenly changed. After all, Canadians have been debating constitutional reform for decades now. What would be the impact on policy in this field if the various proposals were actually implemented? Chapters eight and nine tackle this question in two stages. Since most of the proposed reforms have sought to make government decisions more responsive to the regional nature of Canada, chapter eight asks whether or not there are significant regional differences in attitudes towards income security. On this basis, chapter nine then takes up the implications of specific constitutional reforms, arguing in the end that the direct impact on income security would probably be much less significant than the indirect impact on the fundamental economic and political balance within the Canadian federation.

Finally, Part Four recapitulates, and reflects upon, the major findings concerning the relationships between the structures of the state and the patterns of income security in Canada.

This book can be read in part as a cautionary tale. Because the basic institutions of their government have been under sustained challenge for twenty years, Canadians, and especially Canadian political scientists, are prone to assume that these structures are somehow critical to the major social programs that we take for granted today, and that constitutional change would usher in a new policy world. The evidence of this study, however, suggests that although institutions influence certain aspects of income security, they do not determine its basic principles. While this conclusion cannot be extended automatically to every area of public policy, it does stand as a warning against attributing too much policy significance to political institutions, or holding unrealistic expectations about the extent to which institutional engineering can solve policy problems.

In addition, this book can be read as an extended plea for more comparative policy studies. The nature—indeed the uniqueness—of Canadian political life can be fully appreciated only from a comparative perspective. While this study does not formally compare Canada with another country, it draws heavily on research into the dynamics of the welfare state in a wide variety of nations. Where cross-national comparisons are of little help, the analysis turns to comparisons across time, examining the symbiosis between institutional change and the development of income security in Canada throughout the twentieth century. Certainly, the most important conclusions of the book flow from this comparative approach. The role of the Canadian state is too important to be studied in isolation.

PART ONE

INCOME SECURITY

2 The Canadian Income Security System

In keeping with other industrial nations, Canada has developed a complex network of income security programs. Some of these are government programs, some are private; but all are essentially collective mechanisms through which Canadians supplement the incomes that they earn and protect themselves from periods of financial hardship. This chapter describes the major programs in both the public and private sectors, examines their growth, and assesses the extent to which individual Canadians depend on them.

Public Income Security Programs

The basic public income security system is set out in Figure 1, which categorizes the different programs on the basis of the four income security techniques employed in Canada: demogrants, social insurance, social assistance, and income supplementation.

Demogrants are universal, flat-rate payments made to individuals or families solely on the basis of demographic characteristics, such as age, rather than on the basis of proven need as in the case of social assistance, or previous contributions as in the case of social insurance. Two of the largest income security programs, both in terms of numbers of beneficiaries and the expenditures involved, are the demogrants paid by the federal government: Old Age Security, which is paid to all persons aged sixty-five and over and which in 1980 was $196.83 per month, and Family Allowances, which are paid to all families with children under the age of eighteen and which in 1980 provided an average monthly benefit of $21.80 per child. Both of these programs are financed completely out of general tax revenues, and the benefits are treated as taxable income in the hands of the recipient, a provi-

Figure 1 *The Public Income Security System*

INCOME SECURITY TECHNIQUE	RECIPIENTS	FEDERAL	PROVINCIAL
Demogrant	Elderly	Old Age Security	
	Families with children	Family Allowances	Quebec family allowances
Social insurance	Retired, disabled survivors	Canada Pension Plan	Quebec Pension Plan
	Unemployed	Unemployment Insurance	
	Injured workers		Worker's Compensation
Social assistance	Needy persons		Social assistance
Income supplementation	Elderly	Guaranteed Income Supplement	Various provincial supplements and tax credits
	Families with children	Child Tax Credit	Saskatchewan, Manitoba and Quebec supplement plans

sion which simultaneously reduces the net cost to the government and introduces an element of progressivity into the distribution of the net benefits. The only major provincial demogrant is the Quebec Family Allowance program, which provides benefits for all children in the province and replaces the exemptions for children in the provincial income tax system. Prince Edward Island, however, does provide a modest monthly supplement to the Family Allowance for fifth and subsequent children in any family.

Social insurance programs constitute the next largest component in the income security system. Unemployment Insurance, which was finally introduced in 1940 and was the object of repeated revisions throughout the 1970s, now covers all wage and salary earners, provides unemployment benefits and some sickness and maternity benefits, and is financed partly out of contributions from employees and employers, and partly out of federal tax revenues. Unemployment Insurance has become a major income security instrument in Canada, paying out over $4.7 billion in 1978-79, a figure which represents a much larger proportion of total income security expenditures than in any other western nation.[1]

Canada's contributory pension plans, on the other hand, are more modest relative to those of other western nations. Canada was a late entrant into the world of contributory pensions, with the Canadian and Quebec Pension plans not being adopted until 1965. These two plans now cover all employed persons, are financed by contributions from employees and employers and by the interest earned on the accumulated funds, and provide earnings-related pensions on retirement, as well as death benefits, survivors' benefits, and disability benefits. But the plans are only now beginning to make major payments. Full retirement pensions were delayed for ten years after the establishment of the plans and, as a result, significant benefit flows only began to build up after 1976. Since the two plans are partially funded, contributions and the interest earned by the accumulated reserves have so far always exceeded the benefits paid out. Consequently, as of 1980 the Canada Pension Plan (CPP) had a surplus of around $18 billion. But this happy situation will prove transitory. By the early 1990s the flow of benefits will begin to exceed revenues, and by the early years of the twenty-first century the two funds will be exhausted, unless changes are made well before then. Adjustment of the plans is currently the biggest issue facing the income security system, and the Canadian governments are already locked in serious negotiations over the changes to be introduced.

Worker's Compensation, the third social insurance component of the income security system, has been called the "first stage of the modern era,"[2] as it was the first of the major income security programs introduced in this century. Worker's Compensation falls within provincial jurisdiction, and it was in 1914 that Ontario passed its Workmen's Compensation Act,

Table 2　Distribution of Social Assistance, by Age of Recipient and Reason for Assistance, 1971

	Old age	Permanent disability or chronic illness	Illness or temporary incapacity	Absence of husband	Unemployed	Inadequate earnings	Total
				(Percent)			
Age group							
Under 25	—	4	13	13	26	15	10
25-39	—	11	24	43	34	39	23
40-54	1	33	41	38	27	28	32
55-64	20	42	20	6	13	16	24
65 and over	79	10	2	—	—	2	11
Total	100	100	100	100	100	100	100
Proportion of all recipients	9	41	8	26	13	3	100

Source:　Economic Council of Canada, *People and Jobs*, Table 8-2.

thereby establishing a legislative pattern soon followed closely by other provinces. In each case, a largely independent board or commission pays compensation to workers injured in the course of their employment, and the costs of the programs are borne entirely by contributions from employers. The injured employee, however, loses his right to sue his employer, and consequently Worker's Compensation can also be thought of as a form of social insurance for employers.

Social Assistance is the modern version of the ancient Poor Laws, which in many parts of the country formed part of Canada's colonial inheritance. In the nineteenth century, such local relief was the only form of public welfare provided in Canada, and the development of other income security programs in the twentieth century essentially represented an attempt to reduce the dependence of Canadians on this, the most stigmatized of all forms of income support. Today social assistance is the residual element in the income security system, the last resort for needy Canadians who do not qualify for other income security programs or whose income from those other programs is still inadequate. Benefits are based on an individual assessment of the applicant's current needs and income, and there are strict limits to the assets that a person may retain while receiving social assistance. The largest categories of recipients are the blind, the disabled, and mothers with dependent children, as Table 2 reveals. Social assistance is a provincial responsibility in Canada, and the actual structure and administration of assistance varies from province to province: some provinces have separate programs for the blind and disabled, and assist all other needy persons under a general program; other provinces administer assistance to recipients with long-term needs, such as the aged, the disabled, and mothers with children, while leaving short-term assistance to the municipalities.[3] Benefit levels also vary from province to province, as Table 3 demonstrates.

Whatever the form of administration or the benefit rates, however, the federal government contributes half of the cost of provincial social assistance programs under the terms of the Canada Assistance Plan (CAP), which is a conditional grant program with remarkably few conditions. To qualify for the federal grant, a provincial social assistance program must base eligibility for assistance on need alone, irrespective of its cause, and must not make previous residence in the province a requirement. Otherwise CAP sets no major constraints on provincial discretion; most important, no minimum or maximum benefit levels are specified.

In 1965 Quebec "contracted out" of the Canada Assistance Plan and several other conditional grant programs, to the accompaniment of substantial fanfare about a "victory" for the province and a "weakening" of federal control over social policy. In fact, however, contracting out of CAP proved to be largely symbolic. The original idea was that Quebec would withdraw from the program completely; it would no longer be bound by

Table 3 *Social Assistance Levels by Province and Family Size, 1980**

	NFLD.	PEI	N.S.	N.B.	QUE.	ONT.	MAN.	SASK.	ALTA.	B.C.
One adult	$3,680	$4,070	$4,140	$3,400	$3,610	$3,140	$3,851	$3,940	$3,900	$4,000
Two adults	6,000	5,490	5,780	5,420	5,750	5,400	5,690	5,760	6,300	6,070
One parent, one child	6,080	5,670	5,750	5,520	5,380	5,520	5,730	5,860	5,890	6,550
One parent, two children	6,880	7,020	7,370	6,190	6,360	6,650	7,241	7,460	7,500	8,270
One parent, three children	7,630	8,200	8,710	6,850	7,320	7,930	8,700	9,000	8,810	9,730
One parent, four children	8,410	9,930	10,260	7,510	8,420	9,110	10,470	10,180	10,590	10,950
Two parents, one child	6,780	6,840	7,400	6,230	6,670	6,540	7,210	7,360	7,900	7,790
Two parents, two children	7,540	8,040	8,750	6,890	7,630	7,650	8,660	9,760	9,130	9,250
Two parents, three children	8,320	9,430	10,300	7,560	8,610	8,900	10,080	10,320	10,460	10,470
Two parents, four children	9,070	11,170	11,840	8,220	9,710	10,080	11,910	11,560	12,070	11,690

* Annual Basic Budget Standards, based on assumed rent, fuel, and utilities. Figures include income from other government transfers: Family Allowances and Child Tax Credits and, where applicable, provincial family allowances, refundable tax credits, and income supplement programs.

Source: Data supplied by the National Council of Welfare.

federal standards, and would receive fiscal compensation in the form of a transfer of tax room rather than a direct cash payment. But the actual impact has been much less dramatic. Even the change in the financial relationship between Ottawa and Quebec City has become increasingly marginal, since the revenue derived from the tax room is now only about one-third of the total amount due to Quebec under the agreement, and the province therefore receives the greater part of the federal contribution by way of cash payment.[4] More important, Quebec has not been freed from the CAP program standards. In order to resolve the problems involved in calculating the appropriate tax room to be transferred, Quebec agreed to an interim "transition" period of five years, during which it would continue to meet the federal standards. But the transition period has been repeatedly extended and remains in force today. Quebec is therefore still subject to precisely the same rules as every other province, and must continue to present an annual audit of its social assistance expenditures to the federal government. Viewed from the perspectives of the 1980s, "contracting out" appears to have been a hollow victory for the nationalist forces in Quebec politics.[5]

Income supplementation represents a diverse, but rapidly growing, element in the income security system. Both federal and provincial governments have recently adopted a number of income supplements that provide additional support to various categories of low-income Canadians, but that do so without recourse to the full needs and assets tests associated with social assistance. In part, these supplements have been developed to reduce the need for groups, such as the elderly, to turn to social assistance, the clearest example here being the Guaranteed Income Supplement (GIS), which was introduced by the federal government in 1966. The GIS provides a supplement, which is added to the Old Age Security (OAS) payment, for those pensioners who have little or no other income. In 1980 the maximum monthly supplement was $197.60 for a single pensioner, and this amount is reduced by $1 for every $2 of income over and above the basic Old Age Security payment that the pensioner receives.[6] Originally the GIS was seen as a transitional mechanism, to help elderly people who had little else to live on and who would not benefit from the Canada Pension Plan being introduced at about the same time, and the role of the supplement was expected to diminish sharply when the Canada Pension Plan matured.[7] To some extent this is beginning to happen; but the GIS has proved politically popular, and governments have repeatedly enriched the guarantee levels, most recently after the 1980 federal election, with the result that the expected life-span of the program has been extended significantly. Provincial governments also appreciate the political potential of such supplements, and six provinces now have special supplement programs that essentially "top up" the federal OAS-GIS payment for the poorest pensioners.[8] These supplements are relatively small in comparison with the federal payment, as

Table 4 *Maximum Benefits from Federal Programs* for the Aged and Provincial Supplements, 1980*

	Single Persons			Couples		
	Federal programs	Provincial supplements	Total	Federal programs	Provincial supplements	Total
Newfoundland	$4,350	$ —	$4,350	$7,859	$ —	$7,859
Prince Edward Island	4,350	—	4,350	7,859	—	7,859
Nova Scotia	4,350	176	4,526	7,859	352	8,211
New Brunswick	4,350	—	4,350	7,859	—	7,859
Quebec	4,350	—	4,350	7,859	—	7,859
Ontario	4,350	587	5,524	7,859	1,484	9,343
Manitoba	4,350	117	4,467	7,859	253	8,112
Saskatchewan	4,350	300	4,650	7,859	540	8,399
Alberta	4,350	720	5,070	7,859	1,466	9,325
British Columbia	4,350	467	4,817	7,859	1,196	9,055

* Old Age Security and the Guaranteed Income Supplement.

Source: Data supplied by the National Council of Welfare.

Table 4 reveals, and in 1977-78 the six provincial governments spent a total of only $200 million on them.[9] Yet the political attractions of such plans are tantalizing for provincial governments, providing as they do a visible sign of social concern at modest cost to the provincial coffers.

A final cluster of income supplements and tax credits adopted to help low-wage families represent the first, hesitant steps towards a major extension of the welfare state in Canada. Historically, income security was seen as an alternative to the wage system and the major programs were designed to provide income to those who could not work, whether because of age, disability, or lack of employment. Those in work, on the other hand, were assumed to be able to provide for themselves and their families, and they received no help from the income security system, with the exception of Family Allowances. But work alone is no guarantee of escaping poverty. With the re-emergence of poverty as a political issue in the 1960s and 1970s, the studies of the Economic Council of Canada and other bodies revealed that at least two-thirds of the heads of poor families were in the labour force and over three-quarters of poor families had at least one wage earner.[10] Similar findings appeared in other western nations, and welfare reformers increasingly focused on the need to help these "working poor," with the result that the concept of a guaranteed annual income, or at least some form of income supplementation for low-wage families, gained wide currency in social policy debate.[11]

The last decade has seen much agonized political debate on this issue. The federal government advanced two major initiatives, but without success. In 1970 it proposed to help low-income families by transforming the existing Family Allowances into an income-tested Family Income Security Plan (FISP), but the plan failed to pass the House of Commons before the 1972 election, after which it was dropped. Then in 1976, during the course of the federal-provincial Social Security Review, the federal government proposed the establishment of a new income supplement program, jointly financed and provincially delivered, but failed to gain sufficient provincial agreement to proceed. In the absence of a single, nation-wide program, action has come in bits and pieces. In 1974, Saskatchewan, so often the leader in the history of the Canadian social policy, took the plunge alone and established its own Family Income Plan (FIP); in 1979, after several years of careful study, the Quebec government followed suit with a Work Income Supplement program;[12] and in 1980 the Manitoba government announced its intention to establish a Child-Related Income Support Program (CRISP).[13] Provincial action, however, still has a somewhat tentative quality. For a number of years during the late 1970s, the Saskatchewan government allowed the benefit levels under FIP to be eroded by inflation;[14] and take-up of benefits in the first year of the Quebec program was much less than anticipated.[15] Other provinces have been much less anxious to become involved. In 1973 the British Columbia government did extend its social assistance program to cover working low-income families, but it has consistently failed to publicize the provision and has basically allowed it to wither.[16] Similarly, in 1975 Ontario established a Low Income Supplement Experiment in three of its cities, but the project was discontinued at the end of 1978, with no permanent action planned.[17]

Some initiatives have come, however, through use of the tax system to deliver benefits to low-income Canadians. Following Ontario's lead, several provinces have established special-purpose tax credits to reduce the burden of sales and property taxes on the poor, and to help specific groups, such as the elderly.[18] This approach received a major boost at the federal level in 1978. Following the failure to secure provincial agreement to a joint plan in 1976, federal planners shifted their attention to the tax system, and the Child Tax Credit, adopted in the summer of 1978, represented the first step in that direction. The child credit, first paid in 1979, provides an additional supplement, either in the form of reduced taxes or a cash rebate, for below average income families, according to the schedule set out in Table 5. If federal planners can overcome the administrative problems involved in delivering this benefit on a monthly basis, it could become the prototype for a purely federal guaranteed annual income.[19] But as yet supplementation remains a new and unresolved element in the Canadian welfare state. The extent of such help, and the eventual role of the different levels of government in this area remain to be settled.

A further sign of the unsettled relations on this new frontier is the tension between the Canada Assistance Plan and provincial income supplements.

Table 5   *Child Tax Credit Benefits Payable, 1981*

| | Number of Children | | | |
Family Net Income	One	Two	Three	Four
Under $21,380	$238	$476	$714	$952
22,000	207	445	683	921
25,000	57	295	533	771
28,000	0	145	383	621
30,000	0	45	283	521
32,000	0	0	183	421
35,000	0	0	33	271
40,000	0	0	0	21

Source: Data Supplied by the National Council of Welfare.

The CAP legislation authorizes federal cost-sharing of traditional forms of social assistance only, and consequently most of the new supplements, which have been introduced specifically to eliminate the standard needs and assets tests, cannot be cost-shared directly. Despite complex negotiation between Ottawa and the provinces introducing supplements for the elderly, for example, almost no cost-sharing was obtained. In the case of supplements for low-income families, administrative sleight-of-hand has provided a partial—but controversial—answer to the problem. The Department of National Health and Welfare agreed to share that portion of Saskatchewan's FIP that would have been paid under social assistance anyway. But to qualify in this way, Saskatchewan officials must administer the conventional needs and assets tests to determine shareability, even though the tests are completely ignored in determining the actual benefit paid to the applicant. Under this system, a significant portion of FIP has been shared, especially during the years during which Saskatchewan allowed FIP levels to stagnate. Quebec, on the other hand, has refused to "shadow test" its Work Income Supplement, and has received no federal contribution at all, a fact which has understandably generated anger in Quebec City.[20] This sort of tension is certain to increase in the future as more provinces experiment with "work incentive" programs.

Growth in Public Income Security

Public expenditure on income security has been rising rapidly over the last decade. Table 6 shows the relative size of each of the major components of the system, and the way in which each has expanded since the early 1960s. Table 7, which deals with income security expenditures as a whole, makes clear the way in which, after a decade of relative stability or even slight decline during the 1960s, income security payments rose steadily during the 1970s, both as a proportion of total government expenditures and of the gross national product (GNP). This shift was the product of a variety of forces: conscious decisions made in the early 1970s to enrich several programs, including Unemployment Insurance, Family Allowances, and Old Age Security; the indexation of federal benefits during a period of accelerating inflation; the coming on-stream of full retirement benefits under the Canada and Quebec Pension plans in the second half of the decade; and a protracted economic stagnation which increased demand for unemployment benefits at the same time as growth in the gross national product was slowing dramatically. The political consequence of this expansion of income security expenditures, especially when coupled with the seemingly inexorable growth in the federal government's deficit, has been to make income security more controversial than possibly at any time since

Table 6 *Expenditure on Major Income Security Programs, 1964-78 [excluding intergovernmental transfers]*

	1964	1966	1968	1970	1972	1974	1976	1978
				—millions of dollars—				
FEDERAL								
OAS-GIS	871	994	1,478	1,862	2,430	3,303	4,305	5,244
Unemployment Insurance	344	295	438	695	1,869	2,121	3,332	4,536
Family Allowances	559	606	615	618	611	1,769	1,942	2,224
Canada Pension Plan	—	—	11	78	190	360	775	1,246
PROVINCIAL								
Social Assistance								
Direct Relief	59	143	381	535	751	1,014	1,392	1,732
Old Age + Blind Pensions	116	101	40	18	23	162	334	352
Mothers + Disabled Allowances	93	113	69	41	41	43	64	89
Workmen's Compensation	124	156	177	230	280	415	701	1,080
Quebec Pension Plan	—	—	4	26	58	135	261	455
LOCAL								
Direct Relief	80	89	131	211	244	214	270	283
TOTAL	2,246	2,497	3,344	4,314	6,497	9,536	13,376	17,241

Source: Statistics Canada, *National Income and Expenditure Accounts 1964-1978.*

Table 7 *Growth in Income Security Expenditures, 1964-78**

	Increase over Previous Year	Expenditure as Proportion of Total Government Spending	Expenditure as Proportion of Gross National Product
		(percent)	
1964	—	15.1	4.5
1965	3.7	13.9	4.2
1966	7.2	13.1	4.0
1967	18.5	13.5	4.5
1968	13.0	13.6	4.6
1969	10.8	12.7	4.6
1970	16.5	13.9	5.0
1971	17.5	14.4	5.4
1972	28.1	16.3	6.2
1973	14.4	16.1	6.0
1974	28.2	17.0	6.5
1975	24.8	18.4	7.2
1976	12.4	17.3	6.9
1977	13.8	18.8	7.2
1978	13.2	17.8	7.4

*   Includes only those programs listed in Table 6.

Source: Calculated from data in Statistics Canada, *National Income and Expenditure Accounts 1964-1978;* data on total government expenditure taken from Canadian Tax Foundation, *The National Finances.*

the 1930s. The result has been several attempts to cut back, including the postponement of indexation of Family Allowances in 1976, and several restrictions in benefits under Unemployment Insurance. But, as yet at least, such efforts have not reversed the general pattern of income security consuming a larger share of Canada's resources.

Public Welfare: Private Welfare

Public income security programs are not the only collective mechanism through which Canadians supplement the incomes that they earn and protect themselves from financial hardship. A private welfare system of considerable magnitude has also developed, and one cannot understand the role of public income security without an examination of its private counterpart. Private welfare is focused overwhelmingly on retirement income, and operates through a multiplicity of private pension plans and

Figure 2 *Growth of Occupational Pensions in Canada, 1960-76*

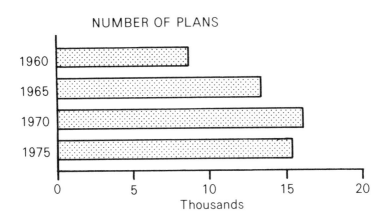

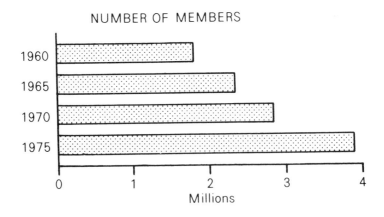

Source: Economic Council of Canada, *One in Three.*

other savings instruments. Occupational pension plans are the most important components of the private retirement income system, and as Figure 2
shows, such plans have expanded rapidly over the last two decades.
Occupational pensions are big business. In 1977 alone these plans took in
contributions of $5.2 billion, more than double those paid into the Canada
and Quebec Pension plans, and the benefits paid out amounted to almost $2
billion.[21] The private welfare sector does provide other welfare benefits, but
much less extensively. Some unions, for example, have been able to secure
supplementary employment benefits as part of their collective agreements
with their employers; such benefits supplement the unemployment insurance payment from the state and thereby guarantee the worker a specified
percentage of his normal pay. And at the upper end of the industrial hierarchy, many executives enjoy low-interest loans or supplementary health
and dental services, all of which convey real benefits and only some of
which the Department of National Revenue is able to track down and
impute as taxable income. But, despite such frills, the real heart of the
private welfare sector is retirement income.

The public and private retirement income systems are locked in uneasy
coexistence, and occasionally sharp conflict emerges over the respective
jurisdictions of these two welfare empires. In part, tension exists because of
the sheer economic power implicit in pensions. By the mid-1970s pension
contributions represented nearly 20 percent of gross savings, and by 1977
the accumulated assets of pension funds were roughly equivalent to one
third of GNP (See Figure 3). Clearly, control over pools of capital of this
size has important implications for control of investment patterns and economic development in Canada generally. Tension between the two sectors
also exists because to some extent they are substitutes for each other.
Indeed, this fact is formally acknowledged in about 40 percent of occupational plans, since they are integrated with the public ones, such that the
private benefit paid takes into account all or part of the payment from the
government plan. And more generally, expansion in one sector depends in
large part on developments in the other;[22] on the one hand, the growth in
the number of occupational plans slowed down after the expansion of the
Canada and Quebec Pension plans; but on the other, any major future
expansion of the two public plans would have to accommodate itself to the
existence of some 15,000 established occupational plans.[23]

The balance between the public and private sectors will undoubtedly
remain controversial. Defenders of the private welfare system contend that
private plans provide greater freedom of choice; they can be better tailored
to the needs and aspirations of various workers through the collective bargaining process; and they provide an essential source of investment for
private industry, avoiding the concentration of these huge pools of capital
in the hands of governments.[24] Critics of the private sector, on the other

Figure 3 *Book Value of Pension Fund Assets as a Proportion of GNP, by Type of Plan, Canada, 1962-77*

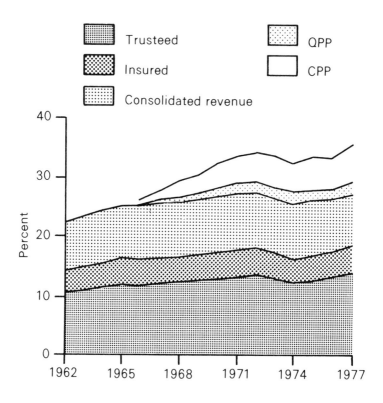

Note: Trusteed and insured plans are using the facilities of a trust or insurance company for the accumulation of assets and disbursement of benefits. Consolidated revenue plans are plans for public employees in which contributions are paid into, and benefits paid from, the consolidated revenue account of the government concerned.

Source: Economic Council of Canada, *One in Three.*

Table 8 *Proportion of Paid Workers in Labour Force Covered by Occupational Pension Plans, by Industry*

	Percentage of Paid Workers in Pension Plans		
Industry	1970	1974	1978
Agriculture	1.3	1.0	0.7
Mines, quarries, oil wells	66.8	70.5	67.6
Manufacturing	43.2	45.7	50.2
Construction	23.5	44.3	47.9
Transportation and communication	49.2	47.5	50.5
Trade	12.9	14.4	15.8
Finance, insurance, and real estate	44.7	42.8	37.0
Community, business, and personal service	25.9	28.7	24.5
Public administration	98.0	98.0	98.0
Total	39.2	40.7	44.1

Source: Statistics Canada, *Pension Plans in Canada 1978.*

Table 9 *Contributors to Occupational Pension Plans, by Income Group, 1977*

Income Group	Percentage Contributing to Occupational Pension Plan
Under $6,000	5.1
$ 6,000 - 10,999	24.1
$11,000 - 16,999	48.2
$17,000 - 24,999	56.7
Over $25,000	62.0

Source: Data supplied by the National Council of Welfare.

hand, point to the selective nature of its coverage. While the Old Age Security and the Canada and Quebec Pension plans provide virtually universal coverage, and the Guaranteed Income Supplement and the provincial supplements help the needy, private retirement provision reflects existing inequalities in income and economic power, providing benefits to the affluent and to well-organized groups of workers. As Table 8 shows, occupational pensions covered only 44 percent of paid workers in 1978, and the extent of coverage varied enormously from industry to industry; only public administration provides anything like comprehensive coverage. And Table 9 confirms that coverage is much more extensive for higher income groups. As well, critics argue that private plans generally have inadequate vesting and portability features, with the result that only a small percentage of those participating in private plans are likely to qualify for maximum benefits, and that private plans cannot adequately protect benefit levels from the ravages of inflation.[25]

Controversy also surrounds the way in which the state subsidizes private retirement income plans by making contributions to them deductible from taxable income. Such tax deductions, or "tax expenditures" as they are now called,[26] are essentially a regressive welfare benefit. Because the value of deductions increases with the taxpayer's marginal rate of tax, they bestow much more generous benefits on those at the top of the income scale than on those at the bottom. Table 10 demonstrates this pattern for the specific case of the tax deduction for contributions to occupational pension plans. In 1974, those reporting incomes under $10,000, who made up 70 percent of tax filers, received a mere 17 percent of the total benefits conferred by the deduction, whereas the 5 percent of tax filers reporting incomes above $20,000 received 26 percent of the benefits. This pattern is even more marked in the case of the newest retirement savings instrument, the Registered Retirement Savings Plan (RRSP), which has shown phenomenal growth since its introduction in 1973. The RRSP is essentially a tax-deferral device through which the state subsidizes personal retirement savings. Under the terms of the Income Tax Act, contributions to such plans and the interest earned by them are exempt from tax so long as they remain in the RRSP, thereby deferring taxation of the income until after retirement when the individual's marginal tax rate is likely to be much lower. As Table 11 shows, participation in the program is largely confined to taxpayers in the upper income levels, and the National Council of Welfare has calculated

Table 10 *Tax Savings Resulting from Deduction of Contributions to Occupational Pension Plans, 1974*

Income	Average Tax Saving	Percentage of All Tax Savings
Under $5,000	$ 1.85	.9
$5,000 - 9,999	21.19	16.5
$10,000 - 14,999	73.26	34.0
$15,000 - 19,999	135.76	22.8
$20,000 and over	225.50	25.8

Source: National Council of Welfare, *The Hidden Welfare System*, p. 25.

Table 11 *Contributors to RRSP's by Contributor's Annual Income, 1976*

	Contributors to RRSP's	
Income	Number	Average contribution (dollars)
Less than $2,000	3,162	358
$ 2,000 - 2,999	3,696	430
$ 3,000 - 3,999	5,822	342
$ 4,000 - 4,999	10,960	397
$ 5,000 - 5,999	15,976	554
$ 6,000 - 6,999	24,302	659
$ 7,000 - 7,999	30,326	676
$ 8,000 - 8,999	41,110	784
$ 9,000 - 9,999	46,203	823
$10,000 - 14,999	302,090	1,053
$15,000 - 19,999	304,420	1,344
$20,000 - 24,999	198,807	1,796
$25,000 and over	304,474	1,638
Total	1,291,348	1,638

Source: Statistics Canada, *Pension Plans in Canada 1978.*

that the highest income decile reaps 70 percent of the benefits conferred by the RRSP device.[27] Clearly, no government would ever openly propose direct cash benefits that were so regressive. But because taxation is still regarded as a conceptually separate compartment of public policy, scarcely a murmur of dissent greets these two "upside-down" welfare programs, which in 1979 cost $2 billion.[28]

Since the depression, then, Canadians have constructed two major welfare systems, one public, one private, each administered by large, powerful organizations, each managing large amounts of money, and each jealously guarding its own jurisdiction. Administrators in each of these systems watch the constant ebb and flow of federal-provincial relations with rapt attention since, as will be examined more fully below, the balance between the two is critically dependent on the structure of Canadian federalism.

Income Security and Individual Canadians

Income security, redistributing as it does billions of dollars each year, is an important component of the political economy of Canada, with significant implications for the broad economic and political contours of the nation.

Table 12 *Number of Recipients of Major Income Security Programs, 1971-76*

Year	Old Age Security	Guaranteed Income Supplement	CPP/QPP	Unemployment[a] Insurance	Family[b] Allowances	Social[c] Assistance
			—thousands—			
1971	1,720	860	331	604	3,024	1,622
1972	1,763	974	449	804	3,063	1,536
1973	1,808	1,045	564	828	3,110	1,373
1974	1,858	1,076	690	828	3,344	1,349
1975	1,916	1,082	822	1,049	3,446	1,438
1976	1,957	1,087	1,008	1,006	3,510	1,501

a. Average monthly number of claimants.
b. Number of families receiving Family Allowances.
c. Number of persons assisted through the Canada Assistance Plan.

Source: Based on various tables in Statistics Canada, *Social Security: National Programs 1978.*

Subsequent chapters investigate some of these: the impact on the structure of income inequality between classes and between regions; the implications for economic management and the labour market; the consequences for the legitimacy and relative power of the governments of Canada. But before the focus shifts to such broad consequences, it is necessary to highlight the importance of income security in the lives of millions of Canadians, including the poorest and most vulnerable groups in our society.

No other area of public policy has such a direct and powerful impact on individual Canadians. Most government policies affect the general public *indirectly* through other institutions: economic policy is felt primarily as it impinges on the behaviour of businesses, financial institutions, labour unions, and other important economic groups; communications policy has meaning only insofar as it alters the patterns of operation in the telecommunications, broadcasting, and publication industries; and foreign policy only when it shifts the actions of other governments; and so on. Income security, on the other hand, is a *direct* exchange between citizen and state, which by-passes such institutional intermediaries. To the recipient, the role of the state in this field is direct, visible and, for many, crucial. In no other policy area are so many Canadians dependent on the state in such an obvious way.

Tables 12 and 13 reveal the dimensions of this dependency. Table 12 shows the number of recipients of the major programs, and the totals are impressive indeed: in 1976 there were over 10 million recipients. Such a figure clearly overstates the extent of dependency on income security at any single point in time. The various recipient categories are not mutually exclusive, as many Canadians benefit from more than one program each year. And the dependence of some recipients is marginal; for many families, for example, the monthly Family Allowance cheque is a welcome supplement rather than a basic component of their income. But the table does identify several large groups of Canadians who are almost entirely dependent on the income security system. First, in 1976 over 1 million pensioners, representing more than half of all pensioners and 4.7 percent of the population, received a GIS payment, indicating that they had little or no income from sources other than their Old Age Security cheque. Similarly the 1.5 million Canadians who benefitted from social assistance represented another 6.5 percent of the population almost wholly dependent on income security. And finally, Unemployment Insurance beneficiaries make up another 4.3 percent of the population; adding their dependents to the figure would push the proportion much higher, although in many cases the recipient is a second income-earner and the family is therefore not entirely dependent on the benefit.

Table 13 gives another view of dependence on the income security system. In 1978 over 20 percent of Canadian families and unattached indi-

Table 13   Composition of Income of Families and Unattached Individuals, by Income Groups, 1978

Income Group	Number	Wages and Salaries	Net Income from Self-Employment	Investment Income	Transfer Payments	Other Money Income
	(000)			Percent		
Under $3,000	472	36.7	-16.8	-2.2	79.4	3.1
$ 3,000 - 4,999	765	18.6	2.5	7.2	66.2	5.6
$ 5,000 - 6,999	562	31.5	4.8	8.1	49.2	6.4
$ 7,000 - 8,999	549	44.8	5.1	7.3	34.8	7.9
$ 9,000 - 10,999	517	54.9	7.4	8.6	21.7	7.3
$11,000 - 11,999	238	63.9	5.6	8.4	16.0	6.0
$12,000 - 12,999	230	67.7	7.7	5.1	14.4	5.0
$13,000 - 13,999	245	69.0	5.1	6.6	14.5	4.9
$14,000 - 14,999	262	73.7	4.6	5.7	12.3	3.7
$15,000 - 15,999	261	79.0	7.0	3.5	7.9	2.7
$16,000 - 16,999	253	81.1	3.8	4.0	8.4	2.6
$17,000 - 17,999	269	84.0	2.8	3.3	7.0	2.9
$18,000 - 19,999	497	82.7	3.1	4.4	7.2	2.7
$20,000 - 21,999	474	82.6	4.9	3.8	7.0	1.8
$22,000 - 24,999	621	86.7	3.3	3.2	4.9	1.9
$25,000 - 29,999	790	87.1	3.4	3.4	4.4	1.7
$30,000 - 34,999	534	85.0	5.5	4.6	3.6	1.2
$35,000 -	842	77.4	9.0	9.4	2.5	1.7
Totals	8,379	76.8	5.5	5.9	9.1	2.6

Source: Statistics Canada, Income Distribution by Size in Canada.

viduals received at least half of the income from transfer programs. Clearly, one in five Canadian families and unattached individuals is basically a ward of the state. Indeed, if one assumes that a person is not really independent of an income source unless it contributes less than 10 percent of his income, then significantly fewer than half of all Canadian families and unattached individuals can be considered independent of the income security system.

Yet in another sense, all of these figures understate Canadian dependence on incomed security, since they all provide a snap-shot view of a single point in time. There is a substantial turnover among the dependent population, so that over time a much higher proportion of the public benefits from each program.[29] Indeed, viewed over the entire life-cycle, income security programs form an important part of the financial expectations of virtually every Canadian. Under existing legislation, every Canadian can look forward to an Old Age Security pension and plan his or her retirement savings accordingly. Similarly, every employed person can look forward to a pension from the Canada or Quebec Pension Plan; by 1977 there were 7.6 million contributors to one or other of these plans, each one with a vested interest in its continuance and financial strength.[30] And of course, programs such as the Guaranteed Income Supplement, Unemployment Insurance, and social assistance provide a degree of social reassurance even to people who do not now rely on them, and hope never to have to do so. Clearly, income security is deeply embedded in the fabric of the Canadian nation. The financial future of almost every Canadian is affected, in a direct and visible way, and governments threaten such universal expectations at their peril.

3 Political Institutions and Income Security: Comparative Perspectives

The social policies of any country have a decidedly mixed parentage. The nature of its economy, its social structure and demographic profile, its cultural and ideological traditions, and its politics all combine to give shape to its income security system. Given such a complex pattern, the independent influence of any single factor, such as the nature of its political institutions, cannot be assessed by viewing it in isolation. An understanding of the other forces at work, and their relationship with those institutional patterns, is also essential, and thus our analysis of the impact of federal institutions on Canadian income security must be rooted in a broader view of the determinants of income security. This chapter surveys the findings of comparative studies in the field and then focuses more directly on the role of political institutions, in order to identify the questions that should constitute an agenda for the subsequent analysis.

Determinants of Income Security

Cross-national studies of income security are a developing field of inquiry and, while the findings to date are often frustratingly inconclusive, they do point to the major relationships underlying the modern welfare state. The findings can be examined under three general headings: economic development; cultural and ideological traditions; and the patterns of political conflict.

Economic Development. The modern welfare state has its roots in the industrial revolution of the nineteenth and twentieth centuries. The transition from an agrarian to an industrial society exposed whole populations to a new and uncertain economic environment, and the industrial wage system left people particularly vulnerable during unemployment, illness, and old age. At the same time, however, traditional social institutions, such as the family and local communities, which had hitherto provided support and protection during periods of economic adversity, were themselves changing in the new urban setting, and were less and less able to cope with the new range of social problems facing the population. In one sense, then, the income security programs developed by the modern state can be seen essentially as a response to the social problems of industrial society.[1]

Support for this line of reasoning comes from cross-national studies of social security in countries at different levels of economic development. For example, when Cutright examined the social insurance experience of seventy-six nations, he concluded that social security coverage was most powerfully correlated with the level of economic development,[2] and Wilensky's analysis of sixty-four nations, ranging in affluence from the United States to Upper Volta, affirmed the central importance of industrialization, leading him to conclude that "over the long pull, economic level is the root cause of welfare state development."[3] In global terms, then, income security protection is the product of affluence rather than poverty. Such comparative studies also emphasize that the welfare state is not the unique creation of democratic politics. The need for new forms of social protection in an industrial setting exists independently of the nature of the political order, and democratic and non-democratic nations alike have responded with often remarkably similar levels of social security spending. Wilensky found that broad political distinctions, such as that between liberal democracy and totalitarianism, contributed remarkably little to the explanation of social security expenditures; and when Pryor compared seven capitalist nations with seven communist nations at comparable levels of economic development, he found that the type of economic system was not a statistically significant determinant of public expenditures on health and welfare.[4]

Canadian experience conforms to this broad pattern. Welfare provision in the pre-industrial Canada of the nineteenth century was minimal, and only modest expansion occurred before the First World War. By the standards of some European nations, Canada in 1914 had hardly started along the road to the welfare state, a fact that has prompted suggestions that Canadian governments were particularly insensitive to social needs or that Canada was somehow "late" in developing its welfare programs.[5] But Canada was late only in the trivial sense of chronology. In terms of the socio-economic preconditions of welfare development, Canada's progress was typical, or even a little "early." Figure 4 examines this issue by relating Rostow's stages of economic development to the introduction of major social security programs in a number of western nations.[6] The arrows in this chart represent the period of economic "take-off," that is, the beginnings of rapid industrial development and relatively sustained economic growth.

Figure 4 *Industrialization and Welfare*

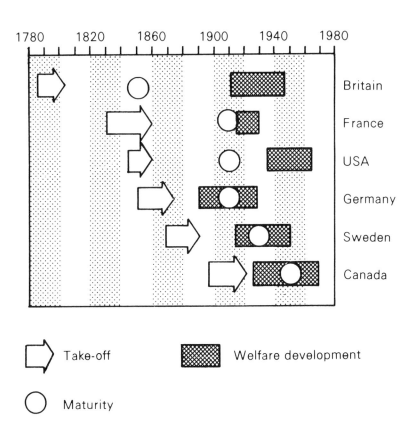

Sources: Adapted from W.W. Rostow, *The Stages of Economic Growth.* Dates of welfare
development derived from various sources.

The circles represent economic "maturity," when industrial processes predominate in a wide range of productive activities and the transition to an industrial economy has been largely completed. Finally, the bars represent the period in which major health and social security legislation was introduced. Thus, in the Canadian case, take-off is depicted as beginning in the late nineteenth century, maturity in the 1950s, and social security development between the late 1920s and the late 1960s.

While there is perhaps room for argument about the precise dates that are appropriate for any country, the broad pattern is perfectly clear. The lag between industrial take-off and the introduction of major health and social security programs was dramatically shorter in Canada than, say, Britain, a country often regarded as a leader in welfare state development. As the Canadian economy developed and became more complex after the First World War, and as the population increasingly settled in urban areas, income security became a major political issue and, in a series of bursts of action spread out over the middle decades of the twentieth century, Canada laid down the basic lines of its version of the welfare state.

The relationship between economic development and income security policy is far from perfect, however. When attention narrows to the policy differences between countries at similar economic levels, other factors naturally assume greater importance. Western democracies, for example, display fascinating differences in their social policies, differences that cannot be explained by relative affluence. In the first place, they devote dramatically different portions of their national resources to social security, as Table 1 above, revealed. Clearly, differences in income levels cannot explain why Austria, the Netherlands, and Belgium devote twice as much of their GDP to income maintenance as Canada or the United States. Such impressionistic conclusions are confirmed by more rigorous analyses; studies by Aaron, Taira and Kilby, and others, all confirm that different levels of income cannot account for differences in the size of social security expenditures in industrial nations.[7] Second, western nations differ in the way in which they distribute their expenditures between different social security programs. As Table 14 shows, in 1972 Canada devoted far more of its resources to unemployment benefits and social assistance, and far less to old age and invalidity pensions, than did other OECD nations. This particular spending mix reflects, among other things, Canada's unemployment rates and its demographic profile, as the elderly make up a smaller proportion of the population than in other OECD nations; and Canada's expenditure mix will undoubtedly become less distinctive as the Canadian population ages and the benefits from the Canada and Quebec Pension plans expand.[8] But the fundamental point remains. Economic development alone dictates neither the size nor the distribution of a nation's income security budget.

Table 14 Expenditure on Main Items of Income Maintenance, 1972 or Near Date

In percent of total income maintenance expenditure

	Old age and invalidity pensions	Child allowances	Sickness cash benefits	Unemployment and related benefits	Social aid	Other
Australia (1971-72)	62.9	14.8	1.9	1.8	—	18.7
Australia (1973)	79.5	11.4	3.6	1.7	—	3.8
Belgium	52.2	21.9	15.3	5.0	2.3	3.3
Canada	39.4	8.0	3.7	26.6	19.6	2.7
Denmark	64.5	15.5	10.8	5.7	2.9	0.5
Finland	70.4	7.3	11.8	3.6	2.8	4.0
France	56.2	20.0	11.4	1.5	4.4	6.5
Germany (1973)	72.4	2.7	7.8	3.3	4.0	9.9
Ireland (FY 1971)	46.8	12.9	14.0	16.8	2.9	6.6
Italy	67.1	11.2	10.7	3.1	0.7	7.1
Japan (1973)	65.4	2.5	15.4	8.7	5.8	2.2
Netherlands (1973)	54.3	15.1	13.7	5.2	11.7	—
New Zealand (FY)	55.9	27.5	1.7	0.4	5.9	—
Norway	68.0	15.6	9.6	1.9	1.7	3.2
Sweden	61.8	14.0	17.5	3.6	3.0	0.1
United Kingdom	62.9	7.1	11.9	8.9	9.2	—
United States	73.0	—	4.1	7.1	12.1	3.8
Dispersion[a]	9.8	7.0	4.9	6.4	5.0	4.6
Average[b]	62.4	12.2	9.7	6.1	5.2	4.3

Notes: Old age and invalidity pensions include survivors, widows, early retirement and disablement pensions. Sickness cash benefits include maternity allowances and industrial injury benefits.

a. Measured by standard deviation.
b. Arithmetic mean.

Source: OECD, Public Expenditure on Income Maintenance Programmes.

Finally, western nations also differ in the structure of their income security programs. Differences in the scope, coverage and organization of programs may well be more important to the public than simple differences in expenditure levels. As Marmor and his colleagues have argued in the health field, "since neither the quality of medical care, nor the mix of medical care services is determined by per capita expenditures, it is not clear that we learn anything crucial about *care* when we explain per capita expenditures."[9] So it is with welfare. The income security programs of western nations differ markedly in the scope of protection that they provide, the mix of income security instruments that they utilize, the distribution of costs and benefits of their programs and, consequently, the extent of income redistribution that they create. To take but one dimension, OECD nations differ in the extent to which they rely on social insurance as the primary instrument of income security:

> On the one hand is a group of countries which largely consists of Members of the original EEC but could also include the United States, in which the State's role can, very broadly, be likened to that of a national insurance company . . . . On the other is a group of countries, frequently of Anglo-Saxon culture, and including Scandinavia, which provides benefits to all the eligible population almost by right, financing such transfers not only through social security contributions but also through general taxation.[10]

Clearly, then, economic development has an important, but limited, role in shaping the welfare state. Industrial development has been a basic precondition of income security expansion, generating a new set of social problems as well as new resources with which to respond to them. But economic development has not determined specific policy contents, and certainly has not dictated the specific size and shape of welfare programs in any particular country. In the context of Canada, then, the key to the existence of some sort of income security is to be found in the elemental facts of Canadian economic development, rather than in the particularities of its culture, politics, or governmental institutions. But to understand the structure of that income security system, its size, the distribution of its costs and benefits, and the mix of instruments through which it operates, attention must shift to the beliefs and politics of Canadians.

Cultural and Ideological Traditions. The diversity in the social policies of the industrial world in part reflects the varying cultural and ideological traditions of the nations within it. Historically, the rise of the welfare state was the consequence not only of the transition to an industrial economy, but also of an accompanying evolution in beliefs about the legitimate role of the state, and about the rights and duties of citizens in western nations.[11] Certainly, the promptness with which the state responded to the social disorders generated by economic change depended on the ideological traditions dominant at that time, as Rimlinger emphasized in his study of the alternative paths to social security in Europe, America, and Russia:

> Where the liberal concept of society triumphed (in England, France and America) social protection was slow to develop. In Germany where liberalism and individualism struck only shallow roots, the chances for social protection were that much better. Indeed, the traditions of the Prussian patriarchal state and the paternalistic environment of the semi-feudal pattern of German industrialization facilitated the pioneering of Imperial Germany in social insurance.[12]

Countless other commentators have emphasized the impact of cultural traditions on the policy patterns that eventually did evolve in industrial nations. Shonfield and King, to cite only two among many, have explained the nature of economic management, the limited extent of public ownership, and the relative underdevelopment of social security in the United States as the consequence of an enduring American commitment to the values of individualism and liberalism.[13] And, in a similar vein, Woodsworth has argued that the impressive differences in the scope and organization of social security in Sweden, Yugoslavia, and Japan "can only be explained by national political goals and values."[14] Similarly, in Canada the individualism of a pioneer community and the conservatism of Catholic Quebec were undoubtedly important in the evolution of income security programs. Bryden, for example, has argued strongly that individualist values, which he terms the "market ethos," delayed the establishment of public pensions and shaped the nature of pension policies that were finally adopted.[15]

Yet cultural values alone cannot explain the social policies of a nation, or the policy differences among nations. There is a potential circularity in such arguments: an assertion, for example, that a country has a limited social policy because the inhabitants of that country want a limited social policy does not advance our understanding very far. In addition, cultural patterns have an impact only through specific groups of people who bring particular values to bear on policy decisions, and this is undoubtedly important in complex societies, which are seldom, if ever, blessed—or cursed—with a single, well-integrated and universally accepted set of traditions. Industrial societies have complex cultures, consisting of an amalgam of traditions, many in conflict with each other, and the particular set of values that predominates within a given policy field depends on the configuration of political life and the relative political power of contending groups.

The Patterns of Political Conflict. Although differences in social policy cannot be separated from differences in political forces, there is no agreement on the combination of forces that lie at the heart of the welfare state. Marxist and radical writers, on one hand, insist that western governments implemented social security programs in the hope of easing the class conflict inherent in industrial society, integrating the industrial workforce more fully into the existing social order and undercutting the revolutionary potential of the poor. For such writers, social security is essentially an instrument of social control, a "kind of insurance for capitalists and corporations,"[16] and differences in the social policies of western nations simply reflect differences in the class balance in each one.[17] Writers in the liberal and pluralist schools, on the other hand, present a less determinist interpretation, in which social policy is the product of the interplay of a host of often contradictory influences: the campaigns of intellectuals and social reformers, the lobbying of business and labour unions, the hidden efforts of civil servants, the electoral calculations of politicians, and so on. Such interpretations also suggest that the particlar combination of political influences underlying social security expansion has varied enormously from country to country, especially in the early years of development: in some countries, the early initiatives came from parties of the right rather than the left; trade unions were strongly supportive of welfare initiatives in some countries, but decidedly hostile in others; and so on.[18] There was thus no standard political configuration—no common inner logic—to the origins of the welfare state in industrial nations.

Now that the welfare state has become an established fact in the life of western nations, there does seem to be a somewhat more common pattern of political conflict over its further expansion, with business and right-wing parties opposed, and labour and social democratic parties in favour. Although the growing body of cross-national studies is still tantalizingly inconclusive on the importance of such political divisions, recent findings do reveal a relationship between social expenditures and the extent of income inequality on one hand, and the political dominance of parties of the left or right on the other.[19] Certainly in Canada, conflict over income security increasingly conforms to such a pattern. Bryden found that, whereas in the early years of the century advocacy of public pensions came from a surprising variety of sources, the debate in recent decades has settled into a more conventional mould, with business spokesmen, and for the most part the two traditional parties, most concerned about the long-range cost implications of pension provision, and with the trade unions and the New Democratic Party (NDP) most committed to expansion of pension benefits.[20] Similar findings come from a 1977-78 survey of the social policy attitudes of 600 senior decision-makers in Canadian government, business, labour, agricultural organizations, the media, and the academic community. The results show business and labour leaders occupying polar positions, with labour leaders much the most supportive of existing or higher welfare expenditures, and with business leaders most opposed to welfare expansion and most ready to use social policy as an instrument of economic management. Other elite groups were arrayed between these two extremes, although the views of the political and bureaucratic elites were, on average, much closer to business than labour opinion.[21] Clearly, the relative political strength of elites with such divergent views has important implications for the further evolution of income security in Canada.

The Role of Political Institutions

Given the importance of such a variety of influences in shaping the social policies of western nations, what is the role of political institutions? There can be no simple answer to this question, in part because institutions on their own have no substantive policy implications. Their influence operates exclusively through their interaction with the economic, cultural, and political patterns of a country, and this interaction proceeds at two levels.

First, political institutions themselves influence the basic economic and cultural patterns of a nation's life, and thereby exercise an important *indirect* influence on the social policies that it chooses to adopt. Stable political arrangements were an important precondition of the economic development in western nations over the last two centuries; the creation of large common markets within the borders of nation states, the building of tariff barriers and other systems of protection, and the elaboration of an increasingly complex array of economic policies had an important influence on the pace, scope, and nature of industrial development. Indeed, in some countries, industrialization was largely a state-directed phenomenon. Thus, the existence of strong political institutions themselves helped set in motion the economic changes that generated subsequent social pressures for income security, pressures to which the state then had to respond. Certainly in nineteenth-century Canada, the shape of the Canadian economy was heavily dependent on institutional design. The act of Confederation itself was, in part, an economic strategy, the creation of a political instrument through which to develop an integrated Canadian economy, to extend that economy across the continent, to encourage the formation and importation of capital, and to populate vast stretches of territory. Clearly, the nature of economic expansion and, as a consequence, many of the attendant social problems that emerged on the northern half of the North American continent were underpinned by the structure of political institutions.[22]

Political structures have a similar impact on the basic cultural and political complexion of a nation. Taking the Canadian example again, it is often

argued that the regionalized nature of Canadian society and politics is not
simply the consequence of an underlying economic, ethnic, and linguistic
diversity, but also the consequence of Canadian political institutions, which
accentuate the territorial dimensions of Canadian life and minimize the
salience of other differences within Canada.[23] The federal system creates a
set of provincial governments with a vested interest in heightening the
distinctiveness and importance of regional concerns. At the national level,
the electoral system exaggerates regional differences in voting, providing
incentives for parties to emphasize region in their policy platforms and
electoral strategies, and regularly producing governments with virtually no
representation from important parts of the country. In addition, the cabinet
system of government, with its strict party discipline and secretive deliberations, reduces the capacity of central governments to represent in a clear,
public manner the full diversity of regional interests, thereby further
enhancing the role of provincial governments as spokesmen for regional
interests, even in areas of federal jurisdiction. Of course, the relative importance of institutions in creating regionalized politics cannot be measured
precisely. But at the very least, the Canadian federal structure of government does seem to accentuate regional conflicts and subsequent chapters
will have to investigate whether or not this influences the definition of social
problems and redistributive goals, and therefore the relative priority of
income security policy in Canada.

At a second level, political institutions have a more *direct* link with the
substance of public policy. The most visible role of a constitution is to
specify the basic decision-making processes of the state, the principles
according to which government is organized, the allocation of legal authority among its various units, and the procedures through which laws are
formally proposed and adopted. In setting these basic procedures, the institutional framework has a number of important consequences for the substance of policy that emerges from it, three of which deserve attention here.

Institutions and the Scope of the Public Sector. Many political scientists
contend that the extent to which legal authority is concentrated in one institution on the one hand, or divided up between a number of separate, politically independent institutions on the other, has important implications for
the capacity of government to introduce new policies and to coordinate
existing ones. The basic proposition is that the greater the institutional
fragmentation of power, the greater the difficulties in reaching agreement
on policy, and therefore the broader the political consensus required before
innovations occur. Conventional wisdom holds, for example, that whereas
the cabinet system of government facilitates agreement on clear lines of
policy, the American congressional system, with its checks and balances
and multiple veto points, increases the likelihood that any given proposal

will be rejected or compromised to death, and that immobilism will result.[24] The differences between cabinet and congressional government can easily be overstated, as Neustadt has emphasized, and certainly the congressional system is not a complete explanation of the more limited role that government plays in the United States, as King has emphasized.[25] But at the very least, the congressional system does seem to require a broader political consensus before major action can be undertaken.

Federalism represents another form of institutional fragmentation, another version of checks and balances, which has important implications for the capacity of government to introduce and coordinate a large public sector. In the nineteenth and early twentieth centuries, federal government was widely judged to mean limited and therefore weak government,[26] and this doctrine is not without contemporary relevance. Historical studies of the growth of the welfare state, such as that of Birch, insist that the complications of federalism inhibited the development of social legislation in countries such as Canada, Australia, and the United States;[27] and Heidenheimer's more recent comparative studies of health and education policy continue to point to the importance of the larger number of access points which federalism provides in West Germany and the United States for those wishing to block the extension of state activity.[28] A revisionist interpretation of the relationship between federalism and policy expansion has developed in recent years, with some commentators arguing that in an era of activist government, federalism contributes to growth in the public sector by multiplying the number of governments with expansionist tendencies. But whatever the relevance of this argument in Canada, a matter discussed more fully below, such expansionist tendencies have not offset the restrictionist side of federalism generally. One of the firmest conclusions to emerge from cross-national studies of expenditure levels is that government expenditure is positively associated with the degree of centralization in government. Cameron discovered that the rate of increase in the public sector as a whole during the period 1960-75 was lower in nations with a federal structure of government than in those with a unitary structure,[29] and the findings of both Wilensky and of Castles and McKinley agree that, other things being equal, countries with federal systems devote a smaller proportion of their national resources to welfare than do those with centralized political systems.[30] Clearly, the relationship between federalism and the expansion of income security in Canada over the last forty years is an important issue to be pursued in subsequent chapters.

Institutions and Redistribution. Political institutions not only influence the size and coordination of the welfare state, but they also influence the distribution of the costs and benefits of social programs, and therefore their redistributive impact. Just as, according to Lowi's famous dictum, policies determine politics,[31] political institutions also determine political interests.

The institutional framework of a country specifies the boundaries of the political constituency relevant to decision-making in each policy field, and therefore the range of interests at stake and the configuration of political forces likely to come into play. As Leslie has argued, reallocating power over a policy problem from one level of government to another redefines the political community relevant to policy-making and often brings a new or modified set of political interests to bear on government decisions.[32] Probably the most important consequence of shifting levels of responsibility is to change the range of income differentials within the relevant policy jurisdiction, and therefore the redistributive interests at stake. The importance of this can be most readily appreciated at the local level. Every student and practitioner of municipal politics attests to the importance of jurisdictional boundaries in distributing the costs of basic municipal services between the city core and suburban communities; a shift from municipal to regional responsibility for such services, for example, can radically alter the redistributive consequences of this sector of state activity.[33] For precisely the same reasons, the redistributive consequences of income security depend in part on the range of incomes within the boundaries of the relevant political constituency. The redistributive consequences of the steady centralization of responsibility for income security in Canada over the last forty years should be added to the agenda of important issues to be investigated below.

Institutions and the Balance of Political Interests. The consequences of institutional arrangements that have already been mentioned—the apparent sensitivity of federalism to regional claims, the relationship between fragmentation and the scope of the public sector, the importance of jurisdictional boundaries for redistributive patterns—could all be seen simply as specific illustrations of the more general proposition that the institutional framework influences the opportunities available to different political interests to shape policy decisions. Because the institutional framework expands or contracts the circle of critical decision-makers, structures the nature of political competition, and specifies the form of representation of the wider public, it necessarily conditions the access of different political interests to policy-makers, smoothing the pathway of some and raising obstacles to others. In Schattschneider's oft-quoted phrase, "organization is the mobilization of bias."[34] What then are the biases implicit in Canadian federal institutions?

Two inter-related propositions about the structure of Canadian federalism deserve special attention here. The first is that the Canadian structure of government ensures that the interests of governments, as governments, assume an unusual importance in decision-making. The second is that the complexity of our system insulates decision-makers from public pressures and that policy, as a consequence, is often unresponsive to the wishes of the public. Clearly these are important charges in any state that claims to be a democracy. The following chapters will have to investigate carefully whether, in the income security field, the structure of Canadian government has responded more to public preferences, elite preferences, or the interests of governments as governments.

Institutions and Income Security: The Agenda

Cross-national studies of income security, however inconclusive they may be, do provide a basis for focusing the analysis of the relationship between federal institutions and income security in Canada. On the one hand, such studies, emphasizing as they do the complexity of the forces underlying the emergence of the welfare state in western nations, stand as a warning against attributing too much importance to political institutions alone. Certainly the fact that industrial nations with often radically different political systems have all made collective provision for a comparable range of welfare needs suggests that the existence of an income security system in Canada does not depend on our particular form of government. On the other hand, comparative analysis also highlights the ways in which the income security systems of western nations differ. The scope of welfare coverage, the proportion of national resources devoted to the task, the balance between public and private programs, the mix of policy instruments utilized, and the redistributive consequences of the welfare state all display fascinating differences, and it is here that political factors, including the institutions of government, are undoubtedly important.

The discussion in this chapter also suggests an agenda, a set of questions, focusing particularly on the role of political institutions in shaping these aspects of income security in Canada. Some of the issues raised, such as the extent to which the institutional structure is responsible for economic development or regionalism in this country, will not be dealt with here, and probably cannot be fully resolved at all. But the more direct relationships are amenable to examination. Has federalism restricted the extent of income security in Canada? Does the apparent sensitivity of Canadian institutions to regional claims alter the definition of redistributive goals in ways which lower the salience of income security? Has the centralization of power over income security changed the actual redistributive impact of income security? Has the complexity of federalism insulated welfare policy from public pressures?

These questions are taken up in Part Two of this study. Chapter four begins by describing the evolution of the division of responsibility for income security between different levels of government, and measures the extent of centralization that now prevails in this policy sector. Chapter five looks at the relationship between centralization and the growth of expenditures on income security, as well as the problems of coordination in the field. Chapter six then examines the implications of federal institutions for the definition of social problems and redistributive goals in Canada, and the impact of centralization on the actual redistributive consequences of income security in Canada. And chapter seven analyses the complex relationships between institutions, elite discretion, the interests of governments as governments, and income security in this country.

PART TWO

FEDERAL INSTITUTIONS AND INCOME SECURITY IN CANADA

4 The Constitutional Division

The emergence of the welfare state posed a major constitutional dilemma for Canada. The British North America Act, in its original form, was clearly a nineteenth-century document, reflecting nineteenth-century assumptions about the appropriate role of state activity. Welfare in the Canada of 1867 was a private matter for the individual, his family, or his church, and the state's role was largely confined to rudimentary poor relief administered at the municipal level. Not surprisingly, such a minor function of government did not attract much attention either in the debates that preceded Confederation or in the BNA Act itself, and certainly such twentieth-century phrases as "income security" and "social services" did not appear in the list of jurisdictions parcelled out to the two senior levels of government. Hence the constitutional dilemma which agonized Canadian politics for the better part of half a century. Which level of government had the legislative authority, and hence the often unwanted political responsibility, of responding to the social problems of an industrial society?

The response to this dilemma has come slowly and awkwardly through a variety of mechanisms of constitutional adaptation. In part, jurisdiction over this new area of government action was simply inferred by both political and judicial authorities from other powers in the constitution; in part, informal arrangements circumvented the formal constitutional structure; and finally, in contrast to every other policy area, the formal division of power over income security was repeatedly amended. Over the course of a half century these adaptations have radically changed the jurisdiction and power relations in the income security field. From an area of virtually absolute provincial dominance in the 1860s, income security has emerged as an area of decisive federal dominance in the 1980s.

In 1867 provincial jurisdiction in the health and welfare field could be inferred from the specific headings of section 92 of the BNA Act that

granted them authority over "hospitals, asylums, charities and eleemos-
ynary institutions," "municipal institutions," "property and civil rights,"
and "all matters of a merely local or private nature in the province." Federal
jurisdiction, on the other hand, would have had to be inferred from more
general grants of power, such as the power to make laws for the "peace,
order and good government" of Canada and its general spending power.*
Given the local, private, and municipal complexion of welfare in the 1860s,
provincial responsibility seemed clearly based in the constitution, and this
pattern was seldom challenged until after the First World War. In the early
decades of the new century, judicial decisions confirmed the authority of
provincial governments to regulate commercial insurance plans and to
establish Worker's Compensation programs, and the federal government
was quite content to accept provincial responsibility for welfare, and to
restrict its initiatives in the field to assistance for its own client groups, such
as veterans in the aftermath of world war.

The inter-war years, however, changed these assumptions for ever. The
period witnessed the beginnings of Canada's transition to an industrial economy, the emergence of welfare as a political problem of the first order, and
the erosion of agreement on the appropriate responsibilities of the various
levels of government for it. As both the scope of the social problems confronting the country and the difficulties facing a purely municipal and
provincial response to them became clearer, advocates of greater action,
including many provincial governments, focused their pressures on the
federal authorities. The federal response was gradual, often grudging, and
initially at least constitutionally cautious. The first stages of intervention
came in the form of grants to the provincial governments, such as the *ad
hoc* grants-in-aid of unemployment relief in the early 1920s and again
during the 1930s,[1] and the conditional grant for means-tested old-age
pensions introduced in 1927. Major unilateral action was not attempted
until 1935, when the Conservative government passed legislation to establish a national social insurance program as part of Bennett's New Deal. But
this legislation was struck down as *ultra vires* of the federal government by
the Judicial Committee of the Privy Council in 1937, and the constitutional
balance in income security remained unresolved at the outbreak of the
Second World War.

The balance that emerged during and after the war can best be examined
in two different categories, social insurance programs on the one hand, and
non-contributory income security programs on the other, since the constitutional position differs with the income security technique in question.

---

* In addition, the federal authority over certain special groups, such as the military, Indians,
and aliens has usually been taken to include the power to legislate for their health and welfare.

Social Insurance

The principles enunciated in the judicial decisions that struck down the 1935 unemployment insurance legislation shaped the subsequent course of constitutional development concerning all social insurance. The decisions determined that social insurance programs, which are financed in whole or in part by premiums paid by or on behalf of the potential beneficiary, fell within provincial jurisdiction.[2] The majority of the Supreme Court declared: "Insurance of all sorts, including insurance against unemployment and health insurances, have always been recognized as being exclusively provincial matters under the head 'Property and Civil Rights', or under the head 'Matters of a merely local or private nature in the Province.'" And the Privy Council concurred: " . . . in pith and substance this Act is an insurance Act affecting the civil rights of employers and employed in each Province, and as such is invalid."[3]

The judgments had eliminated the possibility of any social insurance programs being operated by the federal government but, atypically in Canadian experience, the provincial governments proved willing to surrender some of their jurisdiction through constitutional amendment. In 1940 the BNA Act was altered, with the consent of all provinces, in order to assign to the federal Parliament exclusive legislative authority over unemployment insurance, and a national program was finally established in the same year. In the 1950s and 1960s, attention turned to contributory pensions, and again constitutional uncertainties complicated program design. The federal government wished to establish a direct link between a new pension program and the taxes or contributions used to finance it, but this was precisely what was precluded by the 1937 judgements.[4] However, the provinces again agreed to constitutional change. In 1951 section 94A was added to the BNA Act in order to allow the federal government to operate old age pensions, and in 1964 another amendment extended the federal power to include supplementary benefits such as survivors' and disability benefits. On the basis of these amendments the federal government established Old Age Security in 1951 and the Canada Pension Plan in 1965.

Unlike Unemployment Insurance, however, federal control over pensions is not absolute. At the insistence of Quebec, the 1951 amendment retained provincial paramountcy, stipulating that no federal pension plan "shall affect the operation of any law present or future of a provincial legislature in relation to any such matter." Because the courts have never been called upon to clarify the precise meaning of this clause, there is substantial uncertainty about its full import.[5] Past judicial decisions with respect to the doctrine of paramountcy have involved the regulatory activities of government, and have tended to restrict its applicability to instances of explicit contradiction, that is, to cases in which compliance with the law of one level of government necessarily involves breach of a law of the other level of government.[6] If this strict test were transferred to the income security field, the paramountcy provision of section 94A might have only limited effect, since a citizen might well be able to contribute to, and receive benefits from, duplicate federal and provincial pension plans.

Given such uncertainty, provincial governments have been unwilling to rely solely on this section of the BNA Act, and have negotiated much more specific powers over contributory pensions. In return for provincial agreement to the 1964 constitutional amendment on supplementary benefits, the federal government had to promise to write explicit provincial rights into the proposed pension legislation. As a result, sections 3 and 4 of the Canada Pension Plan Act confirm that any province may opt out and establish its own plan, in which case the CPP ceases to operate generally in that province. This provision was exercised at the outset by Quebec, but it remains an option for other provinces in the future. In addition, section 115 of the act provides that substantive amendments to the Canada Pension Plan must be approved by two-thirds of the provincial governments representing at least two-thirds of the population. Authority over contributory pensions is thus shared in a rather complex manner.*

Nevertheless, despite the limitations in the case of pensions, the federal government has been granted impressive jurisdiction in the field of income insurance through the vehicle of constitutional amendment. Precisely why provincial governments relaxed their otherwise eternal vigilance and surrendered some of their most precious asset, constitutional jurisdiction, in this field—while they steadfastly refused to yield an inch in any other field—has never been adequately studied. The intrinsic importance of the issue, the weakness of provincial revenue bases, the desire for uniform standards across the nation: none of these explain this uniqueness, since each was true of many other policy areas as well. Undoubtedly part of the explanation lies in the particular historical circumstances of the 1940s and early 1950s. Those years represented an era of federal political dominance and, with the memories of the depression still fresh, federal expansionism in income security placed provincial governments firmly on the defensive. In

---

* Another instance of a provincial government refusing to rely on the ambiguous words in section 94A was the rejection of the Victoria Charter by Quebec in 1971. During the negotiations over constitutional reform that led up to consideration of the charter, Quebec had pressed hard to have control of federal income security programs transferred to any province that so wished. The charter, however, simply adopted the language of section 94A, proposing that the federal government retain the power to make laws with respect to old age pensions and supplementary benefits and to family and occupational allowances, provided that such legislation did not "affect the operation" of provincial laws in this field. The proposal was obviously a deliberately vague compromise. Its meaning was never clarified and, in the end, Premier Bourassa rejected the charter, citing the ambiguity over income security as his reason.

particular, Quebec, normally a steadfast opponent of centralization, found it politically difficult to oppose federal initiatives in this field, for reasons more fully explored in chapter eight. Yet this cannot be the entire story, since provincial resistance to centralization in other policy fields was both more intense and more successful.

Perhaps a central element in the explanation lies in the special nature of income security as a direct exchange between citizen and state, which by-passes other social institutions. The contrast with health insurance is revealing. Health insurance was being debated at the same time as income insurance; it was equally important and costly; it posed similarly formidable administrative problems, especially given the mobility of the population; it too would require significant inter-regional transfers to ensure comparable standards across the country; and yet it remained defiantly an area of provincial jurisdiction, with federal involvement restricted to the shared-cost mechanism. Surely the critical political difference between health insurance and income insurance was that health insurance implied substantial control over the entire health complex, including hospitals, the medical profession, and a wide range of community programs. Provincial and municipal governments in many parts of Canada were already deeply involved in health care by mid-century; and until the 1960s the Quebec hospital system was a religious one, and was strongly opposed to the state control that national health insurance would entail.[7] In comparison, transferring responsibility for income insurance to the federal government in 1940 and 1951 made a much smaller cut into the sphere of operations of provincial governments and of those social institutions under their jurisdiction.[8]

Whatever the full explanation for the unique constitutional adjustments in this field, the result is that legislative jurisdiction over income insurance is divided in Canada. Unemployment Insurance is a matter of exclusive federal jurisdiction; Worker's Compensation is a matter of exclusive provincial jurisdiction; and contributory pensions, including supplementary benefits, are a concurrent jurisdiction, with provincial paramountcy in law and shared control in practice. The constitutional status of social insurance programs is thus relatively clear; unlike some areas of jurisdiction, the constitutional rules of the game are understood and respected by decision-makers at both levels of government.[9] This does not mean, however, that constitutional conflict over social insurance is necessarily a thing of the past. There is no reason to assume that western nations will freeze their existing welfare coverage in perpetuity, as demands to socialize the costs of other common risks through social insurance are bound to emerge. When they do, the same constitutional issues will re-emerge with them, and constitutional amendment may reappear on the agenda of the nation once again.[10]

Non-Contributory Programs

The federal-provincial balance in other income security programs has been determined, not by constitutional amendment, but by the distribution of financial and political power between the two levels of government. The provincial power to make welfare payments to individuals has never been in doubt, and historically the issue has been the right of the federal government to do so. Successive federal governments have claimed an untrammeled authority to make such payments to persons, and in a 1957 case, *Angers* v. *Minister of National Revenue,* the courts sustained the federal Family Allowance program, insisting that Parliament could enact such a program under its general power to legislate for the "peace, order and good government" of Canada. Given the general trend of judicial opinion, however, this use of the general power was somewhat exceptional, and the federal government tends to justify such programs primarily in terms of its spending power.[11]

The spending power has become a prominent feature of recent constitutional controversy, and it is important to understand its significance for the income security system. According to the federal view, the spending power allows the federal government to make payments to individuals, institutions, or other governments for purposes on which Parliament does not necessarily have the power to regulate. That is, it claims the power to give money away, and attach conditions if it wishes, even if the purposes involved fall clearly within provincial jurisdiction, as specified by the BNA Act. The constitutional status of this claim has never been settled authoritatively.[12] Some authorities have argued that such a power is inherent in the Royal Prerogative, and therefore resides in both provincial and federal governments. The federal government, however, tends to argue that its power is derived from section 91(3) of the BNA Act, which empowers it to raise money by any mode of taxation, and section 91(1A), which empowers Parliament to deal with "public debt and property," and which the federal authorities construe broadly so as to include all federal assets, including the Consolidated Revenue Fund. Judicial decisions remain ambiguous as to what qualifications, if any, constrain this power. In 1936 the Supreme Court insisted that "Parliament, by properly framed legislation, may raise money by taxation and dispose of its public property in any manner that it sees fit. As to the latter point, . . . the Dominion may grant sums of money to individuals and organizations and that gift may be accompanied by such restrictions and conditions as Parliament may see fit to enact." But the Privy Council, while agreeing with the general principle, added the following:

> But assuming that the Dominion has collected by means of taxa-
> tion a fund, it by no means follows that any legislation which

disposes of it is necessarily within Dominion competence.

> It may still be legislation affecting the classes of subjects in s.92 and if so would be ultra vires. In other words, Dominion legislation, even though it deals with Dominion property, may yet be so framed as to invade civil rights within the Province, or encroach upon the classes of subjects which are reserved to Provincial competence.[13]

As the federal government acknowledged in 1969, "it cannot be said that there is universal agreement among constitutional lawyers in Canada as to the precise meaning of these and related decisions."[14] Federal spokesmen claim that Parliament can make grants for any purpose, even those within provincial jurisdiction, provided that the program does not amount to regulation. Others, such as Quebec's Royal Commission on Constitutional Problems (the Tremblay Commission) have challenged this sweeping claim. "What would be the use of a careful distribution of legislative powers," its report asked, "if one of the governments could get around it and, to some extent annul it by its taxation methods and its fashion of spending?" The Commission's answer was unequivocal: "The right claimed by the federal government to spend money as it sees fit in the provinces' sphere of activity must be rejected as being unfounded, contrary to the federative principle, and to the Canadian Constitution itself." Failure to restrain the federal spending power would result in the "complete destruction of the true federative system."[15] This attack applied to both federal conditional grants and federal income security programs such as Family Allowances.

Despite such controversy, a vast edifice of public spending has been constructed largely on the basis of the spending power. In 1969 the federal government invoked this power as the primary constitutional basis of payments to individuals, including Family Allowances; payments to institutions and industries, including the National Welfare grants which fund administrative improvements, experimentation, and research in welfare agencies and universities; conditional grants to provincial governments, including the Canada Assistance Plan; and unconditional transfers to the provinces, such as equalization grants.[16] At the time, these programs accounted for about 32 percent of all federal expenditures. Since then, Old Age Security also has become a candidate for inclusion in this already formidable list. When this program was established in 1951, benefits were paid from an Old Age Security Fund, which was sustained by specially earmarked taxes, and under those conditions the program found its constitutional footing in section 94A of the BNA Act. But by 1975 both the earmarked taxes and the special fund had been abolished. Old Age Security and the Guaranteed Income Supplement are now paid directly from the Consolidated Revenue Fund, and it is therefore arguable that their primary constitutional basis has shifted to the spending power.

The spending power is critical not only to the present structure of Canada's income security system but also to its future development. The issue exciting the greatest attention in recent years has been a guaranteed annual income, operating through income supplementation of low-wage families and, as noted earlier, the federal government advanced proposals for such a scheme during the Social Security Review. One of the possibilities seriously considered by federal planners at an early stage was to have at least some of the income supplements delivered by the federal government through its Manpower offices; the other alternative, which was eventually offered to the provinces, was for a conditional grant program with complete provincial delivery of the supplements. Either of these approaches, if adopted, would represent a significant extension of the Canadian welfare state, and both would be virtually completely dependent on the spending power for their constitutional legitimacy.

The Present Federal-Provincial Balance: A Bifurcated Welfare State

The constitutional rules and understandings that underpin the Canadian income security system have changed dramatically from the days of provincial exclusivity. Authority over social insurance is divided, and authority over other income security programs is largely concurrent, with no clear provision for paramountcy. These changes have allowed a steady centralization of income security expenditures since the 1940s. "Centralization," however, is not at all a clear concept; and, as Bird has pointed out, there is a variety of ways in which centralization of public finances can be measured.[17] Figure 5 presents three different measures of the degree of centralization of income security expenditures in Canada. Graph A measures centralization by spending government, that is, the government actually paying the benefits out to recipients, irrespective of any intergovernmental transfers involved in the financing of the programs. Even by this standard, the preponderant role of Ottawa in income security is crystal clear: the federal government paid out over 75 percent of all income security dollars during every year from 1964 to 1978.[18] Graph B measures the centralization of income security by financing government, that is, the government actually raising the revenues required to finance income security expenditures; in this case, intergovernmental transfers, such as the Canada Assistance Plan,* are treated as expenditures of the donor government rather than the recipient government. (The proportion of equalization

---

* Only the general assistance portion of the CAP transfers are used, to avoid involving social service expenditures in calculations of income security.

Figure 5 *Degree of centralization of Income Security Expenditure, 1964-78*

GRAPH A
Centralization by Expenditure

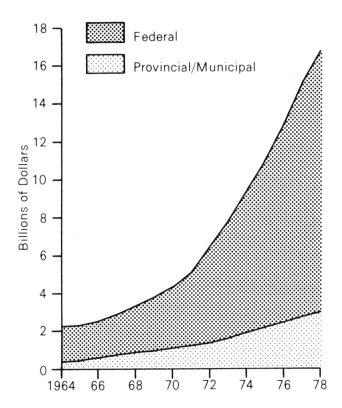

grants devoted to provincial income security costs has not been included.)
By this measure, the income security system is even more centralized, since
the federal government is responsible for raising approximately 85 percent
of all income security dollars, a figure that has varied only a little throughout the 1964-78 period. Clearly, the great bulk of the dollars flowing
through the present system are federal dollars.[19]

However, in some ways, both of these measurements overstate the
importance of the federal government in income security, since Ottawa
does not have exclusive control over the disposition of all those dollars,
even in the case of Graph A, as expenditures under several programs are
subject to varying degrees of provincial discretion. Graph C therefore
measures the extent of centralization by program authority, that is,
according to which levels of government have a legal right to determine, to

Figure 5   *Continued*

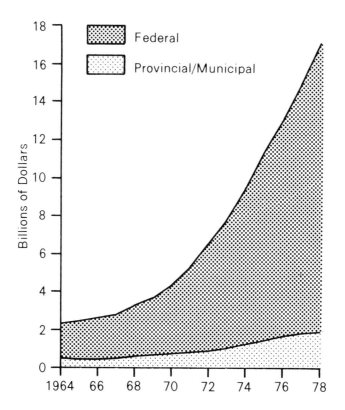

GRAPH B
Centralization by Financing

some degree at least, the disbursement of funds. This generates three categories: *exclusively federal programs* (Old Age Security-Guaranteed Income
Supplement; Unemployment insurance; and—until 1973—Family Allowances); *shared programs* (Canada Pension Plan; social assistance;
and—since 1973—Family Allowances); and finally *exclusively provincial-
municipal programs* (Worker's Compensation; Quebec Pension Plan).
While the two other graphs depict a stable level of centralization over the
whole 1964–78 period, this measurement reveals a clear lessening of federal
dominance in the 1970s, as a result of the acceptance of a provincial role in
the configuration of Family Allowances and the growth of benefits from the
Canada Pension Plan. The exclusively federal share of expenditures
declined from almost 80 percent in 1964 to about 57 percent in 1978.

Figure 5   *Continued*

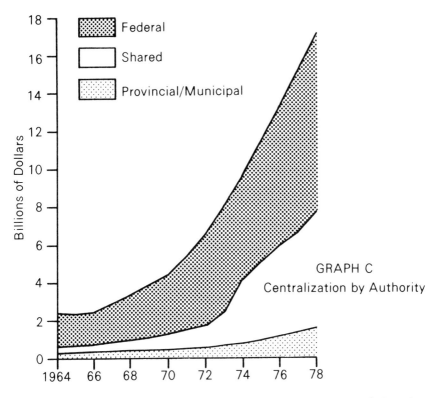

Source: Based on data from Statistics Canada, *National Income and Expenditure Accounts, 1964-1978*.

There is no single measurement of the "true" level of centralization in the income security system, and different graphs are best for different purposes. Graph A is relevant, for example, when discussion focuses, as in chapter seven, on the public visibility of different governments, and the division of the political status or legitimacy that adheres to government as a consequence of the operation of income security. Graph B is relevant when discussing the distribution of the fiscal burden of different governments and the problem of fiscal imbalance in the federation, or when assessing the extent of inter-regional redistribution resulting from income security, as in chapter six. Finally, Graph C is relevant in discussions of the relative influence of the two senior levels of government over income security policy. It is not a perfect measure of the subtle relationships involved, to be sure; the single "shared" category includes both programs over which the federal government has predominant control (such as Family Allowances), and programs in which the federal policy role is much weaker (such as social assistance); and the two "exclusive" categories mask the extent to which such programs are influenced, often decisively, by actions of the other level of government. Nevertheless, Graph C does capture the growing weight of provincial governments in the income security system. While Graphs A and B confirm that so far at least there has been little decentralization of expenditures, this last graph does point firmly to the increasingly complex process of setting national income security policy.

The high level of centralization that still prevails in income security stands in marked contrast to developments in the other side of the welfare state, health and social services. The federal government has always accepted that these policy areas are broadly provincial, and has largely restricted its involvement to shared-cost programs; and recent developments in federal-provincial financial relations represent an even further decentralization of control over such services. The result is that Canada has an increasingly bifurcated welfare state. Health and social services are provincial in theory, and increasingly so in practice. Income security is steadfastly federal, with concessions to provincial assertiveness taking the form of provincial involvement in national programs rather than explicit decentralization. When it comes to welfare, Canada manifests a decidedly schizophrenic personality.

5 Centralization and Expansion in Income Security

The link between political centralization and the expansion of income security, highlighted in comparative studies, does seem at first glance to be confirmed handsomely in Canada. Historically the political dominance of the federal government and the expansion of the welfare state proceeded in tandem during the middle years of the century, and certainly most commentators assumed that the two were intimately related: political centralization was essential to the development of major income security programs, and expanded welfare in turn enhanced the political standing of the central government in the eyes of Canadians. The hopeless inadequacy of welfare provision during the depression had convinced an entire generation of legal scholars and social welfare professionals that strong leadership from Ottawa was the key to the establishment of a modern, coordinated social security system,[1] and the progress of the 1950s and 1960s seemed to drive the lesson home ever more deeply. To this day, many welfare professionals insist that a strong federal role is essential to future expansion of our income security system, and that decentralization would inevitably usher in an age of stagnation and confusion in the welfare world.

Yet the culpability of Canadian federalism during the 1930s was often greatly overplayed. A host of other forces also dictated the slow pace of social development during the interwar years: Canada was still undergoing the transition from an agricultural to an industrial economy; the unionization and political mobilization of an urban workforce was only beginning; left-wing protest was still laying down its foundations in the form of the Co-operative Commonwealth Federation (CCF); Keynesian thinking had not yet cracked the hold of conservative financial orthodoxy over the thinking of government and business elites. As these forces came more fully into play after the Second World War, constitutional roadblocks that had seemed insurmountable during the 1930s proved much less formidable.

More important, the expansion of the role of the Canadian state in other areas has not been limited to the federal government. Provincial governments have also expanded their activities enormously, extending their regulatory reach into an infinite variety of economic and social processes, and mounting an impressive array of public services. Why then assume automatically that centralization was—and is—an absolute prerequisite of welfare expansion in Canada? Indeed, almost twenty years ago, Pierre Trudeau argued forcefully that innovative policies could be introduced *more rapidly* in federal states than in unitary ones.[2] The different regions of a country as diverse as Canada, he pointed out, are always at different stages of economic and political development, and innovative ideas are therefore more socially appropriate and politically acceptable in some parts of the country than others. The genius of federalism is precisely that innovation can proceed promptly in such regions, and that "the seeds of radicalism" can then spread as other parts of the country become convinced by the example. With a unitary system of government, on the other hand, reform must wait until the country as a whole is ready. Could the welfare state have come to Canada through such a process of innovation and diffusion at the provincial level?[3] Or were there constraints at work in this sector, constraints that effectively ruled out the possibility of provincial welfare states?

This chapter examines the relationship between centralization and the expansion of income security in Canada more closely, in order to determine whether or not federalism has restricted the growth of income security. And in a final section, it also takes a brief look at the related issue of federalism and coordination in the income security system.

FEDERALISM AND THE EXPANSION OF INCOME SECURITY

The relationship between the division of power and the expansion of income security in Canada can best be analyzed by examining two distinct stages in the development of the Canadian system: the decentralized welfare system of the interwar period, and the semi-centralized system that has developed since 1940. The obvious problem with this approach is that the radically different attitudes towards welfare in the two periods makes it difficult to sort out the independent influence of the division of powers. Nevertheless, the historical evidence is, as we shall see, suggestive.

Decentralized Welfare: The Interwar Period

The early years of the twentieth century did witness the development of important welfare programs through innovation and diffusion at the provincial level. Worker's Compensation was introduced first in the most industrialized province, Ontario, and then spread progressively, such that when Leonard Marsh's famous report, *Social Security in Canada*, was published in 1943, Worker's Compensation acts, all modelled closely on the Ontario precedent, existed in every province except P.E.I. Similarly Mothers' Allowances, a special means-tested benefit for widowed mothers with dependent children, were first introduced in Manitoba in 1916 and Saskatchewan in 1917, and then spread steadily until, by 1940, all provinces except New Brunswick and P.E.I. provided such benefits. Finally, the inter-war years saw a similar spread of provincial minimum wage laws. Clearly, provincial innovation and diffusion were capable of producing welfare initiatives. But the experience of the interwar period also pointed to major obstacles confronting provincial innovations in income security, the most important of which were fiscal imbalance, and the mobility of capital and labour.

Fiscal Imbalance. An imbalance between the revenue available to each level of government and its spending responsibilities is a recurring phenom-enon in federal systems. It is, de Tocqueville wrote, "as impossible to deter-mine beforehand, with any degree of accuracy, the share of authority which each of two governments [is] to enjoy as to foresee all the incidents in the existence of a nation."[4] And, he might have added, the need to balance the division of revenues with this evolving division of authority magnifies the impossibility tenfold. Fiscal imbalance was a major complication confront-ing the development of the welfare state in a variety of federal systems, since their constitutions usually allocated responsibility over social welfare to provincial or state governments, but reserved the broadest powers of taxation and borrowing to the central government.[5]

In the Canadian case, provincial governments were nervous about the potential burden of welfare costs even during the prosperity of the 1920s, when provincial revenues were reasonably healthy and provincial programs were expanding in a great variety of sectors. Two of the three provincial welfare initiatives of this era, Worker's Compensation and minimum wage laws, did not require public financing at all. Only the third innova-tion, Mothers' Allowances, was wholly financed from provincial revenues, and the costs involved caught the governments very much by surprise. Expenditures greatly exceeded initial estimates, and rose dramatically throughout the 1920s, a fact which redoubled the reluctance of poorer provinces to take the plunge and slowed the spread of Mothers' Allowances in eastern Canada for almost a decade.[6] But, more generally, Mothers' Allowances represented an unwelcome glimpse of the future. The costs of providing support for this relatively small group graphically highlighted the potential costs of grappling seriously with the full range of income security needs emerging in Canadian society.[7] As a result, provincial governments were anxious to avoid welfare commitments, and continued to insist on municipal responsibility for relief efforts. Indeed, most provinces were quite happy to see the end of federal grants-in-aid for municipal relief after 1922 since these had required matching provincial funds;[8] and in the 1930s a number of provinces reversed their original policy and began to insist on municipal contributions to Mothers' Allowances.

But even in the 1920s, it was clear that municipal responsibility would not work indefinitely, especially in the case of pensions. The general problem of dependency in old age was slowly dawning on Canadians and, particularly in the west, provincial concern was accentuated by the demographic profile that had been created by the wave of immigration in the early years of the century. Many of the immigrants had been of mature age when they arrived in Canada and they would be ending their working lives in increasing numbers during the late twenties and thirties, swelling the ranks of the aged poor. "With other problems of public welfare making increased demands," the Rowell-Sirois Commission observed, "the provinces were reluctant to assume such a heavy charge alone."[9] Federal and provincial governments sparred over the responsibility for the potentially enormous costs involved for several years in the mid-1920s, with those provinces keenest on prompt action urging the federal government to accept complete responsibility for pensions, and with the federal government holding back as much for reasons of cost as constitutional propriety.[10]

Finally the federal government's hand was forced by two Labour MPs, J.S. Woodsworth and A.A. Heaps, whose support was critical during the minority Parliament of 1925-26. The resulting Old Age Pensions Act of 1927 represented the first permanent involvement of the federal government in income security. Under its terms, the federal government would reimburse provincial governments for half of the costs of means-tested pensions for those aged seventy and over. Within nine years all provinces had opted in, although the poorer ones in eastern Canada had waited until after 1930 when the federal share of the costs was raised to 75 percent. Later in the decade, the pensions were extended to the blind as well.

The mass unemployment of the depression years completely unbalanced fiscal capacity within the Canadian federal system. "The magnitude of relief costs," the Rowell-Sirois Commission recorded, "hopelessly exceeded the financial capacities of the provinces and municipalities,"[11] and this general imbalance was exacerbated by the regional incidence of welfare needs. Inevitably the depression hit some regions much harder than others, with the result that those with the worst problems had the least resources with which to respond. The federal government was forced to come to the rescue with grants-in-aid of relief efforts and additional loans for the western provinces, the most severely hit. The federal contributions amounted to almost half of total relief expenditures and over 70 percent of expenditures in the western provinces.[12]

Clearly, fiscal imbalance had to be resolved before major action on income security could proceed, and historically the solution chosen in Canada was a massive centralization of responsibility for income security, beginning in a small way with the grants-in-aid during the depression and then accelerating rapidly after 1940 through amendment of the constitution and liberal use of the federal spending power. Logically, of course, this was not the only possible response to fiscal imbalance. As the Tremblay Commission pointed out, fiscal decentralization was another solution. "It is no more difficult," the commission argued, "to add new taxes to the powers of the provinces than to transfer unemployment insurance and old age pensions to the central government."[13] But while fiscal decentralization would have enabled provincial governments to expand their income security programs, this solution would not have produced as large an expansion of welfare as in fact occurred *unless* it was accompanied by a strong mechanism for inter-regional transfers. The reasoning here is familiar. Without such transfers, poor provinces would have faced the unpalatable choice of either below average welfare services or above average taxes, whereas richer provinces would have enjoyed the luxury of below average taxes or above average welfare. The resulting pattern of provincial decisions would undoubtedly not have produced as high a level of welfare expenditures as exists today. Poor provinces would not have opted for taxes sufficiently above the national average to provide income security comparable to that eventually established by the federal government; and even if richer provinces had established more generous programs than the federal ones, it is unlikely that the extra benefits in rich areas would be as large as the deficiency in poor areas. The more probable result, therefore, would have been a welfare system that not only displayed sharp regional disparities but that also provided, on average, less comprehensive protection and spent a smaller proportion of Canadian resources since the 1930s than the present system has.

On the fiscal side, then, the scope for vigorous provincial welfare states quickly becomes a question of the adequacy of inter-regional transfer mechanisms. The Tremblay Commission, which recommended the transfer of all income security to the provincial governments, together with a corresponding fiscal decentralization, was quite sanguine about the prospects of such equalization emerging from the agreement of the provinces themselves.[14] Given the chequered history of the debates over equalization in this country, however, such an assumption was unduly optimistic. Fiscal decentralization plus inter-regional transfers would undoubtedly have been a high risk strategy for poor regions, and the results would almost certainly have been a less expansive welfare state in Canada.

Mobility of Capital and Labour. Even if the problems of fiscal imbalance and inter-regional transfers are surmounted, the ease with which both money and people move about in federations such as Canada also constrains welfare initiatives at the local level. Students who study federations from a rational choice perspective argue that any provincial or state government that establishes new social programs, especially those involving direct employer contributions, places its regions at an economic disadvantage compared to those whose governments do not; established industries are likely to protest vigorously and perhaps transfer some of their operations out of the region, and new investment is less inclined to locate there. On the other hand, provinces or states with superior programs are likely to attract a growing proportion of the nation's indigent, as resident indigents refuse to migrate and new ones arrive from other regions to take advantage of the richer benefit levels.[15]

Mobility was certainly a concern of provincial leaders during the 1920s and 1930s. In 1924, for example, the Saskatchewan government emphasized the problem in its comments to a House of Commons committee on pensions;[16] and in 1927 the premier of Manitoba wrote to the prime minister on the subject of unemployment in the following terms: "If any City or Province singly adopted plans to solve unemployment, that City or Province would become the mecca to which the unemployed in other cities or provinces would drift; for this reason and many others which might be advanced, the assistance of the Federal Government is respectfully urged."[17] Such concerns became even more pronounced during the depression, and underpinned the recommendations of social planners at both the provincial and federal levels. In 1933 the Quebec Social Insurance Commission, for example, accepted the desirability of a wider range of income support policies but clearly felt that an individual province had little latitude in such matters. Although French Canadians had shown considerable interest in Family Allowances, the commission concluded that a provincial program "would perhaps place our manufacturers in a disadvantageous position with reference to other provinces";[18] and six months later, the commission dealt similarly with unemployment insurance:

> . . . ordinary prudence suggests that unemployment insurance should be federal in character. It is very advisable to spread the social responsibilities over the whole country, for otherwise the provinces which participate find themselves in a condition of inferiority with respect to the non-participants. It must not be forgotten that the expenses involved in social legislation would be incorporated into the net cost of production . . . .
>
> Moreover . . . the establishment of unemployment insurance in only one province would prove a great attraction to the unemployed in other provinces.[19]

The commission set as its highest priority the development of a truly contributory system of pensions, yet even here it did not recommend unilateral action, urging instead that the Quebec government take the lead in convincing other Canadian governments to shift the existing pensions to a contributory basis.[20]

The same logic underlay the recommendations for federal jurisdiction over unemployment insurance that repeatedly came from federal advisory bodies. The Rowell-Sirois Commission, for example, summed up the case for federal jurisdiction thus:

> The principal reason . . . lies in the readiness of industry in one province to complain if it is taxed for social services which are provided out of general taxation in other provinces or are not provided at all in other provinces. Even if there are offsetting advantages by way of the better health of employees, or their freedom from anxiety, and even if in the long run the employer's contribution may in the course of wage bargaining come to fall on the employees, the employer is . . . placed in a position of competitive disadvantage in comparison with employers in provinces where there are not contributory social services.[21]

The commission invoked the same line of reasoning in support of federal jurisdiction over contributory old age pensions as well.[22] Clearly, social planners at both levels of government were impressed by the logic of the mobility of the factors of production in the Canadian economy.

Mobility would also create considerable administrative complications for provincial social insurance plans. On one hand, each province would wish to tailor its program to the social needs and financial resources of its population, the political strategies of the party in power, and perhaps even the capital needs of the provincial government itself. On the other hand, provincial governments collectively would face considerable pressure to maintain relatively uniform provisions across the country in order to minimize the problems created by citizens who move from one province to another. The potential complications would be greatest in the case of contributory pensions. Since interprovincial migrants would still wish to receive retirement pensions based on their life-time earnings, there would be considerable pressure on the provinces to negotiate reciprocal arrangements so that the plan paying the final pension would be reimbursed by any other provincial plans to which the individual had contributed during his working life. Such arrangements, however, work easily only if the plans are largely the same. If the provincial plans diverged increasingly, interplan agreements would become much more complex and perhaps, in the extreme, might even collapse.[23] In that case the interprovincial migrant would find himself in the same position as people face with respect to their occupa-

tional pension when they change employment. Either they would eventually draw partial benefit from more than one provincial plan, or they would
have to withdraw their accumulated balance from the one plan and then
buy into another retirement savings vehicle, perhaps the pension plan
operated by their new province of residence. Such arrangements would not
be impossible, but they would be more complicated for government and
citizen alike.

None of this means that provincial welfare states are—or were—an
impossibility. Rational choice theory provides no final answer, beyond
noting that welfare levels that would develop under provincial jurisdiction
would depend on the "propensities of rich and poor to migrate, the extent of
altruism, the extent to which altruism is specific to one's neighbourhood or
ethnic group, and the proportions of incomes in the different provinces
attributable to immovable factors of production."[24] In the Canadian case,
mobility of the factors of production did not prevent the diffusion of
Worker's Compensation, nor at a later date the establishment of health
insurance in Saskatchewan. Indeed, the Tremblay Comission dismissed the
concern about mobility, arguing that the lack of provincial innovations
during the 1930s could "be explained much more fully by the financial
concepts of that time than by any fears of competition,"[25] and the Rowell-
Sirois Commission gave some credence to such arguments in its acceptance
of provincial jurisdiction over health insurance. Despite the realization that
"it may result in inequalities of taxes on industry as between provinces," the
report optimistically assured its readers:

> . . . experience with provincial social welfare legislation in the
> past has been that once an important reform is instituted in one
> province it has been adopted relatively quickly by others. This
> was the case with workmen's compensation; it might well be the
> case with health insurance and, if so, any inequalities of tax
> burdens as between provinces resulting therefrom would soon be
> evened out.[26]

But if mobility of capital and labour does not preclude provincial welfare
innovations, it does complicate the process, and undoubtedly reduces the
likelihood that provincial diffusion would create as complete a system as
would emerge under more centralized political arrangements. Rational
choice theorists are "fairly certain that there would be less redistribution in
total under provincial than under federal jurisdiction."[27] In the Canadian
case, the growth of social insurance programs in particular would have been
more difficult, and provincial governments would have probably relied
more heavily on demogrants and means-tested benefits to achieve their
social policy objectives. But it is doubtful that heavier reliance on these
instruments would have provided the same range of income security as has

developed under federal jurisdiction. Throughout the western world, governments of all persuasions have found social insurance to be a remarkably useful political compromise in the battle over the welfare state, enabling them to provide broad social protection as a matter of right, without recourse to means tests, but also to minimize the extent of any income redistribution between social classes. Deprived of the full benefit of the political magic of social insurance, provincial governments would have been hard pressed to provide as extensive a system of income security as the federal level has managed with it. If this is the case, provincial jurisdiction would have resulted not only in a welfare state constructed with different instruments; the final structure would have been smaller in size.

Support for this line of reasoning comes from the battle over contributory pensions in the mid-1960s. Simeon argues that if contributory pensions had been a provincial responsibility in the 1960s, "it is most unlikely that a plan comparable to the CPP would have been enacted."[28] Provinces would most likely have followed Ontario's proposal to rely on regulation of the private sector to expand pension coverage, with employers of a certain size being required to provide pension plans meeting specified conditions.[29] The public income security system would thus have been smaller; Canadians would have had to rely more heavily on the private sector; and the federal government would have had to rely exclusively on other instruments, such as Old Age Security and the Guaranteed Income Supplement, to provide rudimentary income protection for those with inadequate pensions.

Decentralized Welfare: A Summary. The logic of fiscal imbalance and of inter-regional mobility point in the same direction. A provincialized income security system was—and is—not impossible, and certainly the marked centralization of income security in Canada was not the only possible route forward after the 1930s. If the depression and the Second World War had not drastically altered the political and financial contours of Canadian politics, a much different federal-provincial balance might have emerged in the income security field. But there is certainly a relationship between centralization and the *extent* of income security growth. Fiscal relations and the problems that mobility would have generated undoubtedly would have meant that provincial income security systems would have provided a less expansive welfare state in Canada, and Canadians would have had to rely more heavily on the private sector.

Semi-Centralized Income Security: 1940 and After

In the twenty-five years following the trauma of the depression, Canada moved to a relatively centralized income security system. In doing so, it skipped nimbly over a number of intermediate points, which found favour in other federal systems or in other Canadian policy areas. In the United States, for example, unemployment insurance is a state responsibility, with federal intervention limited to a tax-offset device. If an employer is paying contributions to an approved state unemployment insurance plan, he may credit 90 percent of his contributions against his federal tax liability; since the taxes would be paid anyway, the device neatly reduces the problems posed by the mobility of capital.[30] Other federal systems provide an even richer variety of possible arrangements in this field.[31] Or more conventionally in Canadian practice, federal intervention in unemployment insurance might have taken the form of conditional grants, as in the case of health insurance; indeed, this approach was assumed in most discussions of unemployment insurance during the 1920s.[32] But given the political dominance of the federal government during the 1940s and early 1950s, it was able to secure a much more decisively centralized income security system than that.

In view of the frustrations of the 1930s, what is remarkable about the postwar period is the ease with which the complications of federalism were overcome in the field of income security. In common with other forms of institutional fragmentation, federalism did raise the level of consensus required for innovation, and occasionally even programs widely regarded as desirable were delayed as a consequence of being linked with other federal-provincial disagreements. But certainly, income security was less restricted than was health insurance, the tangled history of which runs from the Green Book proposals presented by the federal government to the Reconstruction Conference of 1945 until Quebec's decision to opt into medicare beginning in 1971.[33] In comparison, only four years elapsed between the 1937 judicial decisions and the successful introduction of Unemployment Insurance. Old Age Security was in place within six years of the collapse of the Reconstruction Conference, and less than three years separated the federal government's original proposals for contributory pensions and the inauguration of the Canada and Quebec Pension plans. Indeed, in his recent history of pensions, Bryden relegated federalism and the provincial governments to the lowly rank of one among several "subsidiary actors" in the policy process.[34]

Admittedly, federal involvement in social assistance did grow more slowly after the Green Book proposal for direct federal responsibility for all unemployed employables came to naught. But even here, recurring provincial pressures on Ottawa produced a pattern of incremental expansion of the federal role through shared-cost programs, with assistance for the aged in 1952, for the disabled in 1955, and for general welfare recipients through the Unemployment Assistance Act in 1956. In introducing this last piece of legislation, the minister of National Health and Welfare, Paul Martin, proudly proclaimed that it would

> . . . write *finis* to the deadlock which has existed in this country
> for a decade or more on the subject of the responsibility of the
> several governmental jurisdictions for what we call residual assist-
> ance . . . . By this legislation we will eliminate the obstacles pre-
> sented in the past by the fact that each jurisdiction has argued that
> responsibility belonged to another level of government.[35]

Finally, a decade later, these three initiatives of the 1950s were consolidated
and, again under provincial urgings, expanded in the Canada Assistance
Plan, negotiations over which have been called a model of federal-provincial cooperation and accord.[36] Federalism has produced moments of high
drama in income security, and the failure of the proposals for income
supplementation of low-wage families in 1976 stands as a salutary reminder
of the frustration occasionally visited upon social reformers by federalism.
The record of the entire postwar period, however, is at most one of delay
rather than permanent blockage.

But if federalism has not prevented the emergence of the welfare state in
Canada, has the expansion of income security programs been more limited
than would have taken place under complete centralization of jurisdiction
in this field? This is a complex question, because federalism has both a
conservative and an expansionist dynamic in income security. In some
programs federal relations have clearly restricted the level of expenditures,
while other programs have been expanded as a result of tensions inherent in
divided jurisdiction. These two dynamics can best be illustrated by examining them separately.

The Conservative Dynamic. While every federal planner has his or her
favourite example of expansion opportunities sacrificed to federal-provincial relations, the Canada and Quebec Pension plans are the clearest testament to the conservative dynamic of divided responsibility. Jurisdiction
over contributory pensions is complex, and replete with veto points. First,
to avoid the administrative and political headaches that would emerge if
the two plans diverged sharply, pension planners in both Ottawa and
Quebec City accept that the Canada and Quebec plans should remain
broadly parallel, with neither side making significant changes alone.[37]
Second, as was noted in the previous chapter, changes in the CPP itself are
complex, requiring the consent of at least two-thirds of the provincial
governments representing at least two-thirds of the population. As a result,
either Ontario alone, or a variety of possible combinations of other
provinces, can block changes approved by the federal Parliament. In effect,
then, the CPP rules and the pressure for parallelism between CPP and QPP
create a system of multiple vetoes: Ottawa, Ontario, Quebec, or several

combinations of other provinces, can all stop change.*

These multiple veto points slow the pace of change and insulate pensions from the pressures for expansion inherent in democratic politics. While advocates of expansion must carry the day in Ottawa, Quebec City, and Toronto as well as at least five other provincial capitals, opponents of expansion need win in only one of the three major sites, and so far at least the Ontario government has proven particularly receptive to their cause. The conservative ideology of the Progressive Conservative government, reinforced by the influence of the private pension industry which is largely headquartered in that province,[38] has made Ontario a persistent champion of private provision for retirement income needs. Ever since the original negotiations over the establishment of the Canada Pension Plan in the mid-1960s, Ontario spokesmen have argued that CPP should provide only minimum benefit levels in order to leave ample scope for private plans, and that CPP benefits should be closely tied to actual contributions, since too generous a benefit-contribution ratio might also discourage the growth of private plans.[39] While the Ontario government was not completely happy with the form which CPP finally took in 1965, its success in gaining a veto over future amendments to the plan has left it in a much stronger position to guard against any major expansion of public contributory pensions.

This particular position of Ontario has been powerfully reinforced by a more general provincial interest in resisting the liberalization of CPP benefits. In many countries, political pressures have shifted funded pension plans increasingly to a pay-as-you-go basis, as politicians have increased benefits without making comparable increases in contribution rates.[40] In Canada, however, federalism has created formidable institutional barriers against such pressures. Under the terms of the federal-provincial agreement which established the CPP, the massive surpluses which have built up since 1966 have been loaned to the provincial governments on favourable terms,[41] with each province's entitlement determined by the proportion of contributions made to the fund by its own residents (See Table 15). As the

---

* The formula for amending the CPP contains what must be the most fascinating anomaly in all of Canadian federalism. Despite the fact that the Quebec government operates its own pension plan, it is also included in the two-thirds rule governing amendments to the Canada Pension Plan. While accepting the anomalous nature of the situation, federal officials point out that since federal employees resident in Quebec (e.g. RCMP and Armed Forces personnel) contribute to the CPP, Quebec is entitled to borrow money from the CPP fund and that the amount, while not large, is greater than the borrowings of P.E.I. Quebec's share of the population does not entitle it to an outright veto in its own right, but federal officials agree that Quebec and one other small province could block an amendment desired by every other Canadian government. Even Quebec pension planners seem somewhat uneasy in the situation and, in the words of one official, they "walk on eggs" every time one of the smaller provinces seeks to enlist their expertise against the big guns of Ottawa and Toronto.

Table 15 *Provincial and Federal Securities Purchased by the Canada Pension Plan Investment Fund*

Fiscal Years Ending March 31, 1966-79

Securities of	Purchases					Balance	Per Capita Balance
	1966-76	1977	1978	1979	1979	1979	1979
	—$ millions—					$ millions	$
Newfoundland	183.8	31.0	33.0	36.6		284.4	500
Prince Edward Island	36.9	6.4	6.8	7.5		57.6	472
Nova Scotia	368.9	59.7	62.9	68.2		559.7	666
New Brunswick	278.7	45.2	48.0	53.3		425.2	612
Quebec[a]	51.5	7.7	7.5	7.5		74.2	12
Ontario	5,189.6	812.8	851.1	915.9		7,769.4	920
Manitoba	551.4	86.5	91.1	99.3		828.3	802
Saskatchewan	426.7	65.3	69.3	76.0		637.3	672
Alberta	901.1	150.7	162.0	185.5		1,399.3	717
British Columbia	1,373.2	224.2	237.3	260.5		2,095.2	828
Canada	61.6	10.7	11.4	12.0		95.7	4
Total	9,423.5	1,500.2	1,580.3	1,722.1		14,226.3	606

a Amounts available to Quebec relate only to the contribution of some federal employees in that province—e.g., armed forces personnel and RCMP officers.

Source: Adapted from Canadian Tax Foundation. *The National Finances 1979-1980*. Table 7-11.

CPP Advisory Committee noted as early as 1975, "the CPP has become the backbone of provincial debt financing," contributing more than 30 percent of total provincial borrowing and even more in periods of stress in capital markets.[42] In effect, CPP in these early years has primarily been an instrument for extracting compulsory savings from Canadians and transferring them to provincial treasuries. Ontario in particular has made heavy use of the fund, drawing almost $8 billion by 1979 and using this source to camouflage the full extent of its borrowings.[43] But the day of reckoning draws near. With the number of beneficiaries now growing rapidly, current projections suggest that after 1985 provinces will have to start paying the interest on the money and that after 1992 the principal will be increasingly needed as well. In this situation, provinces have a vested interest in opposing any liberalization of CPP benefits that would speed up the repayment timetable, and in 1977 Ontario, the province with by far the biggest CPP debt, vetoed a benefit improvement that had been passed by Parliament.[44]

The financial basis of CPP and QPP has been the subject of active—and secret—negotiations between the provinces and Ottawa for several years. Provinces facing stiff repayment schedules have a clear interest in pressing for an early and significant increase in the contribution rate, which would make CPP more fully funded and postpone repayment. For several years Ontario advocated a fully funded plan,[45] but it now appears to be backing off. A fully funded plan would, in the words of one official, "take an enormous amount of money out of the economy and place it in the public sector for investment purposes; and this raises opposition in some parts of the Ontario government." Unless Ontario can find some means of channeling CPP funds into private investment hands, and convince its CPP partners to accept such an innovation, it might well end up advocating a more moderate contribution increase, enough to postpone repayment until well into the twenty-first century but not enough to liberalize benefits significantly as well. Whatever the outcome, one thing is certain. The vested interests of the provincial governments stand as a powerful barrier against the pressures inherent in democratic nations for pay-as-you-go pensions.

These institutional barriers to expansion tend to deflect the impact of electoral competition at the national level away from the Canada Pension Plan. Federal parties simply cannot make election promises to increase CPP benefits; at best they can promise to try. In contrast to British parties, which made reform of contributory pensions a central issue in every election between 1959 and 1974, Canadian parties are virtually silent. "Without the various vetoes," one federal official concurred, "we would certainly see more federal election platforms with CPP items." Electioneering is thus focused even more intensely on exclusively federal retirement programs such as the Guaranteed Income supplement, as the 1980 election demonstrated. A $35 increase in the monthly supplement was almost the only concrete election promise made by the Liberal party, and the increase was actually being paid out within months of its victory, something that simply could not happen with the Canada Pension Plan. But growth in the income-tested supplement is less significant than a similar rate of growth in the much broader CPP. Consequently, the scope of the total Canadian income security package is reduced from what it would otherwise be.

Executive federalism is thus a decidedly conservative force in pension politics. Divided jurisdiction insulates contributory pensions from the expansionist pressures inherent in democratic politics, and more firmly entrenches the existing balance between the public and private sectors in the retirement income field. This does not mean, however, that the role of the private pensions is protected in perpetuity. Institutional obstacles, however real, can be overcome if the pressures are great enough, and the private pension industry may well be facing such a threat over the next decade. Unless inflation recedes, or some method of indexing private pensions is developed (perhaps through government absorbing the costs involved),[46] then the political pressures for a significant expansion of public plans are likely to grow, and perhaps overwhelm advocates of the private sector within the federal-provincial arena. Institutions are never the only factor shaping public policy, and the future balance between public and private in this field remains uncertain. But one thing is clear. Federalism affords the private pension industry with greater protection than it would otherwise enjoy, providing it with more time and political opportunities as it attempts to adjust to a new and harsher economic climate.

The Expansionist Dynamic. Recent years have seen the emergence of a revisionist theory of the impact of federalism on the role of government. In the modern era of activist government, the revisionists contend, federalism contributes to the growth of the public sector by multiplying the number of independent decision-making units with expansionist tendencies. Drawing on Downs, Niskanen, and others, they contend that bureaucracies develop their own expansionist momentum, and that these organizations, together with the ministers who sit atop them, become the primary pressures for program growth.[47] (In fact, support for such propositions can be found in studies of income security; histories of the welfare state repeatedly stress the importance of the day-to-day demands from public officials for incremental expansion of welfare provision,[48] and the findings of statistical analyses of welfare expenditures among industrial nations are at least compatible with such arguments.)[49] Given such assumptions, federalism, which multiplies the number of autonomous bureaucracies and the number of ministers seeking to satisfy the public, seems to offer even greater scope for expansion, especially when one level of government spends money raised by another level of government.[50] Such expansionist pressures are also accentuated because federalism injects competition into intergovernmental relations. Alan Cairns, for example, has argued that "The nature of the federal system with its fuzzy lines of jurisdictional demarcation, and extensive overlapping of the potential for government response, means that in innumerable fields there is, in fact, an intergovernmental competition to occupy the field, and slackness by one level of government provides the occasion for a pre-emptive strike by the other."[51] Similarly, an American commentator, trying to account for the difference between the steady development of welfare spending in Canada and the pattern of stagnation in the United States, has argued that the very severity of strains in the Canadian federation have created expansive pressures: ". . . the imminence [of crisis] places policy-making on an 'around-the-clock' footing. the consequences of stagnation are unacceptable, so with the limits set by federal-provincial politics, compromises are worked out."[52]

Historically such expansionist dynamics have been limited in income security, since the provincial instinct to defend and expand jurisdiction at all costs was weakest here. In general, provincial governments saw an expanding federal role as a means of avoiding income security commitments themselves, and even today most provinces like to see the enrichment of federal programs such as Old Age Security, the Guaranteed Income Supplement, Family Allowances, and Unemployment Insurance, because increases in these programs tend to ease the pressures on their own social assistance systems. (The implications of this are more fully examined in chapter seven.) But some signs of an expansionist element did develop in the 1960s and 1970s, as the rivalry between Ottawa and Quebec City for the political allegiance of Quebecers added a new dimension to the politics of income security. During these last two decades the Quebec government set out to create a comprehensive *provincial* welfare state, and to that end it sought to halt the process of centralization and to recapture territory lost in previous years. This drive generated intense conflict in federal-provincial relations, and inclined both governments to exercise their jurisdiction as vigorously and generously as possible. The first sign of things to come was the competition between Ottawa and Quebec over the design of contributory pensions. During a 1963 federal-provincial conference, the Quebec government created a sensation by outlining proposals that promised broader coverage, more generous benefits, and a more redistributive financial formula than those that had been presented by the federal authorities; and after the final compromises were sorted out, the plans adopted were certainly more extensive than Ottawa had first envisioned.[53] Next came the protracted battle over family allowances. To establish its jurisdiction in concrete terms, the Quebec government established its own general Family Allowance program in 1967, as a precursor to its demand two years later that the federal government transfer its Family Allowances to the provincial level. After several years of hesitancy, the federal government adopted the old sports maxim that the best defence is a good offence, and protected its jurisdiction by exercising it dramatically. Although not the most important factor involved, this "territorial imperative" was one reason behind Ottawa's decision to maintain Family Allowances as a universal benefit payable to every family with children and to triple the benefit levels, rather than proceed with its earlier proposal to restrict benefit levels to low-income families.

Federal Dynamics and Income Supplementation. Both the conservative and expansionist dynamics of divided jurisdiction were clearly illustrated by the controversy over income supplementation during the Social Security Review, which was launched in 1973. The institutional framework certainly opened more channels to reformist opinion, since a number of provincial governments were committed to the goal of a guaranteed annual income. Two years earlier, Quebec had published the massive report of its Commission of Inquiry on Health and Social Welfare (the Castonguay-Nepveu Report),[54] with its sweeping blueprint for reform of both federal and provincial welfare programs in order to establish a guaranteed income for all Quebecers. The report put the federal authorities on the defensive. In the aftermath of the failure of the Victoria Conference, Ottawa was forced to respond ambitiously, if only to demonstrate that federalism did not inevitably doom progress in the income security field.[55] In addition, the federal-provincial process ensured that the three NDP governments had a central place at the table, creating another bloc pushing for major advances towards a guaranteed income. Indeed, Saskatchewan significantly reinforced this pressure by introducing its own program, the Family Income Plan, as a prod to national action.

But federalism also maximized the ideological distance between participants, since some quite conservative provincial governments were also present at the bargaining table. This increased the problems of achieving sufficient consensus for nation-wide action. Ideological divisions complicated the program design stage of the review, fueling a protracted argument between a one-tier and a two-tier program,[56] and delayed final decisions for an additional year, during which time the economic recession was biting deeper and political support for welfare expansion was shrinking. In the end, even the mild proposals advanced by Marc Lalonde, the federal minister, were flatly rejected by Ontario and deferred by several other provinces, dashing the fondest hopes of social reformers in the 1970s.

The problems of low-wage families did not suddenly disappear in June 1976, however. Proposals for major income-supplementation programs have remained a staple of social policy debate in Canada, and federalism has facilitated—perhaps even encouraged—piecemeal progress since. Both Ottawa and Quebec City have taken unilateral actions that stake out their claims to this new frontier of income security. The federal Child Tax Credit now stands as a reminder of the federal role in income redistribution to low-income families, and the Quebec government has staked its claim with the Work Income Supplement Program. Moreover, the recent decision of the Manitoba government to launch a program similar to Saskatchewan's FIP suggests that a broader process of provincial diffusion may be setting in. In the case of the Social Security Review, then, divided jurisdiction increased the access of reformist opinion to national councils, decreased the prospects of achieving consensus on a national program, but facilitated incremental progress thereafter.

Conservative and Expansionist Dynamics: The Modern Balance. Clearly divided jurisdiction has both a conservative and an expansionist side, with the relative impact of each side varying from program to program, and from decade to decade. Certainly, federalism claimed more income security victims during the 1970s than during the 1950s and 1960s. But whether divided jurisdiction is, on balance, a conservative or expansionist force in income security, or whether the two sides are broadly self-cancelling, is more difficult to judge. While cross-national studies repeatedly conclude that federalism tends to dampen the rate of expansion in the public sector generally, and social security expenditures specifically,[57] they cannot answer the question conclusively for any individual federation such as Canada. But perhaps they do suggest that the benefit of the doubt should be given to the conservative side. The impact, however, is not overwhelming. Canada already has a reasonably centralized income security system, and there is no evidence that Canada would suddenly leap up the OECD tables on welfare spending if only jurisdiction over all income security were consolidated in Ottawa.

CENTRALIZATION AND COORDINATION IN INCOME SECURITY

When attention turns from the overall scope of income security to the coordination of income security programs, the complications of federalism become even more evident. Administrators and social workers who actually operate the programs regularly despair over the lack of an inte-grated system, rationally designed and simple to administer. Duplication of programs on one side and gaps in coverage on the other, differing criteria of eligibility, shuffling of needy persons from one office to another: all of these seem to be the unacceptable face of federalism. This professional orienta-tion received one of its earliest expressions in the 1943 Marsh Report.[58] "The task is to visualize the system as a whole, and to integrate the component units," its author insisted; variations in coverage, eligibility rules, and benefit rates that resulted from provincial jurisdiction were regrettable "anomalies," and even well-established provincial programs such as Workers's Compensation were judged weaker for the lack of "a national and unified structure."[59] While Marsh conceded in passing that it was "not essential for every unit [of the welfare system] to be Dominion-operated," he was certain that it would be a "catastrophe" if the federal government dominated some programs while the provinces completely dominated others.[60] The secret to an adequate *system*, Marsh and his contemporaries insisted, was strong central leadership.[61]

Even though the federal government does now dominate much of the income security side of the welfare state, Canadians in need must still face a maze of authorities. As a federal policy paper admitted in 1973:

> At the federal level there is the Department of National Health and Welfare, the Manpower and Immigration Department and the Unemployment Insurance Commission—and rarely are these agencies located in the same buildings. At the provincial level there is the Provincial Department of Welfare, the Workmen's Compensation Board, and sometimes manpower or training departments. And at the municipal level there are the municipal welfare offices and many voluntary agencies. Somehow the poor citizen is expected to coordinate all of these bureaucracies if he is to resolve the problems with which he is confronted—a degree of coordination which even governments themselves have been unable to achieve.[62]

The lack of coordination not only causes problems for individual Canadians, but it also generates endless friction and conflict between governments, as policy shifts at one level complicate life at other levels. Given the relative weight of the two senior levels of government in this field, conflict usually results from federal waves rocking provincial boats. The role of social assistance, and to a lesser extent, the various provincial supplements, as the residual element in the income security system leaves them particularly vulnerable to changes in other parts of the system. Any income that social assistance recipients receive from other welfare programs is normally taken into account when calculating their benefits; and consequently a sudden shift in one of the major income security programs operated by the federal government can necessitate rapid, complex, and often controversial adjustments in provincial benefits. Underpayments, overpayments, confused beneficiaries, angry legislators: these are often the provincial reverberations of federal initiatives.

In the last decade, major conflicts over coordination of income security have erupted in two areas, Family Allowances and Unemployment Insurance. Conflict over Family Allowance between the federal government and the government of Quebec has simmered away since the initial implementation of the benefits in 1944, but it resurfaced with a vengeance in 1968-73, largely in the form of a fight over the power of *planification*. In keeping with a pervasive trend towards wider state planning and rationalization in many aspects of Quebec life during the 1960s, the Quebec government, and especially its forceful minister of Social Affairs, Claude Castonguay, wished to reorganize all social programs in Quebec into a *single, integrated system* of income support. The need for such integration had been a dominant theme of Quebec's Commission on Social Welfare, which Castonguay himself had originally headed,[63] but the goal seemed impossible, as long as key programs, such as Family Allowances, were controlled by the federal government. Quebec's anxiety was considerably increased in 1970 when Ottawa proposed to change Family Allowances into a Family Income Security Plan (FISP), which would have been even less compatible with Castonguay's elaborate plan. As a result, Quebec launched a campaign to wrest control of Family Allowances out of federal hands. The battle quickly assumed much broader constitutional importance, as Quebec chose to make income security its major demand in the negotiations leading up to the Victoria Conference, and it was only after the collapse of the broader constitutional package that a separate compromise was reached, whereby provinces can alter the configuration of federal Family Allowance payments within their borders.[64] But, whatever the uses made of the issue at Victoria, the origins of the conflict lay in the inevitable tension between the logic of planning and the logic of federalism.

The history of Unemployment Insurance is equally instructive. The relationship between Unemployment Insurance and provincial social assistance programs has always been fraught with administrative tensions. Provincial governments, for example, insist that many people who are waiting for their first Unemployment Insurance cheque are forced to turn to them, with the inevitable result of duplication of payments, unnecessary complications in assessing benefits, and many cases of hardship. Provinces are entitled to reclaim duplicate payments from the Unemployment Insurance Commission, but they insist that only a small proportion of overpayments are ever recovered in this way.[65] Such administrative tensions are inevitable when two separate income-maintenance programs are providing assistance to the same target group, but the ongoing frustrations exploded in 1976-78 when the federal government announced a succession of major cutbacks in Unemployment Insurance. Provincial governments feared that the proposed cutbacks would simply transfer much of the cost of relief from the federal program to social assistance, raising their costs by millions, and they protested vigorously. The first phase of the battle, over the lengthening of the eligibility requirement from eight to twelve weeks of employment, was fought passionately by Atlantic MPs in particular, but with a strong chorus of support from provincial governments; and in the end the government compromised by introducing the regionally varied entrance requirement, ranging from ten to fourteen weeks, depending on local unemployment rates. (Even then, the government had to introduce closure in April 1977 in order to fend off parliamentary criticism, largely from its own back-benches.)[66]

But in September 1978, when the federal government proposed further restrictions that would make eligibility more difficult for seasonal workers and repeating claimants, the provincial governments emerged even more forcefully, under the leadership of New Brunswick and British Columbia. The provincial governments utilized every channel available to them: they protested directly to the federal minister and cabinet; they utilized the network of federal-provincial meetings, both at the official and the ministerial level, and in both the manpower and welfare fields; they carried their opposition to the public and the media. The federal minister of Manpower tried to insist that fewer than 5 percent of those cut off Unemployment Insurance ended up on welfare rolls,[67] but provinces were not mollified, and federal figures did predict a total increase in the cost of social assistance of some $55 million.[68]

Recognizing that cuts in Unemployment Insurance were inevitable, given the prevailing public mood, the provinces developed a consensus on an alternative approach, which would have had less serious implications for social assistance caseloads. Essentially the provinces, with the support of at least some Atlantic MPs, proposed a "family approach" to Unemployment Insurance: a family income test to stop second-income earners from receiving benefits while another family member earned a healthy salary, or at least a lower benefit level for single earners with no dependents and second-income earners.[69] While this position was presented as an issue of basic equity by some, its prime attraction to provincial governments was that it would swell local welfare rolls less than the federal proposals. In the end, while making a number of minor concessions, the federal cabinet rejected the "provincial option," as it came to be called. The provinces did continue to protest, even to the point of presenting their alternative to the committee of the House of Commons that was considering the legislation, and calling upon Atlantic area cabinet ministers, in particular, to do their duty.[70] Although their appeals failed, the extent to which provincial governments sought to force their way into the federal policy process during consideration of an exclusively federal program stands as a visible symbol of the coordination tensions inherent in the federal division of welfare.

Provincial resentment of federal unilateralism peaked in 1978, and led to the appointment of an interprovincial task force to examine the complexity of the income security system. Its report, published in 1980, highlighted the

continuing series of provincial adjustments to federal changes during the
1970s; in addition to the repeated shifts in Unemployment Insurance, provincial welfare authorities had to cope with four changes in Family Allowances, the introduction of the Child Tax Credit, and finally the enrichment
of the Guaranteed Income Supplement. "Within the provinces," the report
concluded, "considerable time and effort have been devoted recently to
reacting to federal initiatives," with the inevitable consequence that less
time was available for improving social assistance itself.[71] But the authors
could see no solution to this tension. Since "there is no agreement on what
level of government should co-ordinate and integrate social security programmes," they could only recommend that "future reforms should be
undertaken with sensitivity to their consequences within the whole
system."[72] The history of federal-provincial relations offers scant reassurance to such pious hopes.

　　Yet federalism alone is not responsible for all of Canada's coordination
problems. Tensions would exist between social assistance and other income
security programs even if they were all operated by the same level of
government. Changes in the British National Insurance and Child Benefit
programs, for example, necessitate similar adjustments in their social assistance system, which is called Supplementary Benefits. Because all income
security is operated by the central government, administrators of Supplementary Benefits are perhaps caught off guard less often, and may be able
to exert greater influence over the timing of changes in other programs than
their counterparts in the provincial welfare departments in this country. But
the essential adjustment dynamic is similar. Indeed, one of the biggest
differences may be that administrators of the British Supplementary Benefits must suffer in silence, while provincial officials and ministers can
protest in public.

　　More generally, concentrating all income security at one level of government does not guarantee a fully integrated system. Any cabinet government
can be thought of as a quasi-federal system in itself, composed of major
departments of state, each led by an ambitious political head and each
jealous of its jurisdiction. Coordination across interdepartmental boundaries can be every bit as difficult as coordination across governmental ones.
Again the Social Security Review provides a classic example. One of the
prime reasons for launching the review was to solve the lack of coordination in our "patchwork quilt" of programs, according to the federal government's position paper.[73] Yet this goal was doomed from the outset by interdepartmental barriers at both levels. Critical income-related programs that
did not fall under the immediate jurisdiction of welfare ministers, such as
Unemployment Insurance, taxation, Workmen's Compensation, and minimum wage laws, were simply not "on the table" for discussion and inclusion
in an integrated system.[74] Comprehensive coordination proved a chimerical
goal even before the first federal-provincial meeting.

Perhaps the best evidence that those who yearn for the apparent simplicity of a single locus of jurisdiction are deceived comes from the response of the British government to the problems of poverty in the 1960s and 1970s. There was never any single, coordinated response to the problem, and each department developed its own policies to assist families living on low wages. The result was a proliferation of income-tested benefits: poor people could receive income supplements from the Department of Health and Social Security, free school meals for their children from the Department of Education, rebates on their rents, property taxes, and energy costs from the Department of the Environment, and so on. Each of these programs was politically attractive in its own right, and each was reasonably inexpensive since the benefit was reduced as the recipient's income rose. But the cumulative impact was as dramatic as it was unanticipated. Low-income families could find any increase in their own earnings virtually nullified by the withdrawal of the various benefits; indeed, in theory at least, for some families, an increase in earnings could actually reduce their final standard of living. Well-intentioned but uncoordinated policies have succeeded in creating a "poverty trap."[75]

Given the size and complexity of the modern state, program coordination is always a problem. The additional jurisdictional boundaries do complicate the process even further, but there is no perfect system. Indeed, federalism's primary contribution may be to the visibility of coordination failures. Canadians may be more concerned about coordination precisely because coordination problems are often translated into highly public intergovernmental disputes rather than hidden from view in the privacy of the cabinet room.

FEDERALISM, EXPANSION, AND COORDINATION: A SUMMARY

Canadian experience does confirm the relationship between political centralization and expansion of income security identified in cross-national studies. Federalism has been—and remains—a conservative force in welfare politics. The link between centralization and expansion is weaker than many of the federal government's champions claimed during the middle decades of this century, since provincial responsibility for welfare was not the only, or even the most important, factor inhibiting the growth of income security during the interwar years. But the problems posed by fiscal imbalance and the mobility of capital and labour did complicate attempts to cope with the social needs of the time, and reduced the likelihood that comprehensive social security would have emerged from a steady spread of the "seeds of radicalism" from one part of the country to another. Undoubtedly, some progress would have been made during the 1940s and 1950s, even if the federal system had not been profoundly transformed by war. But the semi-centralized system that did emerge after 1939 generated a larger expansion of income security than Canadians could have expected from the constitutional alternatives confronting them during those critical years.

In the modern era, the link between federalism and expansion has become more complex, since divided jurisdiction today has both a conservative and an expansionist dynamic. Federalism can still jeopardize the introduction of new programs; and it restrains the growth of the Canada Pension Plan, thereby helping to protect the interests of the private sector in the retirement income field. But during the last two decades this conservative dynamic has been offset in part by the rising political tensions between the federal and provincial governments, particularly the government of Quebec. In this climate of intergovernmental warfare, governments have been inclined to exercise their jurisdiction over income security more extensively, in order to occupy as much of the disputed territory as possible. As a result, federalism today probably has only a modestly depressing impact on Canada's overall commitment to income security.

The same forces that have made federalism's impact on welfare *expansion* more ambiguous have, at the same time, made its impact on welfare *co-ordination* more visible. The rising tensions between federal and provincial programs in recent years have been the product of two trends. First, the pace of change and experimentation in income security has quickened, as governments at both levels have sought to diversify their programs with new supplements and credits at the same time as they have been under pressure to tailor other programs to a harsher economic environment. Second, while the pace of change has accelerated, bureaucratic and political tolerance for the coordination problems that change inevitably creates has been declining. Increasing sophistication of social policy planners has raised bureaucratic expectations about systematic integration and coordination in income security; and the rising political tensions in Confederation generally have occasionally tempted politicians to escalate program rivalries into intergovernmental battles of the first order. But these coordination problems, while real, must be kept firmly in perspective. Coordination is a problem in all modern states, unitary and federal alike. In the Canadian case, federalism undoubtedly adds to the difficulties. But to a large extent federalism itself is responsible for its image as the primary culprit in this area. The politics of executive federalism focus the full glare of government and public attention on *intergovernmental* coordination failures. In comparison, *intragovernmental* failures languish in the twilight of cabinet discretion.

6 Centralization and Redistribution

Redistribution lies at the heart of modern politics. Virtually all public policies alter the distribution of the nation's product in some way, and political conflict in modern societies largely revolves around the extent to which, and the way in which, redistribution should be carried out. Income security is one important focus in this battle, and here again the institutional framework of government can have important consequences, both for the definition of redistributive goals and for the actual redistributive impact of income security. In the Canadian case, however, the influence of federal institutions on redistribution has been the subject of much misleading discussion. Contrary to conventional wisdom among students of Canadian politics, federalism has not significantly altered Canadian redistributive goals, and has not diverted significant resources away from redistribution between individuals through the income security system. Rather, the much more important consequence of federalism concerns the actual redistributive impact of income security. The centralization of responsibility for income security has not only increased the overall size of the system that has emerged over the last generation; it has also transformed income security into a major instrument of inter-regional redistribution, equal in importance to the equalization grant system.

The Definition of Redistributive Goals

A persistent structure of inequality exists in every industrial nation, and in this Canada is no exception. Subject to the problems always inherent in making such international comparisons, Canada seems to fall mid-way between the OECD nations with the most, and those with the least, unequal distribution of incomes.[1] In addition, this particular distribution has proved

Table 16 Distribution of Income of Families and Unattached Individuals, by Quintiles, 1951-78

	1951	1957	1961	1965 (percent)	1969	1973	1976	1978
Lowest quintile	4.4	4.2	4.2	4.4	4.3	3.9	4.3	4.1
Second quintile	11.2	11.9	11.9	11.8	11.0	10.8	10.7	10.4
Third quintile	18.3	18.0	18.3	18.0	17.6	17.7	17.4	17.6
Fourth quintile	23.3	24.5	24.5	24.5	24.5	25.2	24.7	25.2
Highest quintile	42.8	41.4	41.1	41.4	42.6	42.4	42.9	42.7

Source: Statistics Canada, Income Distribution by Size in Canada (Ottawa: Minister of Supply and Services, various years). The data for 1951 through 1961 are for non-farm units only. The data for 1965 and later years are for farm and non-farm families.

remarkably stable over the last quarter century; as Table 16 reveals, there has been no significant narrowing of the spread between the upper and lower income groups.[2] Since the figures reported in this table include transfer income derived from welfare payments, the expansion of income security expenditures as a proportion of GNP has hardly been the harbinger of an ever more equal society, as many had hoped or feared, as the case may be. Clearly this must rank as one of the great social phenomena of the post-war era. Despite major changes in the structure of the economy and a major expansion of the role of the state, with public expenditures reaching more than 40 percent of GNP in the late 1970s, the distribution of income has changed marginally, if at all. Moreover, this basic pattern is repeated in a variety of other western industrial nations, such as the United States and Britain.[3]

The sheer facts of inequality do not, however, determine the way in which they will be perceived and defined in political life.[4] Nations with similar levels of inequality often differ markedly in which dimensions of that inequality are considered illegitimate, and therefore defined as social problems to be reduced or eliminated through redistributive instruments. In many western nations, controversy over inequality centres on the distribution of the nation's wealth between social classes, but in Canada, this conception of the social problems of industrial society is supplemented by controversy over the distribution of income, wealth, and opportunity among different regions and between the two major language groups. In Canada the inequalities revealed in Table 17 are often considered as salient in political terms as those in Table 16, and an impressive array of initiatives are geared to equalizing regional incomes through economic assistance to depressed regions and equalization payments to the governments of poor provinces.*

This intermingling of redistributive goals in Canada is neatly illustrated by debate over the role of the Department of Regional Economic Expansion (DREE). In 1972, for example, the DREE minister, Jean Marchand, insisted on the need for expanding his department's efforts "so that, in time, the great inequalities in wealth and opportunity which have persisted in this country for so long will be greatly reduced"; and later his colleague, John Turner, then minister of Finance, expressed the same conception of inequality when he told the House of Commons that "the reduction of regional disparities—or better put, the growing equality of economic opportunity—has been a high priority of this government."[5] More is at stake here than a choice of language,[6] for there is a major difference between the goals

---

* Interestingly, while inequality between income classes has remained frustratingly stable, the calculations of standard deviation at the foot of Table 17 suggest a moderate decline in the extent of regional inequality over the last fifteen years.

Table 17   *Index of Per Capita Personal Income, by Province, 1964-78*

(Canada = 100)

	1964	1968	1972	1976	1978
Newfoundland	57	61	64	68	66
P.E.I.	61	64	66	69	69
Nova Scotia	76	77	80	79	80
New Brunswick	68	70	74	75	74
Quebec	90	89	90	93	95
Ontario	117	117	116	109	109
Manitoba	96	97	94	94	93
Saskatchewan	85	85	79	100	92
Alberta	96	100	98	103	104
B.C.	113	108	109	109	109
CANADA	100	100	100	100	100
Standard Deviation	7.6	7.0	6.7	5.7	5.9

Source: Calculated from data in Statistics Canada, *National Income and Expenditure Accounts 1964-1978*, Table 36.

of equalization among regions and equalization among individuals. Although poorer regions do have a somewhat higher proportion of poor people in their populations, Table 18 suggests that perhaps a majority of poor Canadians live in the three richest provinces, Ontario, Alberta, and British Columbia. As a result, the reduction of regional disparities is a very different objective from the elimination of poverty. Indeed, one analysis of the redistributive impact of DREE, to take one example, concluded that:

> . . . the lower income classes benefit to a much lesser extent from DREE expenditures than would be expected from the policy objectives of the program. The richest *tenth* of family units receive about the same total benefits as do the lowest *half* of family units . . . . In all regions the relative economic position of the poor would improve much more with increased federal transfers to persons (perhaps in the form of a guaranteed annual income) than it does with the existing DREE program.[7]

Clearly, the relative priority of these two redistributive goals is critical to the impact of Canadian public policy, and it is now conventional wisdom among students of federalism that the structure of Canadian institutions ensures that territorial claims will predominate in redistributive battles. The regionalized nature of Canadian institutions, they argue, channels reformist

Table 18   *Low Income in Canada, 1978*

Region	Regional Incidence of Low Income		Distribution of Low-income Units	
	Families	Unattached Individuals	Families	Unattached Individuals
		(percent)		
Atlantic Provinces	14.5	41.8	12.4	8.5
Quebec	12.0	36.4	31.1	24.5
Ontario	8.8	34.9	31.4	36.1
Prairie Provinces	10.2	33.0	16.4	17.9
B.C.	8.3	31.6	8.8	13.0
CANADA	10.3	34.9	100.0	100.0

Note: Regional incidence of low income measures low-income families and individuals as a proportion of all families and individuals in each region. Distribution of low-income units measure the proportion of all low-income units that lives in each of the various regions.

Source: Statistics Canada, *Income Distribution by Size in Canada: 1978.*

energies and social expenditure into regional programs, energies and money that otherwise might well be devoted to interpersonal redistribution through the income security system. Alan Cairns, for example, argues that our institutions focus attention on regions rather than classes, with the result that "the poverty of the Maritimes has occupied an honourable place in the foreground of public discussion," while "the diffuse poverty of the generally underprivileged has scarcely been noticed."[8] Similarly, Canadian institutions, according to Simeon, ensure that "policy-making will focus primarily on the territorial dimension. Thus discussion of poverty tends to be transmuted into the problem of regional disparities."[9] Moore concludes that "the federal form of government is an historical misfortune" that has diverted redistributive efforts from standard conceptions of social equity.[10] And when Smiley asks "Why is Ottawa so much more preoccupied with the reduction of regional economic disparities than with redistributive measure on an interpersonal basis?", he finds the answer in the federal structure, which:

> . . . "organizes into politics" the interests of governments and those private groupings which are territorially concentrated . . . .

One of the results of the continuing conflicts between Ottawa and
the provinces is to displace other conflicts among Canadians,
particularly those between the relatively advantaged and those
who are less so. So long as the major cleavages are between
governments, inequalities *within* the provinces are buttressed.[11]

Such examples could be multiplied almost endlessly.[12]

In fact, however, the evidence of actual expenditure patterns suggests
that our federal institutions have *not* diverted an unusually large share of
resources in this way. In the first place, there is no reason to assume that a
unitary system of government would devote any less effort to inter-regional
redistribution. MPs in unitary governments still have a political incentive to
appeal to depressed regions through special development schemes, and
comparative evidence confirms that they do so. Despite the alleged sensitivity of our institutions to territorially-based claims, Canadian efforts to
reduce differentials in regional incomes are not especially impressive in
international terms; as a proportion of GDP, spending on regional development programs in the early 1970s, for example, fell behind that even of
Great Britain, a country with a unitary system of government and a class-
based politics.[13] The Canadian system of equalization payments is
undoubtedly an important component of intergovernmental fiscal relations,
but these grants are large precisely because the federation is relatively
decentralized. More centralized governments produce the same inter-
regional transfers automatically through national programs that provide
uniform standards of public services in rich and poor regions alike. Again
Great Britain provides an example, as Table 19 reveals.[14]

In the second place, despite the regionalized nature of its institutions,
Canada still devotes vastly more of its resources to income security than to
programs designed explicitly to alleviate regional disparities. In 1977-78 the
federal government budgeted about $4 billion for equalization grants,
DREE, and Oil Import Compensation. In the same year the federal government allocations for social welfare programs of all kinds amounted to over
$15 billion; and if the proper comparison is with all social policies, includ-
ing health care, the federal total was well over $21 billion.[15] Admittedly,
there is a variety of additional inter-regional transfers built into other
federal-provincial programs, but the point remains. The welfare state is a
much greater spending priority for Canadian governments than is regional
equality.

There is nothing incompatible between regionalism, federal institutions,
and priority for interpersonal redistribution through income security.
People in deprived regions who look to redistributive instruments in order
to raise their incomes, or those of people in their community, do not look
solely—or even primarily—to DREE and equalization grants. They also

Table 19   *Inter-regional Redistribution through Government Programs, United Kingdom, 1964*

Region	Relative GDP per head	Beneficial Government Expenditures minus Tax Receipts
	Percentage of UK figure	£ per head
South East	113	−39
West Midlands	109	−22
Yorkshire and Humberside	99	+13
North West	98	+ 5
East Midlands	98	+14
South West	88	+25
Wales	88	+45
East Anglia	87	+37
Scotland	86	+32
North	85	+31
Northern Ireland	66	+82

Source: Great Britain, Commission on the Constitution, Research Paper (10), *Financial and Economic Aspects of Regionalism and Separatism,* Table 35.

look to interpersonal redistribution through income security. As will be seen in more detail in chapter eight, support for welfare and income redistribution between income classes is somewhat higher in low-income regions, such as Quebec and Atlantic Canada, than elsewhere; and, more revealing, Atlantic Canadians and Quebecers give greater support to proposals to expand help for the poor and the elderly than they give to expanded efforts to reduce regional inequality. To some extent the income security policies of the federal government represent a compromise, not only between the interests of high and low-income Canadians, but also between high and low-income regions. Regionalism not only focuses effort on regional development; it also feeds into the welfare debate in Canada, reinforcing the priority of interpersonal redistribution.

Centralization and the Redistributive Impact

While federal institutions have not altered the balance between redistributive goals in Canada, they have had a tremendous impact on the actual redistributive consequences of income security. The expansion of the federal role in this field may not have resulted in welfare policies that are powerfully redistributive between income classes, as a growing body of evidence now confirms.[16] But centralization has had a dramatic impact on the distribution of income security benefits among the various regions of the country. The establishment of national programs that provide equal benefits for all Canadians, together with the expansion of shared-cost schemes that help finance provincial welfare programs, have resulted in large, hidden transfers of income between rich and poor areas of Canada. In effect, Canadian political institutions have tended to help poor regions, not by channeling an unusually large proportion of national resources into special regional programs, but by transforming the income security into a powerful instrument of inter-regional redistribution.

Once again the consequences of federal action in income security can best be appreciated against the backdrop of interwar experience. The most striking feature of the welfare programs that did exist at that time was the sharp variations in the scope and generosity of coverage between regions. Undoubtedly the municipal basis of relief exacerbated the problem, as provision varied enormously even *within* individual provinces. Municipalities differed in their eligibility rules; some smaller municipalities either gave no relief or very inadequate relief; and all municipalities varied widely in the amount of food, clothing, fuel, shelter, and medical care provided.[17] Local responsibility also resulted in gross maldistribution of the financial burdens of coping with mass unemployment during the depression. Urban and metropolitan communities, which comprised 32 percent of the total population, faced 75 percent of the total direct relief costs for all of Canada; and as the Rowell-Sirois Commission noted, "exclusive residential suburban municipalities escaped with virtually no additional relief burdens" while "working-class municipalities, on the other hand, in many cases became completely bankrupt."[18] But the financial burden would have been distorted even if provincial governments had taken over unemployment relief completely from their municipalities:

> The costs of relief varied inversely with the ability to meet them. In Western Canada where incomes fell most rapidly, relief costs were relatively the highest. The weight of the burden in Saskatchewan, the province most severely affected, was about five times as great as that in the Maritimes and Ontario, the provinces least affected.[19]

Although unemployment relief highlighted the disparities most dramatically, significant variations also existed in other benefits provided by provincial governments. Mothers' Allowances are the best measure here, since they were financed from provincial revenues and, as Table 20 reveals, average benefits in the seven provinces that had such a program in 1942

Table 20   *Average Monthly Benefit Levels under Provincial Programs,*
            1938-49

	Mothers Allowances	Blind Pensions	Old Age Pensions	
	1942	1938	1938	1949
Prince Edward Island	—	$14.07	$10.63	$34.46
Nova Scotia	$28.55	19.08	14.64	35.33
New Brunswick	—	19.34	13.68	36.01
Quebec	26.64	19.57	17.84	37.63
Ontario	28.91	19.48	18.43	38.05
Manitoba	35.79	18.68	18.66	38.36
Saskatchewan	13.77	19.79	16.45	37.29
Alberta	22.96	—	18.30	37.87
British Columbia	39.19	17.52	19.18	37.26

Sources: A.E. Grauer, *Public Assistance and Social Insurance,* Tables 11 and 25; L. Marsh,
           Report on Social Security for Canada, p. 222; Department of National Health and
           Welfare, "Canada's Old Age Pension Program," Joint Committee of the Senate and
           House of Commons on Old Age Security, *Minutes of Evidence* (1950), Chart E.

varied from $39.77 in British Columbia to $13.19 in Saskatchewan, a ratio
of almost three to one. In contrast, the impact of federal involvement in
income security was already apparent in the case of pensions for the blind
and the elderly. The federal government shared the costs of these programs,
and set a maximum shareable benefit level for each, with the result that
variation in average benefit levels was much less and, in the case of
pensions, declined significantly between 1938 and 1949.

The postwar expansion in the federal role reduced variation in benefits
available to citizens of different regions in two ways: the establishment of
national programs with uniform standards across the country, and the
sharing of the costs of provincial social assistance programs. In both cases,
reduction in regional variations has required inter-regional transfers of
income, increasingly from rich to poor regions.

National Programs. A graphic demonstration of the consequences of
transferring an income security function from provincial to federal jurisdiction took place on January 1, 1952. On that date, the federal Old Age
Security came into effect, paying a uniform pension of $40 a month to every
citizen aged seventy or over, and replacing the different pension benefits
that had existed in the provinces. This standardization was not simply the
consequence of replacing means-tested pensions with a demogrant; if the
provinces had paid universal pensions, the levels would have undoubtedly

varied from one province to another. Rather, the most powerful source of standardization was the intense political pressure on the federal government to treat citizens in all regions equally. In the same way, other federal income security programs provide equal treatment across the country. It is true that in the last few years, slightly greater regional variation has crept into some programs. There is the provision for limited variation in the distribution of Family Allowances, but *average* benefits do remain equal in all provinces. More important, Unemployment Insurance was amended in ways that have particular relevance in poorer regions. Coverage has been extended to self-employed fishermen, the only category of self-employment so covered, and unemployment benefits constitute an important supplementary source of income in fishing communities in Atlantic Canada.[20] More recently, the program was amended to provide regional variation in both eligibility and benefit periods; since 1977 claimants in areas of high unemployment can receive benefit after fewer weeks of employment, and can then remain on benefit for substantially longer than claimants in areas with low unemployment. Thus, unemployment insurance stands out as a regionalized federal income-security program. Otherwise federal programs provide uniform benefit conditions across the country.

The consequence of uniform benefits under programs such as OAS-GIS and Family Allowance is, of course, that the benefits are "worth" more in relation to local living standards in some regions than others. In effect, federal programs bring rich and poor closer together in poor regions than they do in richer ones. As Table 21 indicates, Family Allowances represent a

Table 21   *Family Allowances and OAS-GIS Related to Regional Living Standards, 1974*

	Average Monthly Family Allowance Payment Related to Average Monthly Family Income	OAS-GIS Level Related to Per Capita Personal Income
	(percent)	
Atlantic Provinces	5.0	64.3
Quebec	3.7	51.8
Ontario	3.2	39.8
Prairie Provinces	3.7	47.3
British Columbia	3.3	42.1
CANADA	3.5	45.9

Sources: Statistics Canada, *Social Security: National Programs 1976*, pp. 566-68; and *Social Security: National Programs 1978*, pp. 512-13.

higher percentage of average family income in poorer regions than richer ones, and pensioners in Atlantic Canada are guaranteed almost two-thirds of per capita income in their region, whereas Ontario pensioners are guaranteed less than two-fifths of per capita income in theirs. Undoubtedly this latter set of figures goes a long way towards explaining why provincial governments in Ontario and the four western provinces all provide additional supplements for needy pensioners, whereas in the half of Canada east of the Ottawa River only Nova Scotia does so.

Interestingly, in the 1930s uniformity of benefits was considered a serious drawback to an expanded federal role in income security. In a background study prepared for the Rowell-Sirois Commission, Esdras Minville argued that if the federal government provided unemployment relief with uniform benefits across the country, people living in regions with higher living standards "would probably complain about insufficiency," while those in regions with lower living standards "would be inclined to settle down on relief."[21] Another background study, prepared by A.E. Grauer, was equally worried that ". . . if the Dominion had sole authority over old age pensions, it might find it impossible for political reasons to maintain the differences between average pensions in provinces that exist at the present time because of differences in regional costs of living."[22] Provinces such as British Columbia, which in the late 1930s "had no serious rival to its claim for pre-eminence among the provinces in social welfare,"[23] feared that uniform federal programs would have a levelling effect and, not surprisingly, the B.C. brief to the Rowell-Sirois Commission recommended that, with the exception of unemployment relief, social welfare be left to the provinces, with the federal role limited to research and grants-in-aid.[24]

The prognosis of the 1930s proved correct. When the new federal pensions came into effect in 1951, for example, no serious consideration was given to adjusting the benefit levels to regional costs of living, with the result that their real value varied from region to region.[25] Despite occasional complaints, such as that of the Tremblay Commission, that "too great uniformity can only engender inequalities,"[26] the political pressures on the federal government to provide equal benefits to citizens in all regions have proven irresistible.[27] As one official explained: "Suggestions for regional differentials have emerged from time to time, but they have always been slapped down almost immediately. There is a general abhorrence of the idea. The federal government has to treat all its citizens equally." Only in the case of Unemployment Insurance has this principle been seriously abridged, and only for qualification requirements rather than actual benefit levels.

Social Assistance and Conditional Grants. The growth of federal transfers to provincial governments in the form of conditional grants and equalization payments has been a critical factor in equalizing the capacity of provinces to provide public services, including social assistance. As Simeon and Miller have argued, such transfers break the bond between the strength of a provincial economy and its access to public revenues, and have made possible a substantial convergence in the spending patterns of Canadian provinces.[28] Provincial social assistance programs reveal this pattern clearly. Prior to the introduction of the Unemployment Assistance Act in 1956, relief provisions varied enormously across the country. While the western provinces had already pioneered general social assistance for those in need, Atlantic Canada continued to rely on a grim legacy of poor laws and local responsibility, and in Quebec relief payments were still largely the responsibility of the Church, although its welfare role was financially supported by the provincial government.[29] But since the establishment of federal conditional grants, especially the 1956 Unemployment Assistance Act, provinces across the country have adopted much more similar social assistance programs. Provinces in which there had been no general social assistance programs began such services; more provinces imposed common standards with respect to benefits and administration on their municipalities; and some provinces even began to assume direct responsibility for the operation of social assistance, relieving municipalities of their welfare role, either in whole or in part.[30] This general impact was accentuated by the 1966 Canada Assistance Plan (CAP), which consolidated and expanded existing conditional grants in this field.

More important in this context, provincial social assistance benefits are now far more uniform. During the formulation of the Canada Assistance Plan, key officials in National Health and Welfare wanted to include a provision for reviewing and influencing provincial benefit levels, but they were defeated by a powerful alliance of the provinces, the Department of Finance, and the Privy Council Office.[31] Despite this, however, real per capita expenditure on social welfare by the provinces has converged steadily since the mid-1950s; as Table 22 shows, the ratio of the top spending province to the lowest has declined from 3:1 in 1957 to about 2:1 in 1972. This is not simply the product of changes in relative numbers of recipients, as the basic levels of social assistance have become more uniform. Indeed, these benefit levels are now much more uniform than those in the United States. As the U.S. Advisory Commission on Inter-governmental Relations commented in 1971, "the difference between the high-paying and low-paying Provinces under the Canada Assistance Plan are generally in the range of 1.5 to 1 using their monthly budget standards as the basis of comparison. This contrasts to the ratio of 6 to 1 among the states—four times the Canadian divergence."[32] While the remaining differences in provincial welfare standards are undoubtedly important, the overall pattern is clearly one of convergence, and the growth of intergovern-

Table 22 *Ranking by Province of Real Per Capita Expenditures on Social Welfare*

($ / person)

1957		1962		1967		1972	
Nfld.	34	Nfld.	52	Nfld.	102	Que.	134
B.C.	27	Que.	44	P.E.I.	90	Nfld.	107
Que.	25	B.C.	39	Que.	85	Alta.	92
Sask.	23	Sask.	34	Alta.	68	*Average*	90
Average	19	*Average*	33	*Average*	63	B.C.	90
Alta.	17	Alta.	33	B.C.	61	P.E.I.	90
N.B.	16	P.E.I.	31	Sask.	46	Man.	88
Man.	14	Man.	28	N.S.	46	Sask.	84
P.E.I.	14	N.B.	25	Ont.	44	N.B.	84
N.S.	13	N.S.	22	N.B.	43	Ont.	70
Ont.	11	Ont.	19	Man.	40	N.S.	63

Source: R. Simeon and R. Miller, "Regional Variations in Public Policy," in D.J. Elkins and R. Simeon, *Small Worlds*, p. 258.

mental transfers through the Canada Assistance Plan and the equalization grant system is critical to this trend.

The Canada Assistance Plan has also been an instrument of greater uniformity at the provincial level in several other ways as well. CAP is a relatively flexible instrument, with few strings attached to the federal contribution, but two conditions that were included in the legislation have been influential. The first of these requires each province to establish formal appeal procedures for dissatisfied welfare recipients. Prior to 1966 few provinces had such procedures in place and, even after the establishment of the legal requirement in the CAP legislation, progress was slower than expected, leading the National Council of Welfare and a number of client groups to attack the federal government for not threatening to cut off funds to tardy governments.[33] Nevertheless, despite slow and occasionally half-hearted efforts at the provincial level, appeal procedures are now common, and CAP has been critical to the progress that has been made.

The impact of the second CAP condition, which forbids residency requirements for social assistance, has been more decisive. The history of residency requirements in Canada highlights an important difference between the policy implications of ten provincial welfare systems, on one hand, and one national one on the other. With provincial welfare programs, every indigent entering the province represents an increase in provincial welfare costs, and each province therefore has a clear vested interest in a requirement that restricts benefits to those who have been resident in the province for some specified time. With a federal welfare program, however, interprovincial migration does not represent an increase in costs, and the federal government can afford the luxury of dispensing with such restrictions domestically, although it does face a parallel temptation to restrict access to welfare by recent immigrants from other countries.

Residency requirements for welfare were the norm in Canada throughout the period of exclusive municipal and provincial responsibility. Such requirements were stiffened dramatically during the depression, as municipalities sought to avoid all responsibility for migrants, and "destitute families unable to qualify for residence in a municipality were virtually left to starve, except as assisted by private charity, or were shipped back to their former place of residence."[34] Transient males in search of employment in particular were treated as potentially dangerous vagrants and forced to move on. Some provinces objected strongly to this interprovincial shifting of the welfare burden, and British Columbia, which continually protested that its climate was attracting thousands of transients from the prairies, took a leading role in demanding that the federal government act to co-ordinate residency conditions.[35] Such requirements remained a problem well into the 1950s. A few provinces did develop interprovincial agreements, according to which any welfare paid to a migrant was recoverable from his previous province of residence, but the scope for such accords was severely curtailed by the great variability in the length of residency requirements and by the role played by municipalities in welfare administration in many provinces. Yet as late as 1952 a study prepared for the Canadian Welfare Council could see no better solution than greater uniformity of residence periods, as a first step to more interprovincial accords.[36]

The expanding federal role changed all that. The Unemployment Assistance Act of 1956 stipulated that length of residence could not be a condition of the receipt of assistance, although the rule was never fully enforced and residence qualifications did remain part of many provincial welfare statutes. The prohibition of such tests by CAP, however, was more effective, despite the continued protests of some provinces. British Columbia, which traditionally has one of the highest rates of net in-migration[37] and still believes that a significant portion of its caseload consists of recent arrivals, did resist amending its legislation for some time, and demanded a special "portability grant" as compensation for its additional burdens. But, in practice, B.C. stopped enforcing residency requirements in 1966.[38] The prohibition, it should be noted, does not apply to CAP contributions to *social services* for the needy, and residency requirements remain the norm in public housing, residential care for the elderly, day care, and home-maker services.[39] But in social assistance at least, federal intervention has largely eliminated such tests.

Indeed, the only major residency requirement in the entire income security system is a federal one, aimed at immigrants from abroad. Until recently, the residency requirement for Old Age Security was straight-forward: an individual had to have been a resident for ten years before qualifying. In 1977, however, the requirement was made more complex and more stringent. Even though the last pretense that OAS has a contributory basis was swept away in 1975 when the special fund was eliminated, the full benefit must now be "earned" through forty years of residence in Canada. The minimum requirement of ten years remains in force. But new pensioners who have been here for more than ten but less than forty years receive only a partial benefit, calculated in strict proportion to the length of their residence (one-fortieth of full pension for every year in Canada). Under these new rules, many immigrants who are middle-aged when they come to this country will never receive a full OAS payment. Clearly, on the question of residency requirements, the federal government is not always as tough on itself as it is on its provincial counterparts.

Inter-regional Redistribution: Winners and Losers. National income security programs redistribute income between regions whenever greater proportions of elderly, unemployed or needy people, or children, are found in some regions than in others, or whenever revenues to finance those programs are raised disproportionately from different regions. Both of these conditions are met in Canada and, as a result, the centralization of responsi-bility for income security in the postwar period has transformed it into a major instrument of inter-regional redistribution, equal in importance to the much more publicized equalization grants.

Table 23 shows the beneficiaries of federal programs as a percentage of provincial populations. Clearly, the pattern varies with the type of income security program. The number of recipients of demogrants, such as Old Age Security and Family Allowance, varies with the demographic profile of each provincial population, rather than regional income levels. As a result, while the three Maritime provinces have above average proportions of recipients in both programs, Quebec is below the national average in both, and New-foundland displays a conflicting pattern, with the lowest proportion of OAS beneficiaries but the highest proportion of Family Allowance benefi-ciaries. The Canada and Quebec Pension plans reveal a similar pattern and, so far at least, there is relatively little variation in the proportions of provin-cial populations benefiting from them. On the other hand, programs that are need-related, such as the Guaranteed Income Supplement, Unemploy-ment Insurance, and the Canada Assistance Plan, distribute their benefits much differently. Atlantic Canada and Quebec have above average propor-tions of recipients of each of these three programs; indeed, the only major anomaly here is British Columbia which, despite high average income, also has significant unemployment and social assistance caseloads.

Table 23 Beneficiaries of Federal Income Security Programs as a Proportion of Population: Canada and Provinces, 1976

	Old Age Security	Guaranteed Income Supplement	Canada/Quebec Pension Plans	Family Allowances[a]	Unemployment Insurance[b]	Canada Assistance Plan
				(percent)		
Newfoundland	7.0	5.3	3.0	40.5	9.3	12.2
P.E.I.	11.8	8.4	4.9	34.8	8.1	8.7
Nova Scotia	10.0	6.4	5.4	33.3	5.7	7.4
New Brunswick	9.2	5.9	4.4	35.1	7.8	8.7
Quebec	7.9	4.8	3.8	31.5	5.6	7.7
Ontario	8.8	4.1	4.8	30.9	3.6	5.1
Manitoba	10.6	6.1	5.1	31.9	2.3	6.2
Saskatchewan	11.4	6.2	4.9	33.3	1.9	5.6
Alberta	7.4	4.2	3.7	33.1	1.7	5.2
B.C.	9.6	5.0	4.5	30.1	4.9	7.3
CANADA	8.8	4.7	4.4	31.8	4.4	6.5

a. Based on number of children on whose behalf payments are made.
b. Based on average monthly number of claimants; does not include dependents.

Source: Derived from various tables in Statistics Canada, Social Security: National Programs 1978.

Figure 6 Index of Government Income Security Payments Per Capita, by Region, 1953-78

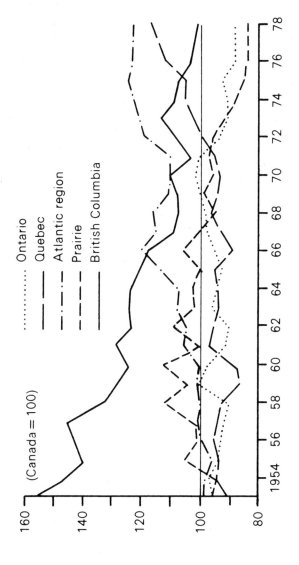

Source: Adapted from Economic Council of Canada, Living Together, Chart 4.3. Index for 1975-78 calculated from data in Statistics
           Canada, National Income and Expenditure Accounts 1964-1978, Table 42.

Total income security payments, which are traced on a per capita basis in Figure 6, show fascinating trends over time. In the 1950s and early 1960s the distribution did not work consistently in an equalizing direction. Atlantic Canadians received below average benefits until the mid-1950s, as did Quebecers until the 1970s; British Columbians, on the other hand, received benefits well above the national average. But in the 1970s, this pattern shifted significantly, with a surge in per capita benefits going to the Atlantic region and Quebec, coinciding with the 1971 revision of Unemployment Insurance. By 1978 the distribution of benefits was compensating for differences in regional incomes in a much more consistent way. Canadians east of the Ottawa River received above average per capita benefits, while those west of the Ottawa received below average, or in the case of British Columbians, average per capita benefits. A breakdown of the same data on a provincial basis for recent years, which is set out in Table 24, shows that only Manitoba and Saskatchewan among the have-not provinces received less than average per capita benefits.

The importance of income security payments in the income structure of different provincial populations can be seen in Table 25. Not only is income security a critical component of total personal income in poor regions, especially Atlantic Canada,[40] but also regional differences in the importance of income security have also grown steadily over the last fifteen years. The difference in the proportion of income derived from welfare between the

Table 24 *Index of Income Security Payments Per Capita, by Province, 1970-78*

	1970	1972	1974	1976	1978
Newfoundland	132	146	151	150	145
P.E.I.	119	123	122	122	121
Nova Scotia	99	108	111	107	110
New Brunswick	105	113	117	119	117
Quebec	93	100	104	113	117
Ontario	102	94	91	89	88
Manitoba	100	97	91	88	87
Saskatchewan	92	95	101	95	94
Alberta	96	98	86	83	84
B.C.	111	108	111	105	100
CANADA	100	100	100	100	100
Standard Deviation	4.1	5.5	6.3	6.5	6.1

Source: Calculated from data in Statistics Canada, *National Income and Expenditure Accounts 1964-1978*, Table 42.

Table 25 *Income Security Payments as a Proportion of Total Personal Income, by Province, 1964-78*

	1964	1968	1972	1976	1978
			(percent)		
Newfoundland	15.6	21.9	27.1	27.6	29.4
P.E.I.	16.4	18.5	22.0	22.2	23.4
Nova Scotia	12.2	13.5	16.1	17.1	18.4
New Brunswick	13.3	15.6	18.2	19.7	20.9
Quebec	8.9	10.6	13.3	15.2	16.5
Ontario	6.9	8.3	9.6	10.2	10.8
Manitoba	9.2	10.0	12.3	11.7	12.5
Saskatchewan	10.4	10.8	14.2	11.9	13.6
Alberta	9.1	9.5	11.8	10.2	10.7
B.C.	9.4	9.8	11.7	12.1	12.2
CANADA	8.5	9.8	11.8	12.5	13.3
Standard Deviation	1.3	1.7	2.0	2.0	2.2

Source: Calculated from data in Statistics Canada, *National Income and Expenditure Accounts 1964-1978*, Tables 35 and 42.

provincial population most dependent on income security and that least dependent doubled between 1964 and 1978. (For the statistically minded, the calculations of standard deviation at the foot of Tables 24 and 25 reveal a similar pattern.) The importance of income security in poorer regions is further enhanced by the inadequacy of private welfare protection there. As Table 26 shows, private pension coverage is much more limited in poorer provinces, primarily because of their dependence on industries such as agriculture and fishing, in which private coverage is weak generally: as Figure 7 shows, the coverage that does exist in Atlantic Canada in particular is heavily concentrated amongst government employees. The balance between the private and the public sectors in income security varies across the country, and in Atlantic Canada, especially, the public sector is critical.

The net inter-regional redistribution through the income security system is set out in Table 27 on a per capita basis. These figures are calculated by subtracting from the benefits paid out in a province the proportion of the revenues gathered in that province, and they reveal that all programs work in a broadly equalizing direction, transferring income from rich to poor provinces. The only partial exception to this pattern is Unemployment Insurance which did not, on balance, transfer funds to Manitoba and Saskatchewan, but did do so to British Columbia. (Manitobans also did not derive net benefits from CAP.) The totals, however, indicate that, overall,

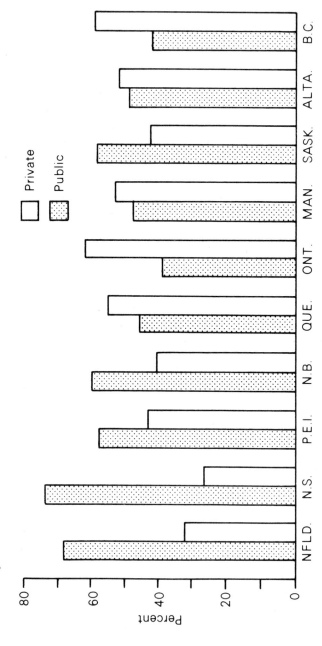

Figure 7 Distribution of Occupational Pension Plan Members Between Public and Private Sectors, by Province, 1978.

Source: Statistics Canada, *Pension Plans in Canada 1978*, p. 16 (as amended in subsequent errata sheet).

Table 26   Membership of Occupational Pension Plans as a Proportion of
            Population, Canada and Provinces, 1970-78

	1970	1974	1976	1978
		(percent)		
Newfoundland	7.4	9.1	9.9	10.3
P.E.I.	7.7	8.9	8.9	9.3
Nova Scotia	12.2	13.4	14.9	15.1
New Brunswick	10.2	11.8	13.2	13.4
Quebec	12.3	15.3	17.3	17.8
Ontario	16.2	18.0	19.0	19.8
Manitoba	12.4	12.8	13.6	16.6
Saskatchewan	9.1	10.6	11.6	12.8
Alberta	11.2	12.8	14.2	15.8
B.C.	11.3	13.6	17.7	19.4
CANADA	13.3	15.3	16.8	17.9

Source: Adapted from Statistics Canada, *Pension Plans in Canada 1976*, Table 2; and
           Pension Plans in Canada 1978, Table 4.

income security is an instrument of greater regional equality.[41] Of course,
even these figures underestimate the full transfer to the economy of each
province, since transfers of this magnitude have important employment-
generating effects. One study of the impact of income maintenance
programs in the three Maritime provinces in the early 1970s concluded that
the unemployment rate in those provinces was reduced, as a result of the
aggregate demand effects of the net transfer, by up to a full percentage
point.[42]

The importance of these net transfers can be emphasized by a comparison
with equalization grants. Table 28 compares the net transfer through
income security with the net transfer through equalization grants, that is,
after deducting the share of the revenues originally gathered in each
province. Clearly, income security is an instrument of inter-regional
redistribution similar in magnitude to equalization grants. Indeed, in
1976-77 federal income security programs transferred more net benefits into
Newfoundland, New Brunswick, Quebec, and Saskatchewan than did
equalization grants; only three have-not provinces derived more net benefit
from the explicit equalization system.

Politically, however, there is an enormous difference between the two
systems. Because inter-regional redistribution through income security is
largely invisible, it is infinitely less controversial than the explicit, visible
transfers involved in equalization grants. Income security has not always
been immune from inter-provincial warfare. The introduction of Family

Table 27 Net Inter-regional Redistribution through Federal Income Security Programs, 1976-77

($ per capita)

	OAS-GIS	Family Allowances	Canada Assistance Plan*	Unemployment Insurance	Total
Newfoundland	64	59	22	233	378
P.E.I.	173	48	15	177	413
Nova Scotia	101	32	6	70	209
New Brunswick	88	37	51	154	330
Quebec	18	11	15	66	110
Ontario	-36	-15	-15	-51	-117
Manitoba	69	12	-8	-67	6
Saskatchewan	92	21	6	-54	65
Alberta	-41	-2	-7	-105	-155
B.C.	-21	-21	-4	7	-39

* General assistance only.

Sources: Calculations for OAS-GIS, Family Allowances and Unemployment Insurance are adapted from unpublished background paper prepared for Task Force on Canadian Unity. Calculations for CAP are based on data for general assistance expenditures in Health and Welfare Canada, *Canada Assistance Plan: Annual Report 1976-1977* (Ottawa: Minister of Supply and Services). Estimates of federal tax incidence by province used throughout are derived from T.J. Courchene, *Refinancing the Canadian Federation*. An unpublished estimate of interprovincial transfers in Unemployment Insurance prepared by Employment and Immigration Canada in 1979 produced results similar to those cited above.

Table 28   Net Inter-Regional Redistribution, 1976-77: Income Security
and Equalization

	Net Income Security Benefits Per Capita	Net Equalization Grant Per Capita
	$	$
Newfoundland	378	364
P.E.I.	413	434
Nova Scotia	209	296
New Brunswick	330	277
Quebec	110	98
Ontario	-117	-111
Manitoba	6	79
Saskatchewan	65	14
Alberta	-155	-104
B.C.	-39	-116

Note: See Table 27 for source of estimate of federal tax incidence by province used in these calculations.

Allowances in 1944, for example, was bitterly denounced by Ontario politicians and newspapers as a blatant bribe to Quebec, to be paid for by Ontario. Premier Drew of Ontario described the scheme as an instrument for taking "money from the pockets of the people of Ontario for the special advantage of Quebec," and insisted that a provincial family allowance program, freed from such implicit transfers, could provide much higher benefits for Ontarians.[43] These basic sentiments were also voiced at the federal level, both in private during Liberal caucus meetings, and in public during parliamentary speeches by some Conservative MPs.[44] But such incidents are exceptional. In general, income security is not perceived as an instrument of territorial redistribution, and is therefore seldom attacked on those grounds. Certainly, any comparison with the chequered political history of explicit transfers to the governments of poor provinces suggests that the regional impact of income security is sufficiently camouflaged to be politically safe.[45]

While the size of the income transfers resulting from the operation of the income security and equalization systems are clear, their actual impact on regional disparities must not be overstated. The Economic Council of Canada calculated that the transfers implicit in income security, conditional grants, and equalization grants together eliminated only one-fifth of regional income disparities.[46] Such an equalizing impact is large enough to be termed significant, but it is also clear that government transfers, including income security, remain a secondary force in the economics of Canadian regionalism.

Federalism and Redistribution: Reflections

Clearly, many of our common assumptions about the impact of our political institutions on redistributive processes in Canada need reconsideration. In particular, the proposition that our federal institutions are particularly sensitive to territorially-based claims, and that they therefore respond more readily to demands for explicit inter-regional redistribution than to demands for interpersonal redistribution is simply not sustained by the evidence. More is involved here than the obvious—but often neglected—point that interpersonal redistribution through the income security system is a much greater spending priority for federal authorities than are special regional programs. More generally, there is no reason to assume that a unitary system of government in Canada would produce less inter-regional redistribution than does our federal one. A unitary government would undoubtedly also be concerned about regional development; indeed, as we have seen, some countries with unitary governments devote proportionately more resources to such programs than does Canada. In addition, the inter-regional transfers that are now delivered through the special equalization grant mechanism would be delivered automatically by a unitary government through national programs that provide uniform standards of public service across the country. Clearly, a much more systematic study of the extent of inter-regional redistribution carried out in different countries would be needed before any final verdict can be rendered. But it remains a possibility that federalism in Canada is an instrument for minimizing, rather than augmenting inter-regional transfers.

The income security field neatly illustrates this relationship between institutional patterns and redistributive processes. The shifting balance between federal and provincial power in this field since the depression has generated a major transfer of income from rich to poor areas of the country. Centralization has transformed income security into a powerful instrument of inter-regional redistribution.

In effect, the growing role of the federal government in income security has shifted the boundaries of the policy community in welfare. Like its social counterpart, a policy community defines the nature and limits of a network of rights and obligations, specifying who is included in the state system of social support, and who may be excluded, who is to contribute to the redistributive process, and who may benefit from it. In the case of income security, the policy community during the early years of this century largely coincided with municipal or parish boundaries; support was due to residents or the faithful, and redistribution took place within the confines of the local economy. But the growing centralization of responsibility for income security has expanded the policy community. The network of obligations extends across the country and the redistributive process now channels resources across the 4,000 miles that separate Newfoundland and British Columbia.

Richard Titmuss has argued eloquently that the system of blood donation and transfusion services is one of the most sensitive of social indicators, revealing much about the nature of human relationships in a society.[47] In the welfare field, the residency requirement is an equally sensitive indicator of the outer boundaries of the network of obligations embodied in income security, defining as it does who is a member of the policy community, who is not a member and therefore—in Titmuss's terms—a "stranger" to whom little is owed, and what the stranger must do to become a full member. In the Canada of the interwar period, residency tests stood as symbolic statements that recognized obligations stopped at the municipal limits. Today they stop at the national borders, and the excluded are limited, in some programs at least, to the recently arrived immigrant.

7 The Policy Process and Income Security

The constitution of a nation specifies the nature of its decision-making processes, and thereby influences the power of different participants within those processes and the interests that bear most heavily on policy decisions. Previous chapters have discussed whether Canadian political structures institutionalize regional concerns in policy deliberations, but the combination of a parliamentary system of government and federalism has other important consequences as well. At both the federal and provincial levels, the parliamentary system concentrates power in the hands of the cabinet and creates a relatively closed policy process. Direct participation in policy-making is limited to ministers, their senior advisors in the civil service, and well-organized interest groups that have established links with these decision-makers. In comparison, Parliament and provincial legislatures, poorly organized groups, and the broad publics can only exhort from outside, or hope that the dictates of electoral politics will ensure sensitivity to their preferences. The Canadian version of federalism reinforces the elitist nature of the process. Divided jurisdiction, and the sheer complexity of federal-provincial policy relations, confuse and weaken the lines of accountability between governments and electors, regularly allowing politicians to take refuge in constitutional ambiguities when things go wrong. In addition, federal-provincial bargaining, through which more and more of the critical issues facing the nation are resolved, is a predominantly closed process. Participation is limited to officials and ministers of the two levels of government; basic agreements are hammered out in secret negotiations, and legislatures are even more than usually constrained not to alter even the details of the delicate compromises that emerge. Thus, the combination of cabinet government and executive federalism has created in Canada a closed, elite-dominated policy process.

This much is not in dispute. But what are the actual policy consequences that flow from this way of making government decisions? Two important consequences are often attributed to this system. First, many commentators insist that the complex and closed nature of the process insulates decision-makers from public pressures and leaves them freer to shape policy according to their own lights. Smiley, for example, suggests that the complexities of federalism discourage "responsiveness of governments to popular demands," and Meisel, among others, argues that public officials regularly initiate programs for which there is no obvious public demand.[1] Such arguments are easily exaggerated by ignoring the extent to which policy initiatives are launched, if not in response to public demand, at least in anticipation of public acclaim, and by ignoring the remains of policy proposals killed off in the secrecy of the cabinet room for fear of an adverse public response. Nevertheless, it remains a reasonable hypothesis that the complexities of federalism enhance elite discretion, and ensure that policy will respond more readily to elite preferences than to contrary public ones.

A second related consequence often attributed to the Canadian policy process is that the interests of governments as governments take on exceptional importance. Governments everywhere are sensitive to the power and standing of the institutions of the state, but in Canada, the argument runs, the continuous struggle for power between the two levels of government over the last two decades has heightened this concern. Every action, every policy option, is scrutinized with infinite care to ensure that it does not weaken that government's hold on its jurisdiction or fiscal base, that it does not weaken its bargaining position in broader federal-provincial negotiations, and that it does not jeopardize its legitimacy in the eyes of the public. More than in many countries, Canadian public policy is continuously shaped—and often mis-shaped—by the interests of governments as governments.

This chapter examines the evolution of income security to assess the extent to which it bears the imprint of these institutional dynamics.

ELITE DISCRETION AND INCOME SECURITY REFORM

If the Fathers of Confederation had carefully designed the institutional framework of Canadian politics so as to ensure that policy decisions faithfully reflected public enthusiasms and intolerances, would the Canadian welfare system differ markedly from its present form? The postwar history of income security suggests a divided verdict. In the case of programs that fall exclusively under federal jurisdiction, while policy elites have often led public opinion, they have also given way whenever clear public opposition to their policies did emerge, and it is difficult therefore to argue that the system reduces responsiveness to public preferences. But in the case of programs under mixed jurisdiction, federalism probably has insulated policy from public preferences, although with contradictory consequences in different programs.

The importance of elite leadership in shifting public preferences is seen clearly in the introduction of Family Allowances in 1944 and of Old Age Security in 1951. Family Allowances were the product of elite doctrine and strategy. The real sources of this innovation were the conversion of federal planners to Keynesian economics and the desire of the Liberal party to undercut the growth of the CCF. While the public was undoubtedly in favour of expanded welfare programs in general, there was certainly no public pressure for Family Allowances as such. There had been some support in French Canada since the 1920s, and both the CCF and the Marsh Report had advocated such benefits in 1942-43, but the labour movement and some social workers opposed their introduction until the last moment on the grounds that they might be used to depress wages. After carefully surveying the debate, Elizabeth Wallace concluded:

> . . . the suggestion had not caught the public imagination, and it had scarcely been discussed at all. The lively newspaper argument was almost entirely confined to the two months preceding the passage of the act . . . . Public interest in the subject was almost entirely developed as a result of the announcement that the cabinet intended to take action in the matter.[2]

Indeed, a Gallup Poll taken in September 1943 found the public evenly divided, with 49 percent in favour of Family Allowances, 42 percent opposed, and 9 percent undecided. Only later, as the federal plan went into action, was there "a marked upswing of public opinion in favour of the scheme."[3] Old Age Security followed a similar pattern. Throughout the late 1940s opinion polls revealed strong public support both for increases in the level of benefits paid under the existing means-tested pensions and for a reduction in the qualifying age; but they also showed that a majority of the public continued to support the means test long after most MPs were convinced that its elimination was essential. As Table 29 shows, even bare majority support for universal pensions did not develop until the fall of 1950, after a summer in which wide publicity was given to the report of a parliamentary committee unanimously recommending such a program; and overwhelming public support did not emerge until after the Old Age Security bill was introduced into Parliament. Clearly, on both the introduction of Family Allowances and the shift to universalism in pensions, elite opinion led public opinion.

Two examples from the 1970s, however, also demonstrate the sensitivity of policy elites when clear public opposition to income security policies does emerge. In 1970 the federal government, in an attempt to make income

Table 29   *Public Opinion on Universal Old Age Pensions, 1946-51*

A. Responses to questions asking whether respondents favoured pensions
    to "old people with no other means of support" or "to everyone who
    reaches old age."

	Nov. 1946	Apr. 1950	Oct. 1950
	(percent)		
No other means of support	58	50	43
All old people	34	38	55
Qualified or undecided	8	12	2

B. Responses to questions: "Next year, every Canadian 70 years of age
    and over will start getting a pension of $40 a month, regardless of their
    (sic) financial position. Do you approve or disapprove of this?"

	Oct. 1951
	(percent)
Approve	81
Disapprove	17
Don't know	2

Source: Canadian Institute of Public Opinion, cited in K. Bryden, *Old Age Pensions and Policy-Making in Canada*, p. 249.

security more redistributive towards low-income families, proposed replacing Family Allowances with the Family Income Supplement Plan (FISP), an
income-related program that would provide larger benefits for low-income
families but eliminate them completely for all families with an annual
income over $10,000. While opinion polls suggested reasonably broad
support for the policy,[4] the intensity of feeling amongst the minority
opposed, especially many middle-class women, stopped the proposal in its
tracks. The mailbag of the minister of National Health and Welfare over-
flowed: as one official recalled: "There was an incredible outpouring of
letters from women who would have lost their cheques. Their willingness to
sit down and write letters of protest produced a steady erosion of political
will." This erosion speeded up during the 1972 election campaign, when
Liberals met the objections on the doorsteps, and shortly thereafter the
policy was radically altered: universal family allowances were retained and
the benefits were tripled in value, although at least some of the original
redistributive aim was achieved by making them taxable. As in any major

policy change, other factors were also involved: the administrative problems posed by the initial proposal; the rivalry with Quebec, which is discussed below; and the attitude of the NDP, on which the Liberal government now depended in the minority Parliament.[5] But the new minister, Marc Lalonde, was clear about the primary reason for the change:

> . . . it's a reaction to the . . . voice of the electorate . . . It's clear that Canadian housewives attach a lot of importance to that Family Allowance cheque, and there was a lot of resistance to the idea that . . . about half of them would be losing that Allowance . . . . That, in large part, was the basis of my recommendation to my colleagues and our decision.[6]

The history of Unemployment Insurance during the 1970s reveals a similar sensitivity to public criticism. In 1971 the program was fundamentally overhauled, with benefit provisions being made much more generous, and once again the reformist impulse came from policy elites rather than the broad public.[7] But as expenditures under the new legislation rose sharply, and as alleged abuses gained widespread publicity, opposition mounted, not only among businessmen, the media, and the Progressive Conservative opposition, but also, according to the polls, among the public.[8] Indeed, so intense was the reaction that many Liberals blamed their near defeat in the 1972 election on the unemployment insurance issue. In this case, responsibility for the policy was unambiguously federal. There were no constitutional complexities among which federal politicians could shelter from the political blast. The result, therefore, was inevitable: benefits were cut, work requirements were tightened, and prosecutions were stepped up.

Divided jurisdiction, on the other hand, would seem to offer greater protection from public pressures, although the consequences vary from program to program. The most powerful impact has undoubtedly been on the Canada and Quebec Pension plans; as the discussion in chapter five has shown, the multiplicity of federal and provincial veto points has insulated the two plans from the expansionist pressures inherent in the politics of pensions in modern democracies. In the case of social assistance, on the other hand, divided jurisdiction has probably facilitated policy expansion in the face of continued public indifference or ambivalence, although its importance here is often overstated. Certainly, the development of federal support for provincial social assistance through the Unemployment Assistance Act and the Canada Assistance Plan was the product of quiet diplomacy between federal and provincial ministers and officials who shared a similar commitment to welfare expansion, and was accomplished with no discernible public pressure behind it. The introduction of CAP, for example, "was an issue that aroused little interest outside of government circles and, in itself, virtually none even in Parliament."[9] Since then, CAP has remained a professionally dominated program, and a variety of commentators have insisted that it has contributed to a steady expansion of provincial social assistance, insulating welfare from potential sources of opposition in several ways.

Until recently at least, welfare officials were unanimous in agreeing that the conditional grant mechanism protected expenditure levels from the knives of treasury officials at two levels of government. Provincial welfare administrators could reassure their own treasury boards that each extra dollar of spending only cost the province fifty cents, while their federal counterparts could insist to treasury officials in Ottawa that they were locked into the agreement with the provinces. It is true that, as the economic recession bit deeper in the 1970s, provincial welfare officials sensed that the protection of CAP was wearing thin, and that their treasury counterparts were remarkably unimpressed by half-price dollars. One of them expressed the prevailing provincial view in the late 1970s thus: "Three or four years ago, having 50 cent dollars really meant something when you went to the Treasury Board here. Now it doesn't mean nearly as much." Federal officials, however, remain somewhat sceptical about this new provincial view. While conceding that CAP could not protect social assistance from the consequences of economic recession completely, they point out that provincial officials still evidence great concern about whether new programs that they are considering would be shareable under the terms of CAP, and are greatly upset whenever the answer is no.

It is difficult to assess such conflicting claims, but Table 30 does raise important doubts about the impact of CAP on expenditure levels over its

Table 30   *Social Assistance Expenditures as a Proportion of all Provincial and Municipal Current Expenditures, 1964-78*

	(percent)
1964	8.8
1966	8.4
1968	8.7
1970	8.1
1972	8.7
1974	8.6
1976	8.8
1978	8.3

Source: Data on social assistance expenditures taken from Statistics Canada, *National Income and Expenditure Accounts 1964-1978;* consolidation of provincial and municipal current expenditures taken from Canadian Tax Foundation, *The National Finances 1979-1980,* Table 2-9.

entire lifetime. Provincial and municipal expenditures on social assistance, including direct relief, old age and blind pensions, and mothers' and disability allowances, have remained virtually constant as a proportion of total provincial and municipal current expenditures since 1964, well before CAP came fully into effect. CAP has undoubtedly contributed towards more comparable standards of welfare in the various provinces, as noted in chapter six, but there is little evidence that, overall, it has enabled provincial welfare officials to capture a larger share of the provincial expenditure pie.

But perhaps CAP's primary contribution has been to protect social assistance from *public* hostility. Christopher Leman has argued vigorously that, in comparison with the American system of government, Canadian institutions have erected barriers between welfare policies and the public, have insulated decision-makers from the type of backlash against deserted or unmarried mothers that characterized American welfare politics in the late 1960s and the early 1970s.[10] The strength of provincial governments not only prevents the federal government from setting detailed standards for CAP-assisted programs, but also from publishing regular, detailed information on the composition of the welfare caseload. While such a closed system undercuts outside groups who might wish to advocate more generous welfare programs, it also helps protect welfare from attack. The United States government publishes a wealth of data, which has become ammunition in the hands of welfare critics, whereas in Canada, according to Leman, controversy over Canadian welfare-mothers is discouraged because information on them is not widely available, reducing the likelihood that a national welfare backlash will develop in the first place. And even when public hostility does manifest itself, the closed and complex world of welfare policy-making helps welfare officials to resist demands for work requirements for welfare recipients or more determined prosecution of fraud and runaway fathers.

Leman undoubtedly overstates the importance of institutional factors in his argument. Even ignoring the distinct possibility of greater cultural support for such welfare programs in Canada,[11] there is a host of other reasons why welfare-mothers have not emerged as a national issue in Canada: social assistance costs have grown gradually in Canada, not explosively as they did in the United States during the late 1960s; mother-headed families represent a much smaller proportion of the caseload in Canada than in the United States; and Canadian welfare recipients are not racially distinct, whereas black families constitute almost half of the American caseload. More important, however, a Canadian welfare backlash does not have to be national to be effective. Despite the 50 percent sharing under CAP, Canada does not really have a *national* social assistance policy; rather, there are ten provincial policies, and provincial ministers of welfare

are the natural, and undoubtedly the most effective, target for welfare red-
necks. Certainly, the record of the 1970s includes restrictions on social
assistance in a number of provinces.[12] Given all of these factors at work, the
independent influence of Canadian institutions is difficult to assess. The
complexity of federal-provincial relationships, the sharing of the costs of
welfare, and the veil of secrecy that has descended over the sector probably
do have some insulating properties, but it is impossible to ascertain their
precise "R-factor."

Clearly, then, at least in the case of exclusively federal programs, Canadian institutions must be acquitted of the slanderous charge of unrespon-
siveness to public pressures. The cabinet system of government has
undoubtedly been important, allowing policy elites to lead public opinion
at critical junctures, by acting in the absence of strong public pressure. But
there is no evidence that the system has frustrated public opposition whenever it developed. In the case of programs with mixed jurisdiction, on the
other hand, institutions probably have insulated decision-makers from the
full force of public expectations and criticisms. The evidence in the case of
social assistance is perhaps inconclusive, but the conservative impact on
contributory pensions is crystal clear.

Income Security and the Interests of Governments

The relationship between the institutions of government and income
security is a reciprocal one. So far the analysis has concentrated on the
impact of federal institutions on the substance of income security programs,
but of course the expansion of income security over the last four decades
has also had an important impact on political structures in Canada, and
especially on the economic and political power that the various governments of Canada wield, both in relation to society generally and in relation
to each other.

Income Security and Economic Power. Income security is the single
biggest component of government expenditure, and a major proportion of
the Canadian tax system is devoted to raising the necessary revenues. Financial flows of this magnitude have important implications for the fiscal
strength of governments, for their capacity to control general economic
activity, and hence for their economic power. The sensitivity of governments to their own fiscal interests in income security debates has already
been demonstrated in the response of provincial governments to the funding
of the Canada and Quebec Pension plans and to the cutbacks in Unemployment Insurance. But the division of authority over income security has a
much broader, reciprocal relationship with the fiscal and economic capacities of government. Chapter five discussed how, historically, responsibility

for income security gravitated towards the federal government because of its greater economic strength, especially its broader tax base and its greater capacity to manage the economy and therefore to grapple with the causes of unemployment. In the middle decades of this century, then, income security flowed to economic power. But the relationship also runs in the opposite direction, and income security has now become a significant component of the federal government's economic power.

On the expenditure side, income security is an important addition to the array of instruments that government can employ to influence the level of purchasing power in the hands of individual Canadians. Programs such as unemployment insurance are what Keynesians call "automatic stabilizers," which increase government expenditures automatically whenever unemployment rises, and governments can also adjust benefit levels in welfare programs as part of their budgetary strategy. Admittedly, income security is not the most politically flexible of economic instruments. *Ad hoc* adjustments in benefit levels usually take the form of increased payments in periods of fiscal expansion, and even here the indexation of benefit levels in the 1970s has further reduced the discretion in the hands of the minister of Finance. Nevertheless, cuts in benefit levels for economic reasons are only rare, not impossible, as the 1976 suspension of indexation of Family Allowances for one year makes clear.

It is on the revenue side, however, that the economic power inherent in income security becomes most visible, as a significant portion of the federal share of tax revenues is committed to, and therefore politically justified by, income security payments. If responsibility for income security were shifted to the provinces, for example, the federal government would face irresistible pressure to provide a fiscal transfer equal to the program costs. In 1969 federal authorities calculated that the transfer required, if the provinces were to take over Family Allowances, Old Age Security, and the Guaranteed Income Supplement, would amount to 32 percent of the basic income tax, plus additional grants of some $500 million; and transferring Unemployment Insurance as well would have pushed the total still higher.[13] More recent calculations are not available, but Department of Finance officials privately suggest that there is no reason to believe that the figures would be substantially less today. Clearly, such a transfer would radically reduce the federal government's capacity to employ the income tax as an instrument of economic management. Thus, on both the expenditure and revenue sides, income security is an important part of federal economic power. As the federal authorities observed in 1969, to transfer income security to the provinces, together with the lion's share of the personal income tax, "would in effect be to transfer to them the major responsibility for the nation's fiscal policy."[14]

Such a transfer would not only require the federal government to rely even more heavily on monetary instruments, but it would also alter the structure of incentives surrounding federal economic policy. As the Rowell-Sirois Commission observed forty years ago: "If the Dominion assumes full responsibility for relief of unemployables, it should have much stronger incentive . . . to adopt vigorous remedial policies and policies to prevent unemployment from arising."[15] Under the current system, with responsibility for economic management and income security lodged at the same level, federal policy-makers know that increases in unemployment will increase their own expenditures. Transferring complete responsibility for income security, and particularly unemployment benefits, to the provinces would simply make it much easier for federal authorities to fight inflation through unemployment, since the social costs would fall elsewhere. Ottawa would be a much more conservative place indeed.

Income security augments federal economic power in one other aspect. The federal government repeatedly complains that provincial governments have created an array of barriers to the inter-provincial mobility of goods, capital, and people through their trade, labour, and language policies. Income security programs can be important to inter-provincial mobility,[16] but this sector is firmly under federal control; as chapter five demonstrated, federal involvement has largely eliminated residency requirements, ensured comparable standards of income security in different regions, and guaranteed portability in public pensions. The actual impact of such policies on inter-regional migration patterns, however, is double-edged. The prohibition of residency requirements and the portability of federal benefits do eliminate barriers that might otherwise arise; but the political pressures to provide uniform benefits in all regions, or to engage in positive discrimination through Unemployment Insurance, also reduces the incentive for those in poor regions to migrate. Courchene, for example, has argued strongly that the inter-regional transfers through both conditional and unconditional grants, and the income security provisions (especially the regionalized eligibility element of Unemployment Insurance), have blunted normal economic adjustment mechanisms, locking both individuals and governments in poor regions into a position of dependency, as "wards of the state."[17]

Income security is thus an important component of federal economic power, and any attempt to alter its jurisdiction in this area confronts much broader opposition within the federal bureaucracy and cabinet than might be anticipated. It is not simply the status of one department, Health and Welfare Canada, that is tied up in this function, but also the capacity of the federal government to influence economic events in Canada.

Income Security and Political Legitimacy. Income security is important to governments for more directly political reasons as well. These are not restricted to the considerable usefulness of such programs as instruments for mobilizing electoral support, through judicious pre-election announcements of new schemes, benefit increases, or campaigns against welfare abuse. More fundamentally, however, political leaders see such social programs as a mechanism for sustaining or enhancing the legitimacy of the institutions of government itself. This is hardly surprising since, aside from the rather painful tax relationship, income security represents the only direct, tangible link between the state and all of its citizens. Ever since the late nineteenth century, when Bismarck introduced social insurance in an explicit attempt to undercut the socialist parties and integrate the German working class into the existing social order,[18] income security has been regarded as an instrument through which governments could secure the allegiance of their populations. In recent years Marxists have been the most insistent advocates of the view that the primary function of social policy is legitimation, but during the 1930s, many liberals also argued that the failure of Canadian governments to respond to the overwhelming social hardship of the depression threatened the foundations of democracy. A.E. Grauer, for example, told the Rowell-Sirois commissioners that failure of governments to deal effectively with the unemployment problem could threaten the democratic system: "It is in this soil that non-democratic movements sprout and flourish. Not only would such governments themselves lose greatly in prestige, but the structure of a democratic federal state would be subjected to severe disintegrating influences."[19]

Modern Canadian politicians view income security, not so much as a means of preserving democracy, but as an instrument of cultural and political integration, as an underpinning of the stability of the federal system, or at least of the role of the central government in it. Some see income security as central to the sense of community in Canada, arguing that the major federal programs are both an indicator of the strength of the Canadian community, and an instrument for its further reinforcement. Thus, in 1969 the federal government argued that:

> The "sense of a Canadian community" is at once the source of income redistribution between people and regions in Canada and the result of such measures. It is the sense of community which makes it possible for Parliament to tax residents of higher income regions for the purpose of making payments to persons in lower income regions. And it is the willingness of people in higher income regions to pay these taxes which gives additional meaning in the minds of those who receive the payments to the concept of a Canadian community.[20]

But, undoubtedly, the strongest statement of the power of income security as a cultural instrument came in the 1950s from Quebec's Tremblay Commission. The expansion of federal income security programs was considered a form of cultural imperialism that threatened the existence of a distinctive French-Canadian culture; such programs, reflecting liberal and socialist traditions of English Canada, represented an intellectual intrusion, injecting alien ideas into the thought of the province. Unless the federal role was checked, the Commission insisted, "in less than a generation, probably, [Quebec's] social system, in its main lines and general inspiration, will be integrated with the rest of Canada . . . . As far as the assimilation of French Canada is concerned, thirty years of social history will thus have had more effect than a century and a half of political history."[21]

While often expressing scepticism that income security is such a powerful instrument of *cultural* integration, Canadian governments clearly assume that it is important to the political legitimacy of the federal government. Virtually all of the social and community services which the public values are provincially delivered; income security is the only beneficial link between Ottawa and the public and, not unreasonably, federal officials consider it crucial to their government's political standing within the federation. As one senior federal official put it: "A government that only taxes its citizens will not be a legitimate government for very long. A government must be more than a device for laundering money. I believe that very firmly."

Simple calculations of the self-interest of citizens would seem to support a connection between income security and political allegiance. Every citizen has a vested interest in the fiscal strength and stability of the government responsible for his or her pension, Family Allowance, or Unemployment Insurance, and under the present regime the income security cheques mailed out of Ottawa every month tie the interests of millions of Canadians to the strength of the federal, rather than a provincial, treasury. If income security were to become a provincial responsibility, this network of client relationships, and whatever political allegiance is generated by them, would be transferred as well. Indeed, the network of interest is even broader than that, as Usher has pointed out.[22] Provincial responsibility for income security would mean that each citizen would have an even greater interest in the prosperity of all industrial and economic activity within the province, as this generates the tax revenues to support social programs, and a similarly reduced interest in the health of the pan-Canadian economy. "Provincial jurisdiction over redistribution creates a community of interests among all residents of the province while federal jurisdiction loosens the bonds between residents of the same province and correspondingly strengthens the bonds between citizens of Canada as a whole."[23]

Income security thus appears to be a potent instrument that can be harnessed to the process of either nation-building or province-building. It is not surprising, then, to find that one of the bitterest battles waged in the income security field during the last forty years involved not the substance of policy but rather the issue of which level of government should control it. During the constitutional negotiations that led up to the Victoria Conference in 1971, Quebec pressed strongly for a constitutional amendment that would have, in effect, entitled any provincial government that so wished to take over federal income security programs, and to receive the fiscal equivalent of the program costs from the federal treasury. The federal government, and especially the minister and Department of National Health and Welfare, strongly resisted the idea. The debate was couched in other terms, with Quebec presenting its case in the language of rationality and efficiency of the Castonguay Report, and federal representatives talking about national standards, equality of opportunity across the country, and economic management. But both governments were conscious of the underlying political potential; Quebec nationalists have often wished to sever the direct cash tie between Ottawa and Quebecers, and federalists have been equally insistent on retaining it. In the end the Victoria Charter did incorporate a compromise on income security, but confusion reigned over its precise meaning, and finally, the Quebec government vetoed the entire Victoria package, citing the uncertainty over the income security clause.[24]

Not all provinces have been as concerned as Quebec to employ income security as an instrument of province-building, but virtually all of them are conscious of the political utility of income security. One sign of this is the rareness of joint delivery systems. The province of Manitoba has arranged for the federal government to mail out its supplement for the elderly, often in the same envelope as the OAS-GIS cheque; and Prince Edward Island's family allowance is delivered through the federal Family Allowance system. In addition, of course, since the income taxes of provinces other than Quebec (and after 1984 British Columbia) are collected by Ottawa, provincial tax credits for low-income groups are simply subsumed in the federal tax system. Delivery integration on this model offers important administrative savings,[25] but political concerns impose a strong limit on such intergovernmental cooperation. Even though all of the other provinces which operate supplements for the elderly also use the federal government's GIS data to determine eligibility for their programs, they insist on sending their separate cheque to the recipient. In addition, British Columbia announced in its 1981 budget that it would withdraw from the Tax Collection agreements and collect its own income taxes, in part so that the provincial government would receive political credit for its contribution to the costs of major tax credits and other tax expenditures.[26] Fights about which government gets to mail out income security cheques may seem petty to some. But in the eyes of governments, they are critical to the wider political balance within the federation.

Summary

Canadian institutions have created a closed, secretive policy process in which power is highly concentrated in the hands of policy elites, and this system has had some influence on the development of income security in Canada. In particular, the concentration of power has allowed cabinets and senior civil servants to introduce new programs, often in the absence of compelling public pressure to do so. Indeed, the entire postwar history of income security can be read as a testament to the influence of reformist elites, especially at the federal level. But the importance of concentrated power is easily, and often, overstated. Another reading of that same historical record emphasizes the sensitivity of policy elites to public reactions to policy innovations, especially in areas of exclusive federal jurisdiction. With the partial exception of programs under joint federal-provincial control, our institutions have not frustrated public desires in income security.

In comparison, the reciprocal impact of income security on political institutions has been much more important. Income security has now become an integral part of the economic and political balance of the federal system. For governments, much more is at stake in income security than simple social justice, their commitment to which varies anyway. Political leaders are convinced that income security is an important part of their capacity to manage their economies and to maintain the allegiance of their populations. For Canadian governments, battles over jurisdiction raise much bigger stakes than do battles over the substance of policy.

PART THREE

INSTITUTIONAL CHANGE AND INCOME SECURITY

8 Regionalism and Income Security

A final way in which to investigate the complex relationships between political institutions and income security in Canada is to ask what would happen to our welfare system if the structure of government were suddenly changed in some major way. Canadians have been debating constitutional reform for almost two decades now and, although major constitutional reform may well remain a permanently elusive goal, an analysis of the impact that it could have on income security reveals much about the importance, and unimportance, of the contours of our political institutions in this area of public policy.

Setting aside the question of an entrenched charter of political and linguistic rights, most advocates of constitutional reform have been concerned to make Canadian government more sensitive to regional interests and attitudes. The Canadian system of government, in its present form, accentuates, even generates, regional conflicts, and the proposals advanced by most aspiring constitution writers have been designed to ease those tensions. As a result, whether such constitutional reforms would result in major shifts in any particular area of public policy depends in large part on whether the basic issues at stake in that policy area are regional in nature. In policy areas where there are no distinct regional interests, and no significant differences in the attitudes of the populations of the various regions, constitutional change along such lines would not likely produce major shifts in policy. Changes in the legislative or financial capacities of the different governments might lead to important differences in detail, but the essential principles of policy would unlikely be challenged. On the other hand, in policy areas where there are distinct regional interests, or where regional publics have decidedly different attitudes towards the issues in question, such constitutional changes would be much more likely to produce changes of significance in the principles of public policy.

Clearly, an analysis of the consequences of constitutional reform for income security must begin with an assessment of the interests at stake. Accordingly, this chapter looks at the nature of regional interests in, and attitudes about, income security. Chapter nine then takes up the implications of specific proposals for institutional change.

Regional Interests and Income Security

In assessing the extent of regional interests in income security, it is important to distinguish between the basic structure of welfare programs on the one hand, and the distribution of benefits within the system on the other. The basic structure of income security does not raise fundamental regional conflicts. While there are undoubtedly many important differences in the economic and social structure of the various regions, they all share the basic social needs to which the welfare state is addressed: the need for protection during unemployment, sickness, disability, old age, and so on. The particular mix of social problems does vary from one region to another, but it is difficult to think of any income security program that is completely unnecessary in any region; nor does any particular region need completely new kinds of income security any more than other regions.

Historically, regional interests were more pronounced. During the interwar years, for example, the prairie provinces, which were leaders in many aspects of welfare policy, had little interest in unemployment insurance programs, because these would have little relevance in an overwhelmingly agricultural economy.[1] Farmers in the west, the growing urban workforce, and the dispossessed generally might find common cause when demanding pensions and better health care, but their interests increasingly diverged as unemployment insurance rose steadily up the political agenda during the 1930s. Indeed, a background study to the Rowell-Sirois Commission commented that "the fear has been expressed in Ontario that if the Dominion contributed to a federal system of unemployment insurance, the Prairie provinces would want it to contribute to a system of crop insurance on the grounds that they gained little from unemployment insurance."[2] But today such divergent regional interests have been muted by the growing diversification of the economy of the prairie region. Unemployment Insurance still benefits a much smaller proportion of the prairie population than other regional populations and, as will be seen, prairie Canadians are more critical of the present program than their fellow countrymen. But Unemployment Insurance is certainly not irrelevant there. In 1979 some 225,000 individuals submitted new claims for Unemployment Insurance benefits in the three prairie provinces;[3] and, as economic diversification proceeds, the number will undoubtedly grow.

Regional interests do emerge, however, when attention is directed to distributional questions. As Table 23 earlier revealed, different proportions of the various provincial populations benefit from each income security program and, as a result, the distribution of the total income security budget between different programs does have regional implications. While the proportions of beneficiaries do not differ dramatically in the case of demogrants, such as Family Allowances and Old Age Security, a decision to enrich programs related to financial need, such as CAP, GIS, and Unemployment Insurance, clearly benefits a greater proportion of Atlantic Canadians and Quebecers than Ontarians and westerners. Unemployment Insurance remains the most regionalized program in this sense; while 9.1 percent of all Newfoundlanders were claimants in 1976, only 1.7 percent of Albertans were, a ratio of over five to one. In addition to the distribution of expenditures between different programs, the distribution of the costs and benefits of the income security system as a whole poses divergent regional interests, since, as chapter six demonstrated, income security has become an important instrument for taking income from rich provinces and transferring it into poorer ones. Thus, while the essential principles and structures of welfare pose no regional issues, distributional questions do so in a decided way.

Regional Attitudes and Income Security: Public, Planners and Provinces

Social needs and economic interests are not the only dimensions of regionalism in Canada. Many commentators insist that cultural patterns also vary across the country, and that Canadians in different regions hold quite different attitudes about governments, and about what they expect their governments to do.[4] It therefore remains possible that attitudes toward income security may vary sufficiently across Canada to constitute regionally distinctive conceptions of the ideal income security system. In fact, however, this is not the case. Attitudes do vary across the country but, whatever else may have been true in the past, attitudinal differences today are not sufficiently dramatic to constitute distinctive approaches to welfare. This holds true at various levels of opinion: public, planners, and provincial governments.

The Public and Income Security. The basic legitimacy of income security is no longer an issue in Canada, at least for the general public. The major programs have become established traditions and discussion about them takes place within a broad consensus on their basic necessity in modern society. Public controversies do, of course, occasionally erupt over welfare,

Table 31   Attitudes Towards Unemployment Insurance, 1977-78

	Agree Strongly or Somewhat				Disagree Strongly or Somewhat			
	Sept. 1977	Jan. 1978	April 1978	Sept. 1978	Sept. 1977	Jan. 1978	April 1978	Sept. 1978
	(percent)				(percent)			
Unemployment Insurance is necessary in today's society	82	86	85	84	11	10	10	10
Stricter controls are needed to ensure that Unemployment Insurance benefits do not go to people who will not take a job	84	86	84	88	6	7	8	5
Many people take unfair advantage of Unemployment Insurance	81	86	80	87	9	8	10	8

Source: Employment and Immigration Canada. *Statistics on Advertising for Unemployment Insurance: Reports of Three Studies* (Ottawa, 1978), and *Fourth Marketing Research Study on Unemployment Insurance* (Ottawa, 1978).

but they focus almost entirely on the extent and nature of the income transfers that result, and seldom challenge the existence or basic principles of income security programs altogether. "Welfare benefits are completely inadequate" versus "Welfare is abused by too many who could take care of themselves": these are the kinds of issues that fuel public controversy over welfare spending. In comparison, acceptance of the need for public provision for the income needs of the retired, the unemployed, and the needy, and probably also of the existing mix of income security instruments, remains the unstated and unchallenged premise. Unemployment Insurance illustrates this vividly. No income security program was more controversial during the 1970s and, as Table 31 indicates, the overwhelming majority of Canadians was convinced that too many people were taking unfair advantage of it and that stricter controls were essential. Yet, the criticism never challenged the basic legitimacy of the program. A similarly overwhelming majority remained convinced that "unemployment insurance is necessary in today's society."

More important for our purposes, this general pattern does not differ markedly from one region of Canada to another. A broad consensus on the basic elements of the existing income security system exists in all regions, and the distribution of opinion on the specific questions concerning the scope and generosity of the system does not differ dramatically among regions. Further, the regional differences in attitudes that do exist are not particularly surprising since, with a few exceptions, the greatest approval of existing programs and the strongest support for their expansion are to be found in Quebec and Atlantic Canada, the regions with the greatest income security needs.

Table 32   *Attitudes of Family Allowance Recipients, by Region, 1974*

Region	Family Allowances are Necessary	I Could Do without Them	Don't Know	No Answer
	(percent)			
Atlantic	64.5	26.4	—	9.1
Quebec	81.4	16.6	1.2	0.9
Ontario	59.2	36.9	2.7	1.2
Prairies	55.8	40.0	—	4.2
B.C.	58.1	38.5	1.6	1.8
CANADA	66.5	29.7	1.4	2.5

Source: J. Laframboise, *A Question of Needs*, Table R-20.

Table 33   *Attitudes Towards Old Age Pensions, by Region, 1974*

Region	Eligibility Should be Lowered to 60	Pensions Not High Enough
	(percent)	
Atlantic	81.4	63.1
Quebec	85.1	63.4
Ontario	75.5	74.3
Prairies	69.6	63.9
B.C.	76.2	80.6
CANADA	77.8	69.3

Source: J. Laframboise, *A Question of Needs*, Tables R-27 and R-34.

Evidence of these regional patterns comes from a number of sources. A survey conducted for the Canadian Council on Social Development in 1974 found that a majority of respondents in every region agreed that Family Allowances were necessary, that the old age pension was not high enough, and that eligibility for the pension should be reduced to age sixty (see Tables 32 and 33). The size of the majorities, however, did differ from region to region. The highest levels of support for Family Allowances and the extension of old age pensions to those in the sixty to sixty-four age category, both questions concerning the *scope* of welfare provision, were found in Quebec and Atlantic Canada. Only on the question of the *level* of benefit under the old age pension program was the pattern reversed, with more respondents in Ontario and British Columbia, regions with higher costs of living, convinced of the inadequacy of existing benefit levels.

A similar pattern emerges from surveys of attitudes towards Unemployment Insurance commissioned by the federal government in 1977 and 1978. Again, the range of differences between regions was limited, and the movement in opinion over the year was in the same direction in all parts of the country, as Table 34 shows. The regional differences in opinion that did exist conform to the anticipated pattern: approval was highest in areas of high unemployment, Atlantic Canada, Quebec, and British Columbia, and lowest on the prairies.[5] Interestingly, as Table 35 demonstrates, this pattern does not seem to have been the result of the adoption of regionally varied qualification periods, a reform that benefitted areas of high unemployment. While awareness of the new classification rules was highest in such areas, approval of the principle of regionally adjusted periods was not; indeed, in the beginning, regions with high unemployment seem to have been rather suspicious of the whole idea.

Table 34   *Attitudes Towards Unemployment Insurance, by Region,*
            1977-78

Region	Percent Saying Program is Very or Fairly Well Run			
	Sept. 77	Jan. 78	Apr. 78	Sept. 78
Atlantic	48	62	71	66
Quebec	49	60	63	55
Ontario	49	54	55	51
Prairies	38	49	56	47
B.C.	48	61	60	56
CANADA	47	56	59	53

Source: Employment and Immigration Canada, *Studies on Advertising for Unemployment*
           Insurance: Reports of Three Studies (Ottawa, 1978), and *Fourth Marketing Research*
           Study on Unemployment Insurance (Ottawa, 1978).

Further evidence comes from two recent academic studies. A survey of Canadian attitudes conducted by political scientists at York University in 1977 discovered the same pattern: support for social welfare and income redistribution was highest in Quebec and Atlantic Canada (although P.E.I. was an exception here), and lower than average in Ontario and the western provinces, as Tables 36 and 37 indicate. The authors of the survey concluded: "It seems clear that attitudes towards income redistribution and social welfare differentiate reasonably well between the 'have' and 'have not' regions of Canada."[6] This pattern is not simply the result of the different income levels of various regions: although support for increased welfare was strongest among lower-income Canadians, *regional differences remained, and indeed predominated, even when socio-economic factors were held constant.*[7] Quebec, in particular, remained highly supportive, followed by Atlantic Canada. Moreover, Table 36 provides support for a point noted in chapter six. Atlantic Canadians and Quebecers give greater support to proposals to expand help for the poor and the elderly than they give to proposals to expand efforts to reduce regional inequality. Clearly, the problem of regional disparities feeds into debate on social policy as well as those over equalization and regional development.

All of the surveys discussed so far were conducted in the mid-1970s, but another study provides a more historical perspective. Blake and Simeon examined questions on public policy issues asked by the Canadian Gallup Poll organization between the years 1949 and 1975.[8] They found that regional differences in attitudes are much less pronounced on economic and social issues, including social security, than on issues relating to the nature of the Canadian community, such as language policy, relations with Britain, and federal-provincial relations. Significantly, they also found that

Table 35   Awareness and Approval of Unemployment Insurance Changes, by Region, 1977-78

Region	Percent Aware of New Qualification Period			Percent Approving of Regionally Adjusted Period			
	Jan. 1978	Apr. 1978	Sept. 1978	Sept. 1977	Jan. 1978	Apr. 1978	Sept. 1978
Atlantic	66	51	51	33	57	58	58
Quebec	46	44	39	44	56	59	58
Ontario	37	33	34	52	54	58	60
Prairies	36	30	23	49	52	50	56
B.C.	38	46	34	43	58	54	61
CANADA	42	39	34	47	55	57	57

Source: Employment and Immigration Canada, *Studies on Advertising for Unemployment Insurance: Reports of Three Studies* (Ottawa, 1978), and *Fourth Marketing Research Study on Unemployment Insurance* (Ottawa, 1978).

Table 36 *Support for Greater Income Redistribution, by Region, 1977*

Percentage of Respondents Favouring More or Much
More Effort

Region	Helping the Poor	Helping the Retired	Assistance for the Unemployed	Workmen's Compen- sation	Decrease Regional Inequality
Atlantic	69.3	72.4	47.6	42.3	60.7
Quebec	73.1	82.5	48.4	68.0	60.7
Ontario	62.4	70.1	35.5	37.1	52.3
Prairies	65.5	69.5	28.3	31.1	58.9
B.C.	66.0	66.5	40.8	36.5	44.9
CANADA	67.5	74.1	41.0	47.8	56.0

Source: Calculated from T. Atkinson, B. Blishen, M. Ornstein and H.M. Stevenson, *Social Change in Canada: Trends in Attitudes, Values and Perceptions—Quality of Life 1977* (Machine readable data file, Institute for Behavioural Research, Survey Research Centre, York University, Downsview, Ontario, 1977).

Table 37 *Attitudes Towards Inequality and Redistribution, by Region, 1977*

Percentage of Respondents Agreeing
or Agreeing Strongly

Region	Too Much Difference Between Rich and Poor	Classes Natural as People are Unequal	High Income Earners Should Pay More Tax
Atlantic	74.4	70.2	58.5
Quebec	70.9	63.7	70.0
Ontario	61.2	74.6	55.1
Prairies	63.8	74.0	53.0
B.C.	58.6	73.8	59.7
CANADA	66.0	70.4	60.7

Source: Calculated from T. Atkinson, B. Blishen, M. Ornstein and H.M. Stevenson, *Social Change in Canada: Trends in Attitudes, Values and Perceptions—Quality of Life 1977* (Machine readable data file, Institute for Behavioural Research, Survey Research Centre, York University, Downsview, Ontario, 1977).

those regional differences that did exist on economic and social questions, including welfare, were declining over time. "The populations of the Canadian regions," they argue, "are becoming more alike in their responses to the issues of the day."[9] Table 38 presents their findings on social policy questions. The figures represent the percentage of respondents approving of various social programs, or supporting their expansion, averaged over all the questions asked about social issues in the two time periods. Again, the figures suggest that regional differences are limited, and the population of Quebec was the most supportive in both time periods.

Table 38 *Attitudes Towards Social Policy, by Region, 1951-75*

	Percentage Favouring Welfare	
Region	1951-69	1970-75
Atlantic	48.3	42.8
Quebec	58.8	50.5
Ontario	57.3	47.1
Prairies	52.7	45.9
B.C.	59.8	45.5
CANADA	54.8	47.3
Average Regional Deviation from National	3.9	2.2

Source: D. Blake and R. Simeon, "Regional Preferences: Citizens' Views of Public Policy," in D. Elkins and R. Simeon, *Small Worlds*.

The surprise in this table is Atlantic Canada. In contrast to the findings of the other studies just cited, this region emerges as the least, rather than one of the most, supportive of welfare. A detailed examination of the actual questions asked by Gallup over the years, however, suggests several possible explanations of this apparent anomaly. The Blake-Simeon study included attitudes towards a wider range of social policies, including a series of questions concerning the introduction of medicare, of which Atlantic Canadians were much less supportive.[10] When attention is restricted to questions about income security, a less anomalous, although somewhat more complex, pattern emerges. Questions that asked whether a particular welfare program was "a good plan" or "good value" regularly found stronger support in Atlantic Canada than in most other regions.[11] But questions about the distribution of benefits (e.g., means tests for pensions, greater selectivity in Family Allowances) usually found the Atlantic region more supportive of, or—to be precise—less opposed to, selectivity in welfare,[12] a position that was classified as anti-welfare by Blake and Simeon. Thus, the picture of attitudes of Atlantic Canadians includes both strong support for existing welfare programs coupled with somewhat greater willingness to restrict those benefits to low-income Canadians, a picture which is not incompatible with the findings of the other studies.

Clearly, Canadian opinion on the welfare state is not uniform. Regional differences in attitudes do exist, and their origins remain a legitimate question for further research. In part, the higher level of support for income security in Quebec and Atlantic Canada is the product of economic self-interest, since income security needs are greatest there. But the fact that regional differences in attitudes do not disappear when income and other social differences among the various parts of the country are held constant suggests a cultural dimension as well, especially in the case of Quebec, where support for welfare is significantly above the national norm. Perhaps this is a modern confirmation of Rimlinger's historical argument, discussed in chapter three, that support for social protection is greater in societies in which the roots of liberalism and individualism are shallow. Nevertheless, fascination with the sources of regionalism in Canada should not obscure the fundamental point that regional differences in public attitudes towards income security are limited, and are declining over time. In income security, regionalism represents variations on common themes, rather than discordant counterpoint.

Relatively broad agreement on the substance of policy, however, does not guarantee agreement on which level of government should run the program. For example, while public support for contributory pensions was reasonably uniform across the country during the 1960s, Canadians in different regions had decidedly different ideas about which level of government should operate the plan. As Table 39 indicates, most Quebecers wanted a provincial plan, while Canadians elsewhere favoured a federal plan by an equally clear majority, a division faithfully paralleled in the Canada and Quebec Pension plans that emerged. Nor do similar preferences on policy ensure that even Canadians outside of Quebec will always prefer federal jurisdiction. In 1972 and 1977 Gallup asked respondents whether they would approve of a larger provincial role, and a smaller federal role, in the area of taxation and social security. The responses, also presented in Table 39, suggested considerable, although not overwhelming, approval across the nation.

The pattern seems clear. The populations of the various Canadian regions do not differ dramatically in their attitudes towards income security. Rather, they share much the same mix of affections and concerns over the welfare state; that is, a broad consensus on the legitimacy of the existing range of programs but disagreements about whether the system should be expanded somewhat or contracted somewhat. On these questions the balance of opinion does vary from region to region, with the greatest support coming from the areas with the greatest income security needs, especially Quebec, but also Atlantic Canada. But this inter-regional consen-

Table 39   *Attitudes Towards Social Policy Jurisdiction*

1) Preferred Jurisdiction over Contributory Pensions, 1964

Region	Federal	Provincial	No Opinion
		(percent)	
Atlantic	55.7	18.6	25.7
Quebec	24.8	58.4	16.8
Ontario	57.4	25.4	17.2
Prairies	68.8	18.0	13.3
B.C.	77.9	13.2	8.8
CANADA	52.1	31.5	16.4

2) Attitudes Towards Larger Provincial Role, 1972, 1977

Region	Approve		Disapprove		Don't Know	
	1972	1977	1972	1977	1972	1977
			(percent)			
Atlantic	35.3	47.4	44.1	33.3	20.6	19.6
Quebec	53.8	59.2	21.0	24.4	25.2	16.4
Ontario	48.7	47.1	30.2	25.8	21.1	27.1
Prairies	55.2	61.4	24.0	21.7	20.8	16.9
B.C.	57.5	57.4	26.0	27.7	16.4	14.9
CANADA	50.9	53.9	27.4	25.6	21.7	20.5

Source: Canadian Institute of Public Opinion (CIPO) 307 (1964), 355 (1972), and 402 (1977).

sus on the broad outlines of income security coexists with public uncertainty and conflict about which level of government should operate the Canadian welfare state.

Planners and Income Security. If regionally distinctive conceptions of the
ideal social security system did exist, one would expect to find their clearest
expression in the books, reports, and background studies that constitute the
intellectual blueprints for Canadian welfare policies. Yet professional
opinion in Canada broadly parallels the pattern of public opinion: increasingly there is a broad consensus on the *substance* of an ideal social policy,
on the necessity for comprehensive income protection, on the range of
problems that remain, and on the options to be considered; but there is still
significant disagreement on *jurisdiction* over this ideal welfare state.

This has not always been true. In the middle years of this century a major
gulf opened up between English and French-speaking social policy specialists. During those years, social planners in English Canada all shared certain

core assumptions: faith in the capacity of government to remedy the social ills of industrial society; advocacy of a welfare state, protecting the population from all major interruptions in earnings; and an insistence on the importance of the central government in building such a system. These propositions formed the foundations of the outpouring of books, reports, and studies in the 1930s, 1940s, and 1950s, including Grauer's study for the Rowell-Sirois Commission, the Marsh Report, the publications of the League for Social Reconstruction, and the writings of individual social workers, such as Harry Cassidy.[13]

In Quebec, however, leading intellectuals elaborated a fundamentally different conception of social security. Social services in the province were provided primarily by the Church, with the role of government largely restricted to subsidizing such private efforts through the Public Charities Act of 1921.[14] Leading French-Canadian intellectuals defended this tradition against the *étatist* inclinations of their Anglophone counterparts. Esdras Minville, a leading sociologist, insisted in a study prepared for the Rowell-Sirois Commission in 1939 that: "The Church lays on the faithful the personal duty of charity . . . It is the bounden duty of each individual to provide, according to his means, for assistance to the destitute and unfortunate, and the state should intervene only when private initiative finds it impossible to supply existing needs."[15] While English-Canadian professionals unanimously advocated unemployment insurance, Minville worried that such programs would hasten the depopulation of rural areas and further undermine traditional French Canada; indeed without "a broad and audacious policy" of rural re-establishment, social policies such as unemployment insurance "might well work more harm than good."[16] Admittedly, professional opinion in the Quebec of the 1930s was not monolithic, and the Quebec Social Insurance Commission did accept the idea of unemployment insurance. But the conservative Catholicism of Minville remained the dominant stream within the Quebec community until the 1960s, and the classic statement of this perspective actually came in the Report of the Royal Commission on Constitutional Problems (the Tremblay Report), published in 1956. In light of subsequent developments, it is important to recall that the Tremblay Commission's opposition to federal welfare initiatives was not simply a call for provincial control of such programs; indeed, it explicitly rejected the notion of a "provincial welfare state":

> For what gives sense and value to provincial autonomy is not that a certain function should be carried out by the Provincial Government . . . but that it should be carried out in a certain spirit . . . . A social policy of Christian inspiration in accordance with traditional forms is thus the only one that justifies respect for its autonomy.[17]

This stark contrast in the ideals of leading English- and French-Canadian intellectuals has given way in the last twenty years to a powerful convergence on the substance of social policy. The ink was hardly dry on the Tremblay Report before its conservatism was overwhelmed by the ideological ferment of the Quiet Revolution. The attitudes of Quebec intellectuals towards the state underwent a profound shift: the state, in the form of the Quebec government, was to become the primary agent of modernization, the instrument through which a modern, urban, technologically advanced Francophone society could be created in Quebec. This new *étatisme* quickly spread to the social security world. In 1963 the *Report of the Study Committee on Public Assistance* (the Boucher Report) insisted that the distribution of government funds through private institutions was outdated. "The theory of the State's supplementary function, the fundamental concept of official social philosophy," was no longer adequate; "the State is the principal and most important distributor of assistance. Its right to this leading role can no longer be challenged seriously."[18] This approach received massive reinforcement a few years later from the voluminous reports of the Commission of Inquiry on Health and Social Welfare (the Castonguay-Nepveu Report), which betrayed no reticence at all in assuming a comprehensive planning role for the state: "Social development requires that the State take the initiative in overall measures aimed at assuring citizens of living conditions adapted to the requirements of their destiny. Only the State has the power and resources necessary to initiate such a vast undertaking."[19] The commission proceeded to outline a comprehensive restructuring of all policies that influenced income security in order to provide a guaranteed annual income for all Quebecers.

This shift in the thinking of a new generation of Quebec professionals and intellectuals has dramatically narrowed the traditional gulf between them and their English counterparts. The Boucher Report and, even more so, the Castonguay-Nepveu reports have been widely read outside of Quebec and have influenced professional thinking throughout Canada.[20] Older ideological differences have given way to a common professional view of social security, and a common language of demogrants, income guarantees, turning-points and the like. Professionals do not always agree, but the debate proceeds within a common frame of reference.

As with public opinion, however, growing consensus on the substance of policy has not generated agreement on which level of government should implement a modern income security system. While English-Canadian social policy planners still look to the federal government to exercise leadership, Quebec planners maintain the Tremblay Report's demand for provincial jurisdiction. The reasoning has changed, since Quebec planners have been drawing the blueprints for the "provincial welfare state" that Tremblay rejected, and the modern case for provincial jurisdiction advanced by bodies such as Castonguay-Nepveu reflects a professional's concern for planning and coordination through a single decision-making unit, together with a nationalist insistence that only the Quebec government can define the social needs of Quebecers.[21] But the effect is the same. While planners throughout Canada have increasingly common conceptions of the ideal social security system, sharp disagreement can emerge over which level of government should implement it.

Provincial Governments and Income Security. This general pattern of broad agreement on the substance of social policy but disagreement about responsibility for it is repeated again in the attitudes of provincial governments, as revealed by their positions in federal-provincial decision-making. Ideological conflict among the governments of Canada over the aims and scope of income security, while not unimportant, tends to be intermittent. As Simeon has argued, "left versus right has not been a salient characteristic of federal-provincial conflict, largely because at this level there has been substantial consensus among the governments. Virtually all Canadian governments have been committed to the notion of the Welfare State, though there have been variations between them."[22] These variations can become important, especially when major *extensions* of the welfare state are under debate; certainly the conflicts over the Canada Pension Plan and medicare in the 1960s, and income supplementation during the 1970s were rooted in part in the diverse ideological orientations of the governments at the table. But the staples of federal-provincial conflict over income security lie elsewhere. Conflicting conceptions of the nature of federalism and the legitimate role of federal and provincial governments have generated intense battles over jurisdiction in the field of income security, and conflicting interests in the distribution of the costs and benefits of the existing programs have generated battles over the financing of welfare, especially the division of the costs between the two senior levels of government.

Quebec and the other provinces differ significantly in the relative importance that they attach to jurisdiction as opposed to financial questions. Most provinces have never evidenced much interest in defending their jurisdiction in income security. Historically they often urged the federal authorities to intervene, they offered minimal resistance to the three constitutional amendments, and they have since shown no interest in recapturing lost territory. This pattern persisted into the 1970s. The power granted to the provinces to vary the rates of the federal government's Family Allowances was not the result of pressure from English Canada, and Alberta was the only English-speaking province to avail itself of the opportunity. During the Social Security Review, there was greater division on the issue of jurisdiction, with the three NDP provinces supporting Quebec's insistence on provincial delivery of the proposed supplements; but others, including

Ontario, much preferred federal jurisdiction over this expensive and potentially controversial program.[23] Clearly, jurisdictional issues have not been
critical to these governments.

For provinces other than Quebec, the real issue in income security is the
financing of it. They lobbied the federal government throughout the 1950s
and 1960s to expand its contributions to their social assistance costs, and
they generally support the expansion of federal programs such as Unemployment Insurance, Old Age Security, the Guaranteed Income Supplement, and Family Allowances. While changes in these benefits may necessitate adjustments in provincial programs, and often generate acrimonious
debates about whether the full benefit of the increased federal payment is
being "passed on" to public assistance recipients,[24] the enrichment of federal
programs generally reduces pressure on social assistance, which understandably brings smiles to the faces of provincial Finance ministers and
treasurers. And, as the battle over Unemployment Insurance revealed, cuts
in federal benefits have the opposite effect on provincial dispositions. The
only exception to this pattern is, as noted earlier, the Canada Pension Plan,
in which case the financial interests of provinces limit the expansion of
benefits.

While the preponderant concern of provinces other than Quebec is financial, their individual financial interests are obviously not identical. Poorer
provinces, such as those in Atlantic Canada, have always been strongly
committed to a major federal role in income security and special treatment
of their welfare needs. This was evident from the very beginnings of the
Canadian welfare state, as the Maritime provinces could not afford to opt
into the 1927 pension plan until after 1931 when the federal contribution
was raised to 75 percent of the cost. The same pattern has persisted since. In
the last fifteen years, for example, Atlantic provinces have repeatedly
fought for differential sharing in social assistance, that is, a financial
formula under CAP whereby the federal government would contribute a
larger proportion of social assistance costs in poorer provinces than elsewhere. But richer provinces and the federal Department of Finance have
insisted that equalization is a separate function to be carried out through the
equalization grant system, and so far the Atlantic region has always lost the
argument in the case of social assistance.[25] Clearly, then, the financial
interests of these nine provinces do not always coincide. But this should not
obscure the fact that the differences are largely over the distribution of
costs, rather than the substance of income security or jurisdiction over it.

In sharp contrast, the primary issue for governments of the province of
Quebec has always been jurisdiction, and the legitimate roles of the federal
and provincial governments in income security. Quebec leaders never fully
accepted the massive federal intervention—or "federal imperialism" to
borrow the Tremblay Commission's phrase[26]—in this previously provincial

domain. Prior to the 1960s, however, Quebec opposition was largely ineffective. Because Quebec governments believed in a limited state role in social matters, they left the field wide open to unilateral federal initiatives, and placed themselves in a vulnerable political position, especially when refusal to participate in federal shared-cost schemes meant that Quebec citizens paid federal taxes for programs from which they did not benefit. Quebec's policy was, consequently, schizophrenic: implacable opposition in principle was often coupled with eventual acquiescence in practice. Thus, the Taschereau regime steadfastly refused to participate in the 1927 pension plan, only to be forced to do so just before the 1936 election by the pressure from the opposition in the legislature, led (ironically) by Maurice Duplessis.[27] In power after 1936, Duplessis did refuse twice to allow a constitutional amendment which would have given the federal government jurisdiction over unemployment insurance; but the succeeding Godbout government, heavily in debt to the federal Liberals for its election, agreed to the amendment in 1940. Even Duplessis, back in power in 1944, soon learned the political impossibility of perpetual opposition. He strongly attacked the federal Family Allowances, even to the point of passing a short bill authorizing the establishment of a provincial plan if the federal government would withdraw. But when Ottawa persisted, tacit submission was inevitable. As Laurendeau, leader of the Bloc Populaire, made clear in the legislature at the time: "Si nous sommes en face de difficultés d'ordre constitutionelle, c'est parce que la Législature n'a pas utilisé les pouvoirs que lui conféraient sa souveraineté at son autonomie pour réaliser elle-même une politique d'allocations familiales."[28]

The lesson was not lost on Duplessis in 1951, when he agreed to the amendment to the BNA Act on pensions. As Bryden concluded: "[L]ike the province's Liberal government of 1936 the Union Nationale government in 1951 had no policy of its own to substitute for the federal plan, and it had long before learned the inexpediency of mere opposition to public pensions."[29] In the end, Duplessis' only qualification was the insistence on provincial paramountcy, so that a future Quebec government could enter the pension field if it so wished. The pattern of eventual accommodation appeared in other areas as well, with Quebec joining the new shared-cost program for the disabled promptly in 1956 and, after a delay of three years, the unemployment assistance program in 1959. The lesson of the Duplessis regime is clear: no government can defend disputed jurisdiction effectively unless it is prepared to utilize it aggressively.

Since 1960, jurisdictional claims of the province of Quebec have become dramatically more effective precisely because the province became intent on creating its own welfare state. Unlike Taschereau in 1936 and Duplessis in 1951, Jean Lesage was able to resist Ottawa's pension plan in 1963-64, not simply because of the constitutional power of the province, but primarily because of his government's firm intention to operate a plan of its own. Not only did the commitment to a provincial welfare state end the political scope for further centralization in income security, but it also generated a strong determination among Quebec politicians, especially in the Quebec Liberal party, to recapture territory lost during the decades of inactivity. Quebec opted out of the Canada Assistance Plan in 1965; during the constitutional discussion of 1968-71, jurisdiction over income security was the major Quebec demand; in 1973 Quebec won the concession on Family Allowance rates; and during the Social Security Review, Quebec insisted upon provincial delivery of any new income supplements.[30] During the most recent round of constitutional negotiations, recapturing jurisdiction over income security has faded as a goal of the Quebec Liberal party. Whether this represents a permanent acceptance of the massive federal role in income security is unclear, and the full implications of this are pursued in the next chapter. But, if the past is any guide to the uncertain future, jurisdiction will continue to be the primary concern of future governments of Quebec.

To what extent has this jurisdictional sensitivity reflected a distinctive conception of social security among the Quebec political elite? Certainly, during the 1940s Quebec leaders could, with justification, claim to speak for a distinctive approach to income security issues, and certainly every provincial leader since then has repeated the Tremblay Commission's warning that federal programs are culturally foreign. Daniel Johnson's brief to the 1968 constitutional conference included a lengthy quote from the Tremblay Report on the cultural importance of social policy,[31] and a year later Jean-Jacques Bertrand supported the demand for the transfer of social policy jurisdiction thus:

> . . . the social policy of a State . . . can influence all the activities of a society; it can create a feeling of dependence where such a thing might have been avoided, or it can destroy family ties. Or again it can discourage or encourage demographic growth, put emphasis on individual or family values. Social policy is the result of the aims of a society whose behaviour it can subsequently influence.[32]

In 1971 Robert Bourassa took up the theme, insisting that "the Quebec community is different" and that income security was integral to it:

> . . . social policy . . . is one of the expressions of a people's way of life. From this point of view, income security is far from being merely a means of redistributing wealth or an instrument of action suited to the circumstances; it touches the very fibre of a culture and may even be its product. The forms this policy takes derive from the culture of a people.[33]

When attention shifts to the specifics of social policy, however, it becomes clear that the aspirations of Quebec leaders differ less from those of their anglophone counterparts than the rhetoric of cultural distinctiveness might suggest. The substantial consensus found at the public and professional levels is repeated here. The Boucher and Castonguay-Nepveu reports have been widely praised in Quebec political circles, and certainly their approach is compatible with thinking in English Canada. Indeed, some Quebec premiers have made this clear. In 1965 Lesage reassured federal and provincial leaders that his demands for greater provincial jurisdiction "should not be taken to mean that we shall inevitably introduce a series of new social measures completely unrelated to those which may exist in Canada . . . . We are inclined to believe that these measures will be comparable, without necessarily being identical."[34] And in 1971 Bourassa similarly acknowledged that, while all provincial social policies need not be identical, they should and would be "consistent."[35]

Undoubtedly there are differences between the social policy ideas of Quebec politicians and those of their Anglophone counterparts. In the first place, income security seems to enjoy a higher priority in Quebec. The strong public support for welfare revealed in opinion surveys is paralleled by the expenditure decisions of Quebec governments: as Table 22 revealed, Quebec spent more on social welfare, on a per capita basis, in 1972 than any other province.[36] Within the welfare field, priorities also differ. Whereas the elderly seem to be the favourite beneficiary group in English Canada, Family Allowances have long enjoyed a particular significance in Quebec. During the 1920s and 1930s the French-Canadian clergy, union leadership, and planning commissions showed active interest in such a program, at a time when English Canadians were either uninterested or hostile.[37] When the federal program was launched in 1944, there was strong criticism in Quebec of the fact that the benefits were reduced for fifth and succeeding children, a provision which was regarded as an insult to the larger families of that province, and Duplessis briefly considered supplementing the payments for larger families. Later in the 1960s, when other provinces were concentrating on developing special supplements for the aged, Quebec developed its own Family Allowance program: in 1960, the province established a School Allowance for students aged sixteen and seventeen; in 1967 the province launched its general Family Allowances; and in 1973 the province used its new power over federal Family Allowances paid in Quebec to alter the benefits in favour of larger families.

The logic of Quebec's interest in Family Allowances has evolved, however. Historically many advocates saw such benefits as support for the critical role of the family in French-Canadian life,[38] and it is true that some nationalists still see the program as an instrument with which to combat the declining birthrate in modern Quebec. But the planners who advocated an enriched program throughout the 1960s and 1970s did not couch their case in cultural terms, and indeed they were quite sceptical about the impact on fertility. Rather, their case was economic: although the birthrate had declined, poverty in Quebec was still highly correlated with family size, and an expanded Family Allowance, weighted in favour of large families, would be a particularly effective anti-poverty instrument.[39] Given this rationale, the emphasis on Family Allowances may well decline as the lower birthrate inexorably alters the demographic profile of the Quebec population, and as poverty among the aged becomes a proportionately larger problem. As the Castonguay-Nepveu Report observed, the future would "lighten the social costs for children and increase them for the aged."[40] But, for the moment at least, Family Allowances remain a high priority in Quebec, and surveys of public opinion, such as that reported earlier in Table 32, indicate that such a stance enjoys strong support in the Quebec population.[41]

Nevertheless, the differences in the social policy goals between the Quebec political elite and those of other Canadian governments are still ones of priority, emphasis and degree, rather than principle. Quebec leaders no longer articulate a completely different approach to social policy; to use Lesage's words, their goals are "compatible without necessarily being identical." Clearly, the drive for greater jurisdiction over income security in the 1960s and early 1970s reflected a desire for greater political self-determination rather than a distinctive cultural approach to the social problems of industrial society.[42]

Conclusions: Regionalism and Income Security

The attitudes of public, planners, and provincial governments point in the same direction. Regional differences in attitudes towards income security are limited: there is broad acceptance of the legitimacy of the existing range of programs in all regions, and there are no clear signs of regionally distinctive conceptions of an ideal social security system. Regional differences in emphasis do exist. The public in poorer regions of Canada is somewhat more supportive of social security programs, and undoubtedly the priorities and emphases of planners and politicians do differ in important details from one part of the country to another. But such differences do not add up to significantly different conceptions of income security. By and large, Canadians share the same mix of affections and concerns about the welfare state from one region to another. Yet, substantial consensus on the substance of policy coexists with disagreement at all three levels of opinion on jursidiction and financing.

Such a configuration of interests and attitudes raises the question whether the most important consequences of jurisdictional change in this area would be for the political system itself, rather than for the income security system that it produces, and it is to this question that the analysis must now turn.

9 The Consequences of Constitutional Reform

Electoral reform, a new Senate, centralization, decentralization, disentanglement, special status, sovereignty-association: a seemingly endless variety of proposals for constitutional change have competed for the attention and favour of Canadians and their governments during the last decade. Only rarely has public debate over the various options moved from polemics and propaganda to careful analysis of how they would actually alter the policies of the nation, and this is perhaps not surprising given the intensely symbolic nature of the issues at stake. But, whatever its relevance to political deliberations about the constitution, an analysis of the likely consequences of institutional reform does serve to heighten our appreciation of the relationship between the *existing* institutional structure and public policy in Canada. This chapter therefore asks what would be the impact of constitutional reform on income security, an area of public policy that is critical to millions of Canadians.

For obvious reasons, any conclusions drawn from such an enterprise must be tentative. But the preceding analyses of the determinants of income security, the impact of the present federal system, and the extent of regional concerns about welfare do provide a basis for discussing the probable consequences of institutional change. At the very least, we can identify pressures and constraints that would emerge or increase under a new constitutional order, even if we cannot predict with certainty how the revised political system would respond to them.

Proposals for constitutional change have followed two basic approaches, the first concentrating on the reform of the institutions of the central government, and the second on a reallocation of the powers of the two senior levels of government.[1] The first approach seeks to make the key policy-making institutions of the central government more representative of, and more responsive to, the full range of regionalism in Canada. Policy decisions made in Ottawa, advocates of this approach contend, should be based not solely on the dictates of majority rule, but on compromises struck between strong and independent representatives of the diverse regions of the country. To that end, they propose changes in the electoral system, the House of Commons, the Senate, the composition of and method of appointment to the Supreme Court and major regulatory agencies, the structure of the civil service, and so on. The second approach to constitutional change, on the other hand, proceeds on the assumption that a central government, however artfully constructed, can never be fully responsive to the needs and aspirations of Canada's diverse regions. Responding to these differences is the role of provincial governments, and the solution to Canada's tensions is therefore to alter the distribution of powers between the federal and provincial governments.

What, then, would be the impact of such constitutional changes on income security? Any answer to this question must be based on an appreciation of the broad determinants of income security policy generally. As chapter three argued, the precise structure of political institutions is far from the most important influence on the shape of the welfare state in western nations. The emergence of the welfare state was primarily a response to the intense social and economic pressures generated by the twin processes of industrialization and urbanization and, under these pressures, countries with dramatically different political and cultural traditions developed a surprisingly similar range of social protections for their populations. The importance of this underlying economic and social transformation stands as a warning against attributing too much significance to the limited forms of institutional change that have been debated in Canada recently. Constitutional reform would not alter the elemental structure of society on the northern half of the North American continent; the basic social needs to which the welfare state was a response would not disappear; and the political pressures of the Canadian state (or successor states) to provide a similar range of policy responses to those needs would not abate.

Consequently, the basic existence of some form of welfare state would not be at stake in any conceivable process of constitutional change. What would be at stake would be the specific structure of that welfare state: the mix of instruments through which it operates, the proportion of the nation's resources devoted to it, and most important, the distribution of the costs and benefits of income security across the country. But even here the specific policy consequences vary sharply with the approach to constitutional reform being considered. Reform of central institutions would have few major consequences for income security. Regional concerns about income security do not differ dramatically, and therefore the adoption of mechanisms designed to heighten the sensitivity of the central government to regional particularisms would be of little moment here. While some of the proposals of this type would also alter the balance of power in Ottawa in other ways that would be of greater importance to income security, the basic thrust of intrastate federalism misses the central political dynamics of the Canadian welfare state.

The second approach, altering the division of power over income security between the federal and provincial governments, on the other hand, could have greater implications for income security in Canada. Change here could influence the instruments of policy, the scope and size of income security benefits, and their distribution among individual Canadians. Yet it is important, even here, to maintain a sense of perspective. In the final analysis, the direct implications for the substance of income security policy itself will likely be less important than the indirect consequences for the broader political and economic structure of the Canadian federation.

REFORM OF CENTRAL INSTITUTIONS

In examining the consequences of this approach, attention will focus on proposals for electoral reform and for a new second chamber to replace or parallel the existing Senate. These have been the most widely canvassed, and probably the most important, of the proposals that fall into this category. Some of the others, such as reform of judicial and regulatory bodies, have less relevance for income security, while others, such as proposals to reform the House of Commons by loosening the bonds of party discipline seem patently politically unattainable. Even if such changes were set in place, it is unlikely that their impact on income security would differ dramatically from that of electoral or Senate reform.

Electoral Reform: Proportional Representation

Reform of the electoral system through which Canadians choose their members of Parliament has emerged as a common prescription in recent years.[2] While most advocates draw back from a complete shift to proportional representation, for fear that the result would be perpetual minority or coalition government, they do opt for a mixed system that would preserve the present basis for electing the House of Commons, but supplement its membership with an additional sixty to one hundred MPs selected on the basis of proportional representation. The case for such a reform is straightforward: greater proportional representation would create national political parties that could serve as instruments of inter-regional accommodation. The major parties would have significant representation from all parts of the country; they would have less incentive to tailor their electoral strategies and platforms to particular regions; and all regions would be represented in cabinet, ending the virtual exclusion of either Quebec or the west from power. As a result, the federal government would be seen to be governing for all Canadians; its policy decisions would be more sensitive to the interests of all regions; and provincial governments would be less able to claim the mantle of sole spokesman for regional concerns. In the words of one advocate, proportional representation is a "prerequisite to revitalizing the central government and harnessing it to serve the common interests of Canadians."[3]

What would be the impact of such a change on income security? The explicit goal of electoral reformers is to make the internal composition of the caucuses of the major parties, and therefore of any cabinets that they form, more representative of all regions. But given the limited nature of regional variation in concerns about income security, a reshuffling of regional voices in the House of Commons could not be expected to alter income security dramatically. There might be some tendency to mute even further the marginal differences that do exist in the two major parties' approaches to welfare. Since the prairie population is now somewhat less sympathetic to welfare programs than are other Canadians, increasing the prairie representation in Liberal ranks might constrain welfare advocates within the party; and as the Quebec population is the most sympathetic to welfare, a sizeable Quebec contingent in the Conservative caucus might, for example, moderate its arguments for greater selectivity in such programs as Family Allowances. But this line of reasoning should not be pressed too far. It was, after all, a Liberal government that proposed in 1970 to eliminate the universal Family Allowances, and replace them with the Family Income Security Plan, an income-tested benefit.

Much more important to income security would be the change in the relative strength of different parties in the House of Commons. While it is impossible to predict exactly what kind of party system would eventually develop under proportional representation, the short-term consequences are clear. The size of the major parties in the House would be reduced, especially when they are in government; minority or coalition governments would become more common; and, most important, the strength of the NDP would be increased. As Irvine has argued, "in addition to cleavages organized around culture and region, class cleavages would be prominently represented in Parliament, as the NDP would be strengthened and would become a potent force in government formation."[4] Such an outcome would undoubtedly strengthen the forces in favour of expansion of income security. The introduction of pensions in 1927, the initiatives of the Pearson regime, and the 1973 tripling of Family Allowances all stand as evidence of the potency of such parliamentary combinations. The impact here depends heavily on the extent of proportionality introduced into the system; a mild "topping up" might still allow one-party majority governments. But the direction of the impact is clearly in favour of the expansion of income security efforts at the national level.

An important assumption of many electoral reformers is that a more representative federal government would be a more powerful federal government vis-à-vis its provincial challengers. If this proved correct, electoral reform would help sustain the dominance of the federal government in income security, preserve the national standards and inter-regional transfers implicit in that dominance, forestall further provincialization of programs along the lines of Family Allowances, and ensure an important role for the central government in any future extensions of income security, such as a guaranteed annual income. The argument, however, is unconvincing. Provincial governments would remain powerful forces in Canadian politics, commanding impressive jurisdiction, financial resources, and bureaucratic skills, and there is no reason to assume that a more representative Ottawa would decisively reduce their legitimacy in the eyes of provincial electorates.[5] Certainly, the ability of MPs selected through a "topping up" system to resist the demands of provincial governments is particularly suspect, as such MPs would face major obstacles in establishing their legitimacy as regional spokesmen.

More important, a review of federal-provincial conflict over income security during the last two decades raises doubts about the link between representativeness and the role of the federal government. Contracting out of the Canada Assistance Plan and other shared-cost programs, the establishment of the Quebec Pension Plan, the provincialization of Family Allowance benefits, and the agreement in 1976 that a new income supplementation scheme should be provincially delivered, were all demanded primarily by Quebec, and were all accepted by a federal government with impressive representation from that province. Obviously, MPs from a province can also become advocates of compromise with "their" provincial government. During the protracted battle between Ottawa and Quebec City over Family Allowances in the early 1970s, for example, leading federal Liberals from Quebec, such as Marc Lalonde, were much more inclined to compromise than others, such as John Munro, who was minister of National Health and Welfare in the early stages.[6] The same point can be made about energy. Which government is more likely to accommodate the Alberta government's position, a Progressive Conservative government with twenty-one Alberta MPs or a Liberal government with none? Clearly, the relationship between the representativeness of the central government and its role in the federal system is a complex one, about which we know too little to prophesy with confidence. Electoral reform does seem a rather thin reed on which to construct weighty expectations about the defence of the federal role.

A New Upper Chamber or a Federal Council

Recent constitutional debate has witnessed the emergence of a fascination
with reforming the Senate, or paralleling it with a completely new body, in
order to ensure greater regional or provincial representation in federal decision-making. While most constitutional thinkers are agreed in not wanting
a directly elected upper house,[7] there have been two sharply conflicting
schools of thought on what basic role a new body should play in the Canadian political system. The first of these schools aims at more effective
regional representation in the deliberations of the central government, and
this approach formed the basis of the Trudeau government's 1978 proposal
to replace the Senate with a new body called the House of the Federation.[8]
Under the terms of the government's Constitutional Amendment Bill, the
power of appointment to this new chamber would have been divided, with
the House of Commons appointing half of the members and the provincial
legislatures appointing the rest. But once appointed, members of the House
of the Federation were to be independent of the federal and provincial
cabinets, and free to defend the interests of their regions of the country, as
they saw them. The new House was to have a suspensive veto over all
federal legislation, and a special role in the particularly sensitive area of language legislation.

The second school of thought advocates a chamber, variously titled a
House of the Provinces or Federal Council, the fundamental purpose of
which would be to represent *provincial governments.*[9] The provincial
governments would appoint the members of the new body; provincial
premiers might choose occasionally to head the provincial delegation; and
members of the chamber would act under instructions from the provincial
government that appointed them. Clearly, these two types of chambers
would perform significantly different functions, and the implications of
each for income security should be examined separately.

House of the Federation. As in the case of proportional representation,
this type of chamber would have few important consequences for income
security. Since regional publics do not differ sharply on income security,
there seems little reason to suppose that the policy preferences of such a
body would, over the long term, differ markedly from those of the House of
Commons or the cabinet, unless an appointed body proved more conservative on social issues than the directly elected Commons, a possibility that
should not be discounted. Advocates of this approach to reforming central
institutions hope that the creation of regional spokesmen, who could be
seen to be fighting in public for the interests of their part of the country,
would generate greater public trust in the federal government and reduce
the role of provincial governments as the only defenders of regional
concerns. While such propositions cannot be disproven conclusively,

important doubts linger. Would renaming the Senate, increasing the number of bodies making appointments to it, and reducing its formal powers really solve the fundamental lack of legitimacy of a non-elected body, a body with no mechanism of accountability to the public, in a democratic system? If not, why should it be any more effective than the present Senate, and why should the people of Quebec, Alberta, British Columbia, Newfoundland, or any other province place their faith in it?

Certainly, such a chamber would be marginal to the life-blood of federal-provincial disputes, since provincial governments would continue to press their claims through traditional mechanisms rather than relying on a chamber that they did not control. Indeed, if a House of the Federation did take an independent line on federal-provincial issues, it would simply complicate Canadian federalism further. Federal cabinets that could not commit the federal Parliament could not negotiate as effectively with the provinces, with the result that the major instrument of intergovernmental accommodation, executive federalism, would be undermined, with nothing of similar effectiveness put in its place. Ironically, the fate of the federal government's Bill C-60, which sought to create a House of the Federation, at the hands of a special Joint Committee of the Senate and House of Commons during the summer and fall of 1978, provides clear evidence of the potential for paralysis in such a system.

House of the Provinces or a Federal Council. A House of the Provinces or Federal Council, on the other hand, could have more important consequences for income security, reinforcing as it would the interests of provincial governments as governments. Anticipating the precise nature of those consequences, however, is complicated by the lack of agreement, even among proponents of such a chamber, on its composition and on the powers to be granted to it. Some, for example, see it exercising a general suspensive veto over all legislation, with perhaps an absolute veto over legislation relating to federal-provincial and language relations, while others see it dealing with federal-provincial issues only. Clearly, some assumptions are required at this point. The following discussion proceeds on the basis of a new chamber in which the provincial delegations are not equal in size, but are perhaps weighted so as to over-represent smaller provinces; and it assumes that the new body possesses a suspensive veto over all federal legislation and an absolute veto over legislation directly relevant to federal-provincial relations, including conditional grant programs.

In effect, such a body would import something like the relationships now governing the Canada Pension Plan into our other income security policies. Indeed one member of the Quebec Liberal party's Constitutional Committee, which proposed such a Federal Council, saw the CPP as a prototype: "The Council would simply be the forum in which such decisions could be ratified." But the consequences of such a body for income security generally would be much different from those for the Canada Pension Plan. Whereas provincial governments have a vested interest in restraining the growth of CPP benefits, they have a financial interest in the expansion of other federal income security programs, as these tend to ease the costs of their own social assistance. Even if the House of the Provinces did not actually become a lobby for higher federal benefits, it would strengthen the provinces' ability to block cuts in federal benefits that might increase their welfare costs. The dispute over Unemployment Insurance during the 1970s is a crystal-clear example. The federal cuts were opposed by virtually every provincial government, and would not have been approved by a House of the Provinces; the prospect of even a suspensive veto would have been an important obstacle to the cabinet, intent as it was on rapid change in the program. The cabinet would probably have modified its approach, perhaps even switching to the provincial "family" approach in the end. In general, then, a House of the Provinces or a Federal Council would tend to consolidate, maybe even enhance, the importance of federal income security programs.

Ironically, the impact of a House of the Provinces or Federal Council on shared-cost programs would probably work in the same direction. There is no doubt that a House of the Provinces would formalize the decline of the shared-cost mechanism as an important tool of federalism in Canada. Such programs would be more difficult to launch; the already minimal ability of the federal government to attach conditions to grants would be further eroded; and firmer guarantees of the right of any province to opt out, with full fiscal compensation, would result. At the same time the federal government would be less able to reduce its contributions to on-going programs; there is, for example, no doubt that had such a body been in place, the federal government would have been bargaining from a far weaker position throughout the negotiations leading up to the 1977 Fiscal Arrangements Act. Such a prospect would undoubtedly diminish even further the federal government's interest in such shared-cost programs.

The consequences of all of this, however, again highlight the bifurcated nature of the Canadian welfare state. While the demise of conditional grants would effectively preclude a significant federal role in health and social services, it would, if anything, enhance the federal role in income security. The Canada Assistance Plan is the only major income security program involved, and in the short term at least the probable role of a House of the Provinces would be to shield CAP from the knives of the Department of Finance in Ottawa, which shows recurring signs of wanting to "cap CAP." The prospects of new conditional grants in this field would, of course, be diminished, but this would not foreclose federal expansion in income security. As the emergence of the Child Tax Credit demonstrated, Ottawa can simply pursue its redistributive goals unilaterally. In the long term, if the federal government were shut out of the health and social service field, it might devote even greater attention to income security, expanding existing programs and developing new ones. After all, Canadians would still look to Ottawa for social leadership, the social reformers among the federal politicians would still want to respond, and income security would be their only avenue.

The existence of a House of the Provinces would not significantly increase the likelihood or effectiveness of provincial resistance to such a pattern. Apart from Quebec, the provinces would probably not resist the further centralization of welfare costs implicit in such a development; and even if Quebec did reassert its traditional jurisdictional claims in this area, a House of the Provinces would not make those claims any more effective than they have been in the past. Indeed, such a body might actually undermine its claims. In 1963-64 Quebec had both the firm intent and the clear jurisdiction to implement a contributory pension plan, and a House of the Provinces would have had little choice but to accept a compromise similar to the one that eventually emerged. During the negotiations leading up to the Victoria Charter, Quebec failed to convince the other governments of Canada of the need for decentralization of jurisdiction over income security, and a House of the Provinces would not have produced a different line-up.

Intriguing questions, however, are raised by the acceptance of contracting out in 1965 and the provincialization of Family Allowance benefits in 1973, both of which were basically special deals between Ottawa and Quebec City. How, for example, would a House of the Provinces have reacted to contracting out in 1965, when such a procedure was not yet accepted practice and would obviously result in special status for Quebec? Many of the English-speaking provinces, including Ontario, opposed the idea at the time.[10] Would they have blocked it if they had had a House of the Provinces or Federal Council at their disposal? Such questions have no answers. But it remains possible that a House of the Provinces would effectively entrench a norm of uniformity in the relations between Ottawa and each province. At the very least, a House of the Provinces would not make jurisdictional claims advanced by one province alone more compelling.

REFORM OF JURISDICTION OVER INCOME SECURITY

Logically, the division of power over income security between the federal and provincial governments could be altered in a variety of ways, ranging from complete centralization of all income security programs in the hands of the federal government to complete decentralization of all programs in provincial hands. But given the present predominance of the federal government in income security and the general trends within the federation over the last two decades, only proposals for decentralization have attracted much interest. Even the federal authorities have primarily sought to defend their present role in this area, rather than to expand it at the expense of the provinces. In 1969 a working paper presented by the federal government to the constitutional conference did propose federal paramountcy in the field of contributory pensions,[11] a provision that could have led to federal control over the Quebec Pension Plan; but this federal assertiveness seems to have been primarily a bargaining chip in the negotiations, since it was surrendered rather easily and not revived thereafter. By contrast, proposals for increasing the powers of provincial governments in income security have been a recurring feature of constitutional discussions over the last decade. There have been two major approaches here: the first proposes granting the provincial governments formal constitutional powers over aspects of federal programs in the income security field; and the second advocates outright transfer of at least some elements of income security to some or all of the provincial capitals.

Provincial Power over Federal Policies

The most important constitutional trend in income security over the last twenty years has been the creation of a formal role for provincial governments in decisions about federal programs such as the Canada Pension Plan and Family Allowances, and some would-be constitutional designers would like to expand this approach significantly. Two possibilities have been advanced to this end. The first is an expansion of the principle of provincial configuration of federal income security payments; and the second is provincial control over the federal power to launch shared-cost programs in provincial areas of jurisdiction. These proposals are seeking, in a carefully defined policy area, basically the same goals as those sought for a wider range of policies by advocates of a House of the Provinces or Federal Council: provincial governments would be able to influence federal policies, resist federal initiatives considered damaging to provincial government interests, and better coordinate federal and provincial programs.

Provincial Configuration of Federal Benefits. The basic idea of provincial configuration is that the provincial governments would have the power to alter, within limits, the rates of benefit paid to their populations by federal income security programs. The first and most sweeping recommendation that this principle be entrenched in the constitution came in 1971 from the Special Joint Committee of the Senate and the House of Commons on the Constitution. The committee recommended that, while jurisdiction over social insurance should not change, there should be what it called "limited Provincial paramountcy" in the case of federal demogrants and means-tested payments:

> ... the Federal Parliament would retain concurrent power to establish programs and to pay benefits to individuals under these programs. However, a Province would have the right to vary the national scheme established by Parliament with respect to the allocation within the Province between various programs of the total amount determined by the Federal Government and with respect to the scale of benefits paid to individuals within the Province according to income, number of children, etc., within each program.[12]

In effect, the federal government would determine the total amount of money available for its income-security programs in each province, and then each provincial government would have the right to alter the distribution of those resources between the different federal programs and between different groups of beneficiaries of each individual program. The committee did recommend limits to this right: Parliament should set national standards for each benefit, and the benefit set by the provincial government could not be less than a specified percentage ("perhaps half or two-thirds") of that standard. And, of course, the program would remain a federal one. Ottawa would raise the revenue and mail out the cheques.

This idea was taken up by the federal government in 1973 in the Orange Paper with which it launched the Social Security Review.[13] The federal authorities proposed such an arrangement for all existing benefits, except the social insurance programs, and for any new income supplements that the federal government might establish. In the end the procedure was brought into force for Family Allowances only. Nevertheless, the principle of provincial configuration has now been established, and could no doubt be extended. Indeed such a step was recommended in 1978 by the Canadian Bar Association's Committee on the Constitution, whose report endorsed the full 1972 proposal advanced by the parliamentary committee.[14]

What would be the consequences of provincial configuration of federal benefits? Potentially it might produce a more flexible, more integrated, and more regionally sensitive income security system. While the federal government is locked for political reasons into uniform programs across the country, provincial governments could vary the payments in ways more relevant to the particular blend of social needs of the local population, and coordinate them more closely with their own social policies. In addition, different social values could be pursued. Quebec, for example, might wish to expand Family Allowances more rapidly than Old Age Security, whereas other provinces might allocate resources in the opposite direction; provincial governments with a more selectivist approach to social policy might emphasize growth in the Guaranteed Income Supplement more than Old Age Security, and so on. In general, then, such a reform might become the vehicle of greater flexibility in income security.

Potential and practice are, however, decidedly different phenomena, and the Family Allowance example suggests that such a system would be complicated, perhaps fatally, by the relentless search of governments for public applause. In 1973, the Liberal government, still struggling to find its feet after the setback of the 1972 election, announced with a grand flourish that Family Allowances would be increased dramatically to $20 per child, and naturally the announcement received headline treatment across the country. The publicity, however, became a political straightjacket for provinces wishing to exercise their new powers to alter the configuration of the federal payments. In a number of provinces, welfare officials advised their ministers that poverty was severest in larger families and that the allowances should therefore be larger for third and subsequent children. But in most cases this could only be done by denying first and perhaps second children, and therefore all one- and two-child families, a significant part of the much-heralded $20 per child. Because Quebec had its own Family Allowance program, it could ensure that, even if the federal payments were altered in this way, the combination of federal and provincial allowances would be at least close to the magic $20 figure for such families. Other provinces were not so lucky. As a result, several provincial cabinets overruled their officials' advice rather than face the political risks of tampering with the increase and, in the end, only Alberta and Quebec exercised their new powers. None of this was accidental. The federal government desperately wanted the political credit, and its publicity basically presented the provinces with a *fait accompli.*[15]

Clearly, the successful operation of an enlarged system of provincial configuration would require great political restraint on the part of all governments. Whenever the federal government wished to inject new resources into income security, it would have to abjure politically attractive announcements about average benefit levels until the provinces made their decisions. But the federal government certainly would not restrain itself if the provinces sought to capture a greater share of the political credit by, for example, announcing provincial benefit levels in advance of the federal authorities. The prospects for stable understandings concerning the intergovernmental division of the public's praise seem remote. In effect, such a reform would import into income security the same political rivalry that has bedeviled the history of conditional grant programs in this country, and there is no reason to assume that the political logic would be any different. Exhortations to abstinence are even less effective in politics than they are in family planning.

If political competition did not render the reform meaningless, then provincial variation might have other important consequences, especially in the area of federal-provincial finances. As with a House of the Provinces, provincial configuration could produce fiscal centralization in income security, with the federal government absorbing an even larger share of total costs in the field. Provincial governments would be sorely tempted to vary federal payments in ways that would reduce their own social assistance expenditures. Indeed, the federal government was sufficiently concerned about this possibility to attach the following condition to its proposal in the 1973 Orange Paper: "The provinces would be required to contribute to the social security system the amount they would otherwise have contributed prior to any changes in the system, and before any changes in the levels of federal allowances or income support payments under any new 'flexibility formula'."[16] But such a requirement is patently unenforceable, and it was not included in the agreement on Family Allowances concluded during the Social Security Review. The best prognosis, then, is that provincial configuration would increase the federal share of income security expenditures above that which would otherwise prevail.

These general consequences, however, are minor compared with those that would flow from actual transfer of income security programs to provincial jurisdiction. Ottawa would still mail out the cheques and an important direct link between the federal government and its citizens would not be severed. Ottawa would still finance the expenditures and therefore retain the considerable tax room associated with income security, thereby retaining an important element of its economic power. The hidden interregional transfers would not be altered. Moreover, as long as the federal government set national minimum standards for each program, benefit levels would not vary sufficiently from one province to another to have much influence on migration patterns in the country. Provincial configuration might be nullified completely by political competition. But if it did not, it might provide a useful element of regional sensitivity in income security, without major secondary consequences.

Provincial Controls over Shared-Cost Initiatives. A second possibility of this sort is to limit the federal government's right to establish federal-provincial shared-cost programs. In 1969, for example, the federal government itself proposed that the federal Parliament should retain the right to contribute to provincial programs, but subject to two important conditions.[17] The first of these, which resembled the Canada Pension Plan formula in general terms, was that there would have to be a "broad national consensus"—or more accurately, a broad *intergovernmental* consensus—in favour of a new program before it could be launched. Any new programs would require the approval of the federal Parliament together with a combination of provincial legislatures representing three of the four regions of Canada.[18] Second, the population of any province that chose not to participate would not suffer, as a grant amounting to the *per capita* federal expenditure in the participating provinces would be sent directly to taxpayers in the province. These proposals were not included in the ill-fated Victoria Charter, but such proposals could resurface in the future, especially if a House of the Provinces or Federal Council is not established.

The consequences of such a proposal would, in general, be similar to those of establishing a House of the Provinces, although much would depend on the method chosen for reimbursing non-participating provinces. The federal proposal to reimburse the public in such provinces would put added pressure on provincial governments to join new programs, and to do so at the outset. Provinces that operated their own programs would have to finance them exclusively from provincial revenues. Provinces that decided to join a shared-cost program after it had been in operation for a few years would, in effect, be depriving their provincial population of an established cash rebate from the federal government. It is hardly surprising, then, that the provincial governments were not enamoured by this approach during the 1969-71 constitutional negotiations,[19] and that Quebec liked it even less when the federal government actually resorted to this device during the 1978 battle over the retail sales tax reduction program.[20] Provincial governments insist that the government of non-participating provinces should receive the fiscal compensation, as in the case of the 1965 contracting-out formula. If they won this battle, then the consequences of provincial control over shared-cost initiatives would parallel the consequences of a House of the Provinces or Federal Council, with veto power over such programs. Shared-cost programs would decline even further as an instrument of fiscal federalism, but the closing off of federal initiatives in health and social services might focus federal expansionism more powerfully on income security programs.

Decentralization of Jurisdiction over Income Security

Income security has had a curious role in constitutional controversy during the last fifteen years. In 1969-71, provincial control over major federal income security programs was the primary demand of the province of Quebec, advanced by both the Union Nationale government and even more prominently by the succeeding Liberal administration of Robert Bourassa. Since then, income security has receded as a critical issue. The victory of the Parti Québécois in 1976 raised constitutional debate to a much more general level, and little attention was focused on the specific consequences of sovereignty-association for individual policy areas like income security.[21] But perhaps even more important has been the de-escalation of the demands of the Quebec Liberal party in this field. This process began with Castonguay's acceptance of the Family Allowance accord in 1973, and has accelerated under Ryan's leadership, to the point that the party now largely endorses the existing federal-provincial division in income security. *A New Canadian Federation*, which sets out the party's constitutional position, explicitly defends the importance of the federal government's role in redistributing income between Canadians in all regions through programs such as Family Allowances and Old Age Security.[22] The original draft of the document did demand provincial jurisdiction over all social insurance, including contributory pensions and Unemployment Insurance, but this has turned out to be unimportant. First, Quebec already has its own Quebec Pension Plan, and no Quebec government is likely to insist that other provincial governments take over contributory pensions when they clearly have little wish to do so. Second, provincial control over Unemployment Insurance, which would have been an important change, generated intra-party conflict. Both the committee that drafted the constitutional document and the workshop at the party convention that considered this proposal were divided over it, and in the end the idea was withdrawn.[23] The result is that the Quebec Liberal party basically endorses the constitutional status quo in income security, a sharp reversal from its position of less than a decade ago.

This retreat from traditional positions has proved controversial in Quebec, and the full reasons for it are somewhat unclear. In part, the prominence of income security in Quebec's demands in 1969-71 was fortuitous, reflecting the interests of several strong personalities in the Quebec government, at both the ministerial and advisory level, as well as strategic decisions about the best means of raising the general issue of the division of powers.[24] After 1971, changing personalities and strategic opportunities shifted Quebec's constitutional demands to other policy sectors, including communications, immigration, and culture. Then more recently under Claude Ryan, the party chose to present a principled defence of federalism as a clear alternative to sovereignty-association, and this approach clearly influenced its position on jurisdiction over income security, especially the specific endorsement of the right of the federal government to make direct transfers to individuals.

More pragmatic considerations were also important. The constitutional committee of the party was impressed by the growing complexity of income security instruments and the attention being given to achieving redistributive goals through the taxation system. In the end, the committee concluded that the introduction of programs such as the Child Tax Credit demonstrated that the redistributive function of the state cannot be clearly allocated to one level of government in a federal system. As one of them put it privately, "you would have to have provincial scrutiny of the federal

budget, with all of its exemptions and credits, as well."²⁵ In the case of
Unemployment Insurance, advocates of provincial control raised the logic
of integration, arguing that the program should be coordinated with manpower, labour, and other welfare instruments, whereas advocates of federal
responsibility argued that the large inter-provincial subsidies hidden in the
present program meant that poorer provinces, including Quebec, could not
afford to maintain comparable standards in a purely provincial program.
While the drafting committee gave priority to program integration, the
convention workshop could only see "all those missing millions of dollars"
and decided that Unemployment Insurance was an enormous "political can
of worms best left in Ottawa."

Whether income security remains off the constitutional agenda in the
future is impossible to foresee. Its sudden rise and then equally sudden fall
suggest that another rise is always possible. If economic growth increases to
the point that income security innovations become leading issues again,
constitutional tensions may well re-emerge. But even if decentralization of
jurisdiction over income security seems unlikely in the near future, an
analysis of the probable consequences of such a change highlights the relationships between institutions and policy today. This section therefore
concludes with an examination of the consequences of two possible forms of
decentralization in income security.

General Decentralization. Of all possible constitutional changes, decentralization of jurisdiction would have the greatest impact on income
security in Canada. While decentralization would not alter the basic range
of social needs being met, it would alter the structure of the response to
them. In the first place, the mix of income security instruments employed
for future developments of income security would be altered since, as
chapter five argued, social insurance is a more complicated tool to operate
at the provincial level. These problems might prove manageable for social
insurance programs that are already well established but, as in the 1930s,
they would probably inhibit subsequent expansion. Inter-provincial migration would create a constant pressure for parallelism among provincial
plans, and necessitate elaborate collaboration between provincial governments. The present requirement for inter-governmental consensus for
improvements in the Canada Pension Plan has isolated it from the expansionist pressures inherent in democratic politics and, although decentralization would eliminate the system of formal vetoes which exists now, the need
to maintain comparability between provincial plans would have a similar
effect, and would extend it to Unemployment Insurance. Decentralized
systems of social insurance are not impossible, as countries as diverse as
Yugoslavia and the United States have demonstrated. But such a system
would be more complex, and provincial governments would find it easier to

respond to new social problems by expanding other income security instruments, such as demogrants and means-tested benefits or by leaving new problems to the private sector and accepting the inequalities of coverage that such a strategy would imply.

Decentralization involving all provinces would probably also lower the total level of resources that Canada would devote to income security in the future. The cross-national studies reviewed in chapter three point firmly to a relationship between political centralization and welfare spending, and chapters five and six pointed to a variety of reasons for suspecting that a decentralized system in Canada would commit fewer resources to meeting social needs. First, as just mentioned, social insurance growth would be inhibited and, in all probability, not all of the difference would be made up through other instruments. Second, provincial governments might again be inhibited by the mobility of capital and labour, as they claimed to be during the 1930s. Third, whatever expansionist tendencies result from intergovernmental competition under the present system would be eliminated if responsibility for income security were consolidated at one level of government.

But perhaps the most convincing reason for anticipating a lower level of spending than would otherwise prevail lies in the regional differences in public attitudes towards welfare. Chapter eight revealed that, while public attitudes towards welfare do not differ dramatically from one region to another, Quebecers and Atlantic Canadians are somewhat more supportive than the populations of other provinces. This has important implications for the nature of the constituency of the federal government as opposed to those of the ten provincial governments. In income security matters, the federal constituency includes two types of regions: those with weak economies, high income-security needs, and greater public support for welfare spending on one hand; and those with stronger economies, proportionately lower income-security needs, and more restrained public support for expanded welfare expenditures on the other. Federal policy is, in a sense, a compromise between these conflicting needs and pressures.

Decentralization would alter the relevant constituencies. The poorer provinces would be even less able to meet the aspirations of their publics than the federal government. Much here would depend on the magnitude of equalization payments that would be established but, for reasons discussed below, the equalization system is unlikely to compensate fully for the massive transfers hidden in federal income security. Given the higher levels of public support for welfare in poor regions, some poor provinces might choose to devote more of their resources to welfare spending, in order to meet their constituents' expectations. But the more likely outcome over the long term is a slower rate of growth than would have flowed from continued federal jurisdiction. If more affluent provinces provided benefits much greater than those that the federal government would otherwise have done, then the total resources devoted to income security might not be affected. But, given the somewhat lower levels of public support for welfare in high-income regions, there seems little reason to anticipate benefit levels significantly above those that would have flowed from Ottawa. By international standards Canada does not devote a large share of its resources to income security, and decentralization of jurisdiction in this area would probably ease Canada a little further down the international league tables.

Even if the impact on total expenditures on welfare was not dramatic, decentralization would undoubtedly alter the distribution of benefits among Canadians. The implicit inter-regional transfers identified in chapter six would end, with predictable results: national standards would soon be only a fading memory, and income security would increasingly reflect, rather than compensate for, regional disparities. In addition, there would be important secondary consequences for the economies of various regions. Even if poor provinces raised their own tax rates in order to provide average benefit levels, decentralization would eliminate an important net injection of resources into the economies of poor regions, which would simply tighten the vicious circle of more pressure on income security but less tax revenues with which to respond.

Advocates of general decentralization contend that these consequences could be offset, perhaps even avoided entirely, by other instruments of redistribution, particularly an enhanced equalization program. The basic problem here lies in the strength of the *political* guarantees that underwrite the two types of inter-regional redistribution. Redistribution through income security is sustained by the intense political pressure on the federal government to treat all of its citizens in all regions equally, a norm from which no federal government has ever deviated, except to provide positive discrimination in the form of easier entry to Unemployment Insurance in areas of high unemployment. The resulting inter-regional transfers are hidden and not especially politically controversial. In comparison, the political guarantees that underwrite the equalization program are much less iron-clad. The unilateral amendment of the formula in the wake of sudden increases in energy revenues in western provinces in the mid-1970s stands as clear testimony to the political vulnerability of the program, a vulnerability that would be greatly increased if decentralization further eroded the federal government's tax base and its general standing in the eyes of Canadians. Writing the commitment to equalization payments into the constitution change little, since no mere constitutional words could provide a *political* guarantee that the federal government could continue to insist on a powerfully redistributive formula. In comparison to the political certainty of the transfers hidden in the federal income security programs, decentralization plus equalization would be a high-risk strategy for poorer regions.[26]

In addition, decentralization would undoubtedly reintroduce residency requirements to the income security system. The first move to restrict access to welfare among recent arrivals would probably come from provinces with the largest net in-migration, such as British Columbia, but retaliation by others would not be far behind. As Guest noted, Canada would then "become a series of welfare kingdoms, each pallisaded with stiff residence and other restrictive laws to repel outsiders."[27] Advocates of decentralization again suggest constitutional entrenchment of a right to basic social benefits for every Canadian who moves between provinces,[28] but provinces with high net in-migration have been reluctant to accept such an open-ended financial commitment without some form of financial compensation. Inter-provincial accords, such as those discussed in the early 1950s, might be possible, but perhaps more feasible would be a special conditional grant to meet the costs of migrants who need social services during the initial period in their new province, an idea proposed by Smiley in 1963 when he was advocating the ending of reliance on shared-cost programs in the social services.[29]

All of these consequences for the substance of income security itself, however, pale in comparison with the impact that decentralization in this area would have on the broader political and economic structure of Canada. As chapter seven discussed, control over income security is an important component of the federal government's economic power and political strength. Transferring the associated tax room to the provinces would make them much the predominant fiscal power in Canada, and require them to assume broad responsibility for the management of the Canadian economy. In addition, an important direct contact between the federal government and individual Canadians would be severed, reducing the importance of federal politics for many, and tying the interests of Canadians even more firmly to their provincial economy and political system. The ripple effects of such a major shift in the federal system would spread into virtually every other area of Canadian public policy.

Special Status. Given the sweeping implications of general decentralization and the traditional lack of interest among Anglophone provinces in recapturing such territory, debate has often centred on the possibility of special status for Quebec. Under such a system, Quebec would assume responsibility for certain programs, while the federal government would continue to operate the programs elsewhere in Canada. The litany of objections to special status has long been entrenched in Canadian constitutional discourse, and need not be repeated in full here. But one conventional argument deserves attention. Opponents insist that special status would place MPs from the province of Quebec in an untenable position. Other parts of the country would object to their voting on policies that applied to all of Canada except Quebec; but if MPs from Quebec did not vote on such items, they would be reduced to second-class status in Parliament and cabinet, and traditional conventions of responsible government would have to be stretched even further to allow for the possibility of a government retaining the confidence of the whole House but losing major pieces of legislation on a regular basis.[30]

Such abstract logic does not, however, square fully with the major example of special status that exists today—the Canada and Quebec Pension plans. The link between the two plans has worked well, and relations between planners in Ottawa and Quebec City are quite amicable; indeed, the CPP/QPP relationship has so far caused the minister of National Health and Welfare much less grief than the relationship with Ontario over changes to the CPP itself. More important, the special status of the Quebec Pension Plan has produced absolutely no political challenge to the legitimacy of MPs from Quebec voting on changes to the Canada Pension Plan. This became crystal clear in 1973-74 when the plan was amended several times. The minister of National Health and Welfare who proposed the changes was Marc Lalonde, a Quebec MP; the cabinet which accepted the proposals contained a major contingent of ministers from Quebec; over half of the Liberal caucus which supported the decision in the House was elected by Quebecers. Yet not once was the legitimacy of such a procedure questioned in Parliament or within the public service.[31] Clearly this is not a perfect test of the tolerance of Canadians for special status, since other mechanisms ensured that the amendments were acceptable to English Canada. The CPP amendments had to be approved by two-thirds of the provincial governments; and since the Liberal government was in a minority in the House of Commons, the amendments also required the assent of other parties, which was forthcoming. Without those checks, the legitimacy of the process might have been challenged. Nevertheless, the total silence on the question speaks volumes about the tolerance of Canadians for asymmetrical relationships as long as they are not raised to the level of principle. (The participation of Quebec in the two-thirds rule for amending the CPP is another sign of this.) Perhaps then there is scope for a modest expansion of the CPP/QPP model into other income security programs.

The consequences of such a change for the substance of income security would depend primarily on the extent of fiscal compensation that would accompany it. If the federal government transferred to the provincial government the full amount that would otherwise have been spent in Quebec on federal income security benefits, then the inter-regional transfers inherent in the system would be maintained, and Quebec would be able to retain comparable levels of income security. Priorities would be altered, without doubt, but as in the case of contributory pensions, the most likely outcome would be broad parallelism. The major exception here is Unemployment Insurance. While the federal government might be persuaded to transfer its own contribution to the costs of unemployment insurance to a Quebec plan, it would be unable—for political reasons—to divert a portion of the employer and employee contributions from other parts of the country to subsidize benefits in Quebec, which is in effect what happens through the present national program. A Quebec plan would therefore have to have higher contribution rates, a larger contribution from general tax revenues, or lower benefit rates.[32]

But once again the greatest consequence of special status in income security would lie in the shift in economic and political power between the federal and provincial governments. Even if income security policy itself changed relatively little, Quebecers would have less reason to look to Ottawa for economic and social leadership, and federal politics would become even less relevant to the needs of the population of that province.

In the income security field, a sovereign Quebec, with or without some form of economic association with the rest of Canada, can be best thought of simply as special status without fiscal compensation. The point can be made again by reference to the Canada and Quebec Pension plans. If Quebec were to become a sovereign state, relations between the two plans would not necessarily change very much, except that Quebec would cease to count in the two-thirds rule for amending the Canada Pension Plan. The present system, in its main outlines, is essentially a relationship between two sovereign states, and it is somewhat surprising that the Parti Québécois did not make more use of the relations between the two plans as proof that association was feasible. In the case of other income security programs, the big difference between special status and sovereignty would be financial, as the inter-regional transfers would stop, a point that was used to good political effect by federal spokesmen, especially Monique Bégin, minister of National Health and Welfare, during the debate leading up to the Quebec referendum. She argued strenuously that Quebec would lose some $680 million in implicit transfers, net of taxes, and that an independent Quebec would have to cut benefits, raise taxes, or increase its deficit. Ignoring the uncertainties surrounding the possible response, Bégin simply plunged on to imply that the result would be the elimination of benefits, especially means-tested benefits, such as the Guaranteed Income Supplement.[33] Whatever the propriety of such tactics, their effectiveness stands as a testament to the political sensitivity of income security in the modern world.[34]

CONCLUSIONS: CONSTITUTIONAL CHANGE AND INCOME SECURITY

Clearly, institutions influence policy, and institutional change would alter the income security system of Canada. While the implications of reform of our central institutions are limited, they all do point in the direction of expanding the commitment of the federal government to income security. Electoral reform would strengthen the role of the NDP in national affairs, and hence the drive for greater equality among Canadians through the income security system. And, paradoxically perhaps, granting the provincial governments a stronger role in shaping federal programs, either through a House of the Provinces or through direct controls over the configuration of benefits and the establishment of new conditional grant programs, would also tend to enhance the centrality of the federal government in the income security system. In comparison, however, decentralization would have a much more decided impact on income security. The basic range of programs now in existence and the general principles that govern their design might not change much, but over time the existing mix of instruments, the general expenditure levels and, most clearly, the distribution of benefits among Canadians in different regions of the country would all be in question.

From the perspective of the millions of Canadians dependent in a major way on income security and of the professionals at work in the field, such changes would undoubtedly be tremendously important. Yet from the historical perspective of the evolution of income security over the last century, or from the comparative perspective of the income security systems of western nations generally, the implications of constitutional reform seem more modest. Intrastate federalism certainly is of little moment here; at most it would nudge Canadian income security somewhat further along the road that it has been travelling for the last forty years. But even the consequences of decentralization would represent important variations on existing policy themes rather than entirely new themes. Indeed, it is difficult to envision any constitutional change that would generate an entirely new approach to the income security needs of Canadians.

As a result, the implications of constitutional reform for the substance of income security would probably prove much less important than the secondary impact on the political and economic balance of Canadian federalism. Decentralization of jurisdiction over income security in particular might not usher in a radically new welfare state, but it would have enormous consequences for the relative economic power and political legitimacy of the two levels of government which compete daily for the loyalties of Canadians.

PART FOUR

CONCLUSIONS

10 State Structures and Policy Patterns

During the last half century, the Canadian state has established a new set of social rights, a set of claims for protection from the insecurities of modern society. As with all social rights, this newest set of rights is never absolute, but rather is in constant flux, expanding in some periods and contracting in others. Nevertheless, it does provide essential support for millions of Canadian citizens. Income security is the largest component of this set of social rights, and indeed represents the largest single element of public expenditure in Canada. It is deeply embedded in the fabric of Canadian life, with important implications not only for the poorest and most vulnerable Canadians, but also for the broad economic and political structure of the country. This book has examined the income security system of this country, and traced the impact of our political institutions on it. The time has come to summarize the major findings, and to reflect on the general relationship between the structures of the state and the patterns of policy in this field.

The comparative view of social policy adopted in chapter three is invaluable in placing the role of political institutions in proper perspective. In one sense, such a broader view stresses the limits of the influence of institutional arrangements on the substance of social policy in modern nations. Certainly, the existence of a network of income security programs in Canada cannot be attributed to any particular genius of our political system. Rather, the origins of the welfare state are to be found in the social strains and pressures generated by the transition from an agrarian to an industrial economy, and industrial nations with widely differing types of government—democratic and totalitarian, centralized and decentralized—have all made some form of collective provision for the income security needs of their populations. In this, Canada has been no exception. Indeed, contrary to suggestions that Canada was a "slow developer" in the welfare field, the pattern found here is reasonably typical of western nations. The lag between industrial growth and the construction of a modern income security system has probably been about average, and certainly dramatically shorter than many other nations, including some which are normally regarded as leaders in the field. The emergence of the welfare state did proceed more incrementally here, involving as it did a long series of small steps rather than dramatic, comprehensive leaps forward such as the American Social Security Act of 1935 and the consolidation of the welfare state in Britain after the Second World War. But in comparative terms at least, the historical record is one of only average delay in responding to the social needs of modern life. Obviously our government institutions had an indirect influence on this process, since a stable political framework was a precondition of economic growth. But the ubiquity of income security throughout the industrial world suggests that the existence of such programs here does not depend primarily on the details of our form of government.

In another sense, however, comparative analysis also highlights those aspects of income security on which institutional patterns do have an influence. The income security systems set in place by industrial nations display fascinating differences in the scope of coverage that they provide, in the policy instruments that they utilize to deliver benefits, and in the redistributive consequences of their payments. When attention focuses on these critical details of income security, the importance of political factors, including the structure of the state itself, is more evident. Institutions have important consequences in three areas in particular: they can influence the *scope* of a nation's income security system; they can alter the *redistributive impact* of income security; and they can condition the *balance of interests* that shape policy outcomes. Accordingly, the central chapters of this book examined the impact of Canadian institutions on these elements of our income security system.

The evidence of those chapters clearly demonstrates that the evolution of federalism is the institutional feature that has had the greatest impact on income security in Canada. Jurisdiction and power relationships in this field have been transformed radically since the 1930s: three constitutional amendments and the vigorous use of the federal spending power has turned an area of virtually complete provincial responsibility at the beginning of the century into one of federal dominance in the postwar era. As the data presented in chapter four demonstrated, this centralization has proved reasonably resistant to the decentralizing pressures that have reshaped other areas of policy over the last twenty years. Quebec has assumed a larger role, primarily through the Quebec Pension Plan and its own family allowance program, and the provinces generally have increased their share of income security spending a little during the last decade. But the federal government remains much the predominant power in income security, and the primary adjustment to provincial assertiveness during the last two decades has been the establishment of some provincial control over changes in two major federal programs, the Canada Pension Plan and Family Allowances. This pattern of continuing federal predominance in income security contrasts starkly with the health and social services, over which provincial control has prevailed. Jurisdictionally, Canada has evolved towards a bifurcated welfare state.

Why provincial governments were prepared to surrender formal jurisdiction in this field, when they steadfastly refused to do so in any other field, is a question that has never been fully answered. The particular political balance of the 1940s and 1950s was undoubtedly important. The federal government was politically ascendant; given the bitter experiences of the depression, it was more firmly committed to action in this field than elsewhere; and it therefore pressed the provinces harder for jurisdictional concessions. In addition, successive Quebec governments, normally the staunchest foes of centralization, were politically unable to resist the pressure, since they were unwilling to introduce welfare programs themselves. No government can defend disputed territory effectively unless it is prepared to occupy it. But these political circumstances of the time cannot fully account for the uniqueness of income security. Part of the explanation must also lie in the special nature of income security as a direct exchange between citizen and state, which by-passes other social organizations. As chapter four argued, compared with the implications of changing jurisdiction over health insurance, for example, transferring major responsibilities for income security to the federal government made a much smaller dent in the functions of provincial governments and bureaucracies, and of institutions, professions, and other groups already operating under provincial authority.

As a result, income security has emerged as one of the few exemplars in domestic policy of the centralist concept of Canadian federalism. While both governments are active in the field, the federal government is the predominant power, establishing the basic national policy framework through major programs which create a direct relationship between the federal authorities and individual Canadians. The provinces (with the partial exception of Quebec) are left to devise local embellishments through a variety of supplements, credits, and allowances, and to cope with residual income security needs through social assistance. In effect, the federal government emerged in the postwar period as the principle guarantor of many of the social rights that stand as a hallmark of the twentieth century.

This centralization of power over income security has had important consequences for both the *scope* of income security programs and their *redistributive consequences*. Cross-national studies have demonstrated a clear relationship between the scope of welfare and political centralization:

other things being equal, countries with decentralized governments devote a smaller proportion of their resources to welfare than do those with centralized governments. In comparative terms, federalism is clearly a conservative force in welfare politics, and the analysis of Canadian experience in chapter five supports this proposition. During the interwar era, when welfare was still primarily a provincial and local responsibility, initiatives were constrained both by fiscal imbalance and by the mobility of capital and labour in the Canadian economy. Theories which suggest that social reform can be introduced more rapidly in a federal system than a unitary one, since innovations can be established in one province and the "seeds of radicalism" can then spread across the nation, underestimate the withering effects of regional disparity and provincial economic competition. In the income security field, centralization of responsibility in Ottawa during and after the Second World War facilitated a larger rate of growth in income security than Canadians could have legitimately expected from the alternatives confronting them in those critical decades.

Divided jurisdiction is still a conservative force in welfare politics, but the impact is more modest today. In keeping with other forms of fragmentation of authority, divided jurisdiction raises the level of consensus required for innovation, and thereby complicates the process of introducing new programs, as the collapse of the income supplementation proposals advanced by the federal authorities during the mid-1970s vividly illustrated. In addition, divided control over established programs can restrain their growth, as in the case of the Canada Pension Plan. The elaborate system of federal-provincial vetoes that governs changes in the CPP, and the provision that any accumulated reserves are loaned to the provincial governments, have combined to insulate pension benefits from the expansionist pressures inherent in democratic politics, displacing the brunt of electioneering into the smaller Guaranteed Income Supplement, an exclusively federal program. By constraining the growth of the CPP in this way, federalism reinforces the existing balance between public and private sectors in welfare and helps to preserve room for the operation of occupational pension plans. Such institutional protection can never be absolute, and the pressures on private pensions generated by an inflationary climate may yet erode these barriers to expansionism in the public sector. But there is no doubt that divided jurisdiction does provide the private sector greater protection from collectivist solutions than they would otherwise enjoy.

During the last two decades, these conservative features of divided jurisdiction have been partially offset by competition between governments. The revisionist interpretation of the relationship between federalism and policy expansion, which contends that federal institutions contribute to the growth of the public sector by multiplying the number of governments with expansionist tendencies, is of limited help in understanding the history of

income security, because the provincial instinct to defend and expand jurisdiction at all costs was relatively dormant here. But since the 1960s, the
heightened political tensions between Quebec City and Ottawa have
provided a mildly expansionist pressure, as both governments have been
more inclined to exercise their jurisdiction vigorously.

On balance, federalism probably still does constrain the growth of
income security spending, but only modestly. Certainly there is no compelling evidence to suggest that centralizing all responsibility for income
security in Ottawa would substantially increase Canada's general commitment in this field, especially in the present period of large deficits at the
federal level. Fiscal imbalance, that recurring "complication of federalism,"
has returned in a new guise to haunt welfare advocates once again.

The impact of federalism on the redistributive processes of the Canadian
state has been more marked, as chapter six revealed. Interestingly, federalism has not altered redistributive *goals* in Canada as much as is often
claimed. The fashionable contention that our institutions render decision-
makers particularly sensitive to regional interests, and lead them to give
higher priority to inter-regional redistribution than to interpersonal redistribution, is simply not supported by the hard evidence of government
expenditures. First, Canada's efforts to reduce regional economic disparities
are not especially impressive in international terms, falling behind even
those of some countries with unitary governments. Second, Canadian
equalization grants are large primarily because the federation is relatively
decentralized; more centralized political systems achieve similar redistributive impacts through the operation of national programs that provide
uniform standards in rich and poor regions alike. And third, our federal
government devotes vastly greater resources to income security than to
regional programs. Despite the alleged sensitivity of our political institutions to territorially-based claims, interpersonal rather than inter-regional
redistribution is a much higher priority for the Canadian state.

Centralization has, however, altered the redistributive *impact* of income
security. Transferring responsibility for welfare to the federal government
does not necessarily produce programs that are more redistributive between
income classes, but it does transform income security into a powerful
instrument of redistribution between regions. As long as welfare was
primarily a municipal and provincial responsibility, the poorest parts of the
country always had the greatest social needs but the fewest resources with
which to respond, a problem that became acute during the depression.
Centralization, on the other hand, has generated major flows of money
from rich to poor regions. National income security programs redistribute
inter-regionally because greater proportions of elderly, unemployed and
needy people, and children, are found in some regions, and because the
revenues to finance those programs are raised disproportionately from

different regions. The resulting net inter-regional redistribution through income security is equal to, or greater than that achieved throught the more publicized system of equalization grants, and income security payments have become a critical part of the standard of living and the general economy in poor regions. Thus, as chapter six concluded, the particular structure of Canadian government has helped poor regions, not by channelling an exceptionally large proportion of our national resources into regional programs, but by transforming income security, the quintessential instrument of interpersonal redistribution, into a potent instrument of inter-regional redistribution.

Not surprisingly, therefore, the income security system itself must respond increasingly to the politics of regionalism as well as to the politics of class. Chapter eight noted that Canadians in poorer regions of the country are more supportive of expanded welfare programs than Canadians who live elsewhere, a finding that persists even when income and other differences between regions are held constant. And elected representatives of the public reflect similar divisions. In most other countries, cutbacks in unemployment benefits would pit the government primarily against organized labour; in Canada such cutbacks pit the federal government primarily against politicians from poor regions. The income security programs of the federal government represent a compromise, not only between the interests and desires of high- and low-income Canadians, but also between those of high- and low-income regions.

Centralization of power within the federal system has thus shaped both the scope and redistributive consequences of income security in important ways. But, as chapter seven demonstrated, the expansion of income security has also had an important reciprocal impact on federalism itself, and especially on the relative power of the federal and provincial governments. During the middle decades of this century, responsibility for income security gravitated towards the federal government because of its greater economic and political strength. But as the new programs expanded, they in turn reinforced the position of the central government within the federation. Income security has become a large part of the federal government's *fiscal* power. These payments represent the biggest single component of government expenditure, and a sizeable portion of the taxation system is devoted to raising the necessary revenues. Control over financial flows of this magnitude is central to the federal government's capacity to influence the Canadian economy. Certainly, if Ottawa were to turn responsibility for income security, together with the associated tax room, over to the provinces, it would in effect be surrendering much of the nation's fiscal policy as well.

But perhaps more important, income security has also become an instrument for sustaining or enhancing the *political* power of the federal government. Since virtually all community and social services are provincially delivered, income security is the only direct, beneficial link between Ottawa and the public, a link that ties the interests of millions of Canadians to the strength of the federal government rather than to their provincial government. Deprived of these client relationships, the federal presence in the everyday life of Canadians would fade even more, and the political legitimacy of the federal government would be further eroded. Income security is thus an important part of the federal government's capacity both to manage the economy and to maintain the allegiance of Canadians. The intensity of the battle between Ottawa and Quebec City during the early 1970s over jurisdiction in the field of income security is more readily explicable if the broader economic and political power inherent in these programs is kept firmly in mind. Income security is not just an instrument of social justice. It is also an instrument of statecraft, and states do not surrender such instruments willingly.

The federal government has good reason to be thankful that it did not lose control over this instrument at the time of the Victoria Charter, since income security has served it well during the constitutional battles of the second half of the 1970s and the early 1980s. Many Canadians active in the constitutional debates that followed the election of the Parti Québécois in 1976 continued to support a strong federal government precisely because of its role in stabilizing the incomes, not just of provincial governments through equalization grants, but also of individual Canadians through income security. Without its role in welfare, Ottawa would have lost an important part of its *raison d'être* in the eyes of many. And during the Quebec referendum campaign, the scare that sovereignty-association would put income security benefits in jeopardy was one effective weapon in the federalists' arsenal. Nor did the political utility of income security end with the defeat of the Parti Québécois proposal. During the subsequent political war with the western provinces over the division of the vast revenues to be derived from Canadian energy resources, federal protagonists often defended their claim to a larger share as essential if the federal government were to remain able to meet its responsibilities in fields such as income security. As long as income security remains the most intimate federal involvement in the lives of Canadians, it will be one of Ottawa's most important weapons in inter-governmental warfare.

In comparison with the centralization of power over income security, other aspects of Canadian political institutions have had only a modest impact on the substance of policy in this sector. The allegation that the closed, elite-dominated nature of the policy process, which results from our blend of cabinet government and federalism, has insulated public policy from the wishes of the broad public requires substantial qualification here. Cabinet government alone is innocent of such charges, since—as chapter

seven found—the postwar history of exclusively federal programs such as
Family Allowances, Old Age Security, and Unemployment Insurance is
relatively free of evidence of insensitivity to public wishes. The concentration of power in the hands of the cabinet has been important, allowing
policy elites to initiate reforms in the absence of strong public pressure to do
so. But the system has also been sensitive to public *reactions* to reforms, and
cabinets have regularly retreated when the public response was hostile. In
democratic systems, the role of the public is akin to that of a theatre
audience, and in the case of federal income security programs, there is little
evidence of indifference to its applause.

Adding federalism to the institutional mix does create buffers between
policy and public. Federal-provincial dynamics can constrain elites from
taking initiatives of which the public would probably approve, as already
noted in the case of the Canada Pension Plan. And the complications of
divided responsibility may have protected social assistance spending from
the knives of treasury officials and the potential hostility of the public, although the evidence here is much less convincing. But, with these exceptions, Canadian political institutions do not appear to have significantly
frustrated public preferences in the field of income security.

The limits of the influence that our institutions have exercised on income
security policy is also illustrated by the proposals for constitutional reform
that have been debated passionately in recent years. Most of the proposed
reforms sought to make government decision-making more sensitive to
regional concerns, either by reforming the institutions of the central government or by decentralizing important areas of policy to the provincial
governments. But such proposals, if implemented, would have limited
impact on income security, since attitudes towards policy in this area do not
vary significantly from one region to another. As chapter eight discovered,
the public, professionals in the welfare field, and provincial governments by
and large share broadly the same mix of attitudes towards income security
from one part of the country to another and, indeed, there has been a
striking convergence in thinking about such social questions between
English and French Canada over the last generation. Regional differences in
the degree of support for income security do exist, and priorities among
different income security programs do vary from one part of the country to
another. But such differences, while more than nuances, do not add up to
distinctive approaches to the social needs of modern society.

Consequently, many of the proposed constitutional reforms would have
little influence on the income security system, as chapter nine found. Certainly, reforming the institutions of the central government would have
limited consequences. By and large such an approach would entrench and
perhaps expand the existing federal predominance in income security.
Electoral reform would expand the ranks of the NDP in the House of

Commons and thereby strengthen the pro-welfare forces at the federal level. And, ironically perhaps, giving provincial governments some power over federal policies through a House of the Provinces or a Federal Council would also increase the federal role in income security. Such proposals, which are usually advanced as means of facilitating a more harmonious intergovernmental interdependence, would in fact reduce joint programs by making them even less attractive to Ottawa. Reformist impulses at the federal level would be channelled away from the health and social services and into purely federal activities, including income security programs. Thus, redesigning the central institutions would—at most—accentuate the existing lines of income security development in Canada.

The only constitutional reform with major consequences for income security would be a decision to reverse the centralization of the last half century, and return responsibility for income security to the provincial level. Even here it is important not to overstate the case, since the basic range of programs now in existence and the general principles that govern their operations might not change dramatically. The overall level of expenditures, the mix of policy instruments utilized in future development, and most important, the distribution of the costs and benefits among Canadians in different regions of the country would certainly be shifted to a new course. But the more profound impact would be on the general economic and political balance of the federation, which would tilt sharply, with the federal government losing much of its fiscal power and one of its few major involvements in the daily lives of individual Canadians. The most important consequences of decentralization in this area would probably be for the political system itself, rather than for the income security policies that it produces.

These findings reinforce the argument advanced throughout this book that, although institutional patterns do influence income security, they are not the only or even the most important determinant of policy. The nature of the Canadian economy, the nation's social and demographic profile, its cultural and political configuration, all leave their imprint on the Canadian welfare state. Even allowing for the fact that the institutional framework itself may influence these other dimensions of Canadian life, we should be restrained in our expectations of the importance of our political institutions, and of constitutional reform, for the patterns of income security in Canada. Centralization of power has been significant for the overall scope and redistributive impact of income security, but otherwise the critical forces shaping public policy in this sector lie elsewhere. The social role of the Canadian state does not depend solely, or even centrally, on the particular structures through which it operates.

This general conclusion about the impact of institutions on public policy cannot be extended automatically to other policy fields. Federal institutions

may well have greater influence elsewhere, especially in policy fields in
which the primary lines of conflict coincide more closely with regional divisions. Language policy and energy policy come to mind easily at this point.
But the evidence in this study does stand as a caution against exaggerating
the importance of political institutions. For over a generation now, federalism has been the most dramatic part of Canadian politics, full of conflict,
tension, and explosive potential. Furthermore, much of this drama has been
played out on the public stage, unlike many other exciting battles that have
remained fully cloaked in cabinet secrecy. Not surprisingly, therefore,
Canadians have been fascinated by the politics of federalism and have
assumed them to be central to the substance of Canadian public policy. But
drama and policy impact are decidedly different phenomena. To some
extent, federal-provincial conflict has simply served to highlight certain
policy areas, without increasing their substantive importance. Two
examples from the earlier chapters illustrate the point. At the level of the
broad functions of the Canadian state, the openness of our institutions to
regional interests and claims has certainly increased the political visibility of
instruments of inter-regional redistribution. But, as we have seen, it has not
had a similar impact on the relative importance of such instruments.
Similarly, at the level of administrative experience, federalism has certainly
focused attention on the problems involved in coordinating federal and provincial programs in the income security field. But this does not necessarily
mean that intergovernmental tensions are more important than intragovernmental ones, or that tensions between the same programs would be
absent in a unitary state.

Paradoxically, overstatement of the influence of political institutions on
public policy can only serve to undermine their legitimacy. Opposition to
policy is transformed into opposition to institutions, and an open invitation
is sent to every constitutional thinker in the land to solve policy problems
through institutional engineering. Furthermore, inflating the importance of
institutions also makes any constitutional changes that are enacted less
likely to succeed. Reforms premised on faulty assumptions are bound to
disappoint their champions. Political institutions are much too important to
have their policy significance exaggerated.

Political science would seem to have a special role in guarding against this
danger, and yet as presently constituted it is not fully equipped to do so.
The study of federalism is a strong and distinguished field in Canadian
political science, but specialists on federal-provincial relations are not
always well placed to evaluate the policy impact of the institutions which
they study. Apart from any natural temptation to stress the importance of
one's own specialty, it is impossible to assess the independent influence of
any single factor, such as institutions, by viewing it in isolation. To some
extent, political science does suffer from what has been labelled "the curse

of expertise in independent variables."[1] The corrective for such a disciplinary "mobilization of bias" lies in comparative studies of public policy. Focusing firmly on public policy as the phenomenon to be explained, treating it explicitly as the product of a variety of factors, and examining it in a comparative context—both across time and across political units—can help to place the role of political institutions in perspective. This book cannot claim to have followed this injunction completely, but it does point to the utility of more vigorous efforts in that direction.

11 Income Security and Federalism in the 1980s

The 1980s have ushered in critical changes in the politics of the welfare state in Canada, as in other western industrial nations. The hopes and optimism that accompanied the rapid expansion of social programs during the postwar decades have eroded rapidly, and intense pressures have built up around the social security system. Nowhere are these pressures more intense than in the area of income security, where powerful forces press simultaneously in opposite directions. On the one hand, the number of families and individuals who depend primarily on the income security system for their well-being has grown dramatically, thus expanding the role of transfer programs in the fabric of the country. On the other hand, income security programs themselves are increasingly coming under challenge; the politics of restraint is pervasive, and proposals for sweeping changes abound.

Pressures for the expansion of the redistributive role of the state are deeply rooted in the economic and social changes of the last decade.[1] The economic record of recent years is depressingly familiar: the rapid growth of the postwar decades, which sustained the development of social programs, gave way to stagnation in the 1970s, deep recession in the early 1980s, and slow, hesitant growth thereafter. Moreover, underlying these cyclical patterns are important structural changes, the long term consequences of which are as yet only dimly perceived—the low productivity growth, technological changes which seem to be eating away at parts of the occupational structure, and intense competition in the international trading system, which threatens to leave Canada in an increasingly vulnerable position.

These economic problems have contributed mightily to the expansion of the role of income security in the 1980s. The national unemployment rate peaked at about 12 percent in 1983, and is not expected to return even to the levels that prevailed in the 1970s until well into the 1990s. The result has been a rapid growth in the numbers relying on social benefits, especially those provided through Unemployment Insurance and social assistance. More generally, however, economic problems have tended to expand the political constituencies that are dependent on the redistributive role of the state and which engage in political action to gain protection from market forces. Governments quickly come under pressure to expand their programs to help individuals, as well as sectors of the economy and regions of the country hurt by economic change.[2]

Social trends have accentuated this pattern. While the Canadian population is younger than that of most western industrial nations, it is aging steadily: the proportion of all Canadians who are sixty-five years of age or older is rising. Demographic projections are highly sensitive to differing assumptions about fertility, mortality and immigration, but most estimates agree that the proportion of elderly people will rise modestly until the end of the century and dramatically thereafter, reaching a level two or three times the current population by the year 2030.[3] This aging of the population creates a steadily expanding political constituency heavily dependent on state action to maintain and improve its income and well-being.[4] The defeat of the federal government's attempt in 1985 to partially deindex the Old Age Security program provides graphic evidence of the political strength of the elderly and their allies.

The evolving role of women has similar implications. In a wide variety of ways, women are dependent on the redistributive capacities of the state to achieve a more equitable position in Canadian life, and the growth of the women's movement has created vigorous political organizations committed to greater social intervention in numerous forms: the enrichment of pensions and family benefits, social services such as daycare, and the regulation of earnings differentials in the marketplace through pay equity legislation. In an era in which other political champions of the welfare state, such as organized labour, have been weakened by economic forces, the women's movement and the elderly have emerged as political bulwarks of the social role of the state.

Yet the economic and political trends of the 1980s are also generating countercurrents that simultaneously work to inhibit the redistributive activities of government. While the economic deterioration of the last ten years has created many more beneficiaries of income security programs, it has also reduced the capacity of the state to protect the victims of change. At the most obvious level, the economic problems of the last decade have eroded the flow of government revenue, contributing to a deficit that is relatively larger than that of most other western nations, and generating intense pressures on governments to curb spending in all sectors, including social policy. More ominously, however, intense international economic competition constrains the use of transfers, subsidies, and regulations to shelter those most vulnerable. As one economist has concluded, "as long as growth remains uncertain, increasingly keen competition in world markets will force governments to place strict limits on increases in tax rates, and, as a result, on the extension of transfer programs."[5] A rapidly changing global economy also places a premium on an adaptable domestic economy, and has stimulated a growing emphasis on the importance of flexible labour markets and the restructuring of transfer programs and other policies that limit labour mobility and wage flexibility.[6]

In the political realm, ideological trends are also challenging major social policy initiatives; the diffuse consensus that sustained their expansion in earlier years has clearly weakened.[7] Throughout the postwar era, the prevailing assumption was that a welfare state would complement the market economy: it would be an instrument of automatic countercyclical stabilization, it would ensure an educated and healthy workforce; and it would provide the complex social infrastructure essential to an urban economy. While such ideas never commanded universal assent, their reign was reasonably secure during the decades of sustained economic growth. The problems of the last ten years, however, have revived older conceptions of a fundamental incompatibility between economic efficiency and social equity. A resurgent conservative critique insists that the modern welfare state and its associated taxes undermine growth by stifling entrepreneurship, distorting the incentive structure, interfering with the operation of labour markets, and reinforcing dependency among the recipient population. This is not to say that Canada has entered a new era of unchallenged conservative ideological hegemony—there is vigorous resistance to any such shift within important elements of the political system, and only a limited resonance in public attitudes as a whole. The basic legitimacy of the welfare state is not an issue for the Canadian public, and the experience of the recession has probably strengthened popular support for many important social programs.[8] Nevertheless, the broad consensus that prevailed in earlier decades has given way to a more polarized debate over the future of social security.

The income security system of the 1980s is thus under strain, pressed in contradictory directions by economic, social, and political trends of the decade. In this, Canadian experience closely parallels that in other western nations. In Canada, however, the balance among these pressures and their impact on social programs is also conditioned by the complexities of the federal system of government. The checks and balances of a federal state present economic and social interests with a complex maze of opportunities and obstacles in their efforts to shape public policy. In addition, the political conflict among social groups is overlain by a system of intergovernmental conflict, in which different governments not only ally themselves with specific private interests but also advance distinctive financial and political concerns of their own. Understanding the evolution of public policy thus requires an analysis of the intersection of the changing balance of political forces and the institutional structures of the state.

The dynamics of Canadian federalism have also changed in the 1980s. Much of the political life of the 1960s and 1970s was dominated by an intense struggle over the future of the federal system itself. The growth of Quebec nationalism and the deepening of regional conflicts generated protracted debates over sweeping reforms to the existing institutional order, and at times the very survival of a single country on the northern half of the North American continent seemed to be at stake. Throughout this period, social policy issues were regularly swept up into the constitutional debate and shaped by it. However, this battle peaked with the Quebec referendum on sovereignty-association in 1980. Thereafter, the adoption of the Constitution Act of 1982 introduced a number of important changes into the constitutional order, and the Meech Lake Accord reached by first ministers in April 1987 proposed to extend those changes in significant ways.

Thus the economic, social, ideological, and institutional underpinnings of the Canadian welfare state have all been shifting during the 1980s, with critical implications for the country's social programs. This chapter surveys these broad changes, and the relationships among them. The first section examines the evolution of the income security system during the 1980s, and its role in the distribution of income and maintenance of well-being in a period of economic crisis. The second section then turns to the relationship between federalism and income security in the 1980s, exploring two key dimensions: the implications of constitutional change for income security programs; and the extent to which the impact of both the economic crisis and neoconservatism on the income security system are shaped by federalism.

Income Security in the 1980s

Political controversy over the welfare state in recent years has focused attention on the policies of restraint, reductions in social benefits, and the growing emphasis on the role of the private sector in meeting important social needs. A closer look at the recent record of policy change, however, reveals a more complex pattern. Although benefit reductions have undoubtedly taken place, other programs have been enhanced, and yet others have been restructured rather than reduced. Moreover, when viewed from a broad societal perspective, the dominant impression is that the role of the income security system in Canadian life has expanded. These conflicting currents can be highlighted, first by examining the trend of specific program changes, and then by shifting to the general role of income security.

Program Changes. The golden age of the expansion of the income security system evaporated rapidly in the latter half of the 1970s, and the actual enrichment of programs has been limited since then. Pensions, however, stand as an exception. The one attempt to reduce a pension program—the 1985 proposal by the federal government to provide only partial rather than full indexation of Old Age Security payments—was withdrawn in response to a nation-wide protest by senior citizens, social groups, the media, and opposition parties.[9] Elsewhere in the pension system, however, a pattern of incremental expansion has continued. The Guaranteed Income Supplement for the elderly poor was enriched three times, with increases larger than those required simply to compensate for inflation. Not surprisingly, these increments all came in election years—1979, 1980 and 1984—testifying once again to the electoral significance of pensions policy. In addition, a Spouse's Allowance for younger spouses of pensioners was introduced in 1975 and extended in a long series of incremental steps in the late 1970s and early 1980s. Finally, the Canada and Quebec Pension plans were amended in the mid-1980s to provide greater flexibility in the age of retirement, enhanced disability benefits, the continuance of survivor benefits after remarriage, and more exacting rules governing credit splitting on marriage breakdown. The federal and provincial governments also agreed to a schedule of increases in contribution rates to these two plans which will double the rates between 1987 and the year 2011.

Admittedly, these enrichments of the retirement income system represent a pale shadow of the expansionist proposals debated in the late 1970s and early 1980s, as will be discussed more fully below. Moreover, the continued enrichment of the Guaranteed Income Supplement and the Spouse's Allowance, but not of Old Age Security, shows an increasing drift toward income-tested rather than universal benefits. Nonetheless, the Canadian system of public pensions is marginally more expansive in the late 1980s than it was a decade before, and a 1986 report from the National Council of Welfare concluded that "elderly Canadians have seen a substantial decrease in poverty over the past several years, thanks in large part to improvements in the retirement income system."[10] This record stands in contrast to both the United States and Great Britain, where pension benefits were trimmed, not expanded, during the 1980s.

The dominant pattern in other areas of income security, however, has been a dreary one of restraint and retrenchment, for the most part incremental, but occasionally more severe. The long-term significance of incremental change is demonstrated by the changes in the system of family benefits, composed of Family Allowances, the Child Tax Credit, and the child tax exemption. Over the last decade, this set of programs has slowly become more redistributive, as resources have been transferred on various occasions from Family Allowances and the child tax exemption to the Child Tax Credit, which is targetted on lower-income families. The 1985 and 1986 budgets, however, have both accentuated and constrained this trend. On the one hand, the redistributive goal has been reinforced, as the child tax exemption is to be reduced substantially between 1987 and 1989, and the Child Tax Credit is to be expanded over the same period and targetted more tightly on poorer famililes. On the other hand, the resources that would otherwise flow into the system have been reduced through partial deindexation. Beginning in 1987, Family Allowances are to be increased only by the amount by which inflation exceeds three percent, and, as a result, the benefit will decline slowly in real terms. Moreover, from 1989 onwards, the Child Tax Credit and the level of family income above which the credit is reduced are also to be partially deindexed.

These complex changes will make the overall system more redistributive but will reduce the value of the benefits over time. The National Council of Welfare has calculated that despite the increase in the Child Tax Credit, many poor and all middle-income families will receive lower net child benefits. The losses will mount with each passing year, and figure 8 shows the impact on two-earner families with two children when the reforms are

Figure 8 *Projection of Child Benefits in 1990, before and after 1985 and 1986 Budgets*

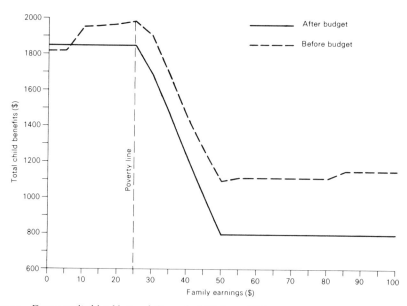

Source: Data supplied by National Council of Welfare, 1987.

complete in 1990. After 1990, all families will receive less than they would have without the 1985 budget, as the child benefit system fails to keep pace with inflation.

In contrast to the marginal enrichment of pensions and the slow, almost surreptitious erosion of family benefits, programs supporting the unemployed have been the target for more serious restraint. Unemployment Insurance was significantly expanded in 1971, but that expansion was moderated in successive rounds of legislative and regulatory change, especially in the late 1970s. The changes affected each major component of the program. First, qualification periods were lengthened: the initial qualification period was extended and put on a regional basis, and a longer qualification period was established for new entrants to the labour force and repeat claimants. Second, benefits were trimmed: the higher benefits for claimants with dependents were eliminated, all benefit levels were reduced from 66⅔ to 60 percent of insurable earnings, and benefits received by individuals with middle and upper incomes were partially taxed back. Finally, the financial basis of the program was revised to reduce the government's contribution and shift the burden more fully onto employers and employees. Restrictions introduced in the 1980s have been milder, although they have included a controversial provision to eliminate or delay coverage of early retirees, a measure that particularly affects military personnel and members of the Royal Canadian Mounted Police.

At the provincial level, the focus has been on social assistance. The impact of the recession on benefit levels varied considerably among provinces, as table 40 demonstrates. The three westernmost provinces, which were hit hardest by the recession and witnessed the largest proportional increases in social assistance caseloads, responded by reducing benefit levels in real terms, in some cases by actually cutting benefits, but most often by refusing to index them to compensate for the effects of inflation. On the other hand, provinces such as Ontario and Newfoundland, which in the past had been among the lowest providers, did increase their benefits marginally in real terms between 1982 and 1985. While the impact on benefit levels was therefore regionally varied, virtually all provinces curtailed other aspects of their social assistance programs: eligibility rules were made more restrictive in various ways, payments for special needs were reduced or in some cases eliminated, and more aggressive monitoring and enforcement procedures were set in place. The strains of the recession highlighted the long-standing problems of social assistance recipients, especially young employables who, as table 40 also demonstrates, had to subsist on very low benefit levels in provinces such as Quebec and New Brunswick. The proliferation of food banks and soup kitchens during the early years of the decade represented a graphic community response to the limits of social security support, especially in western Canada.[11]

Table 40   *Monthly Benefits to Social Assistance Recipients, by Province,*
           1982-85

	1 Adult, 1 Child, Age 4				2 Adults, 2 Children, Ages 10-13			
	1982	1985	Actual Percent Changes 1982-85	Adjusted for Inflation	1982	1985	Actual Percent Changes 1982-85	Adjusted for Inflation
Newfoundland	511	689	34.8	17.3	609	797	30.9	13.9
P.E.I.	548	592	8.0	(6.0)	785	848	8.0	(6.0)
Nova Scotia	572	659	15.2	.3	805	919	14.2	(.6)
New Brunswick	519	609	17.3	2.1	558	671	20.3	4.7
Quebec	536	655	22.2	6.4	750	929	23.9	7.8
Ontario	518	647	24.9	8.7	615	762	23.9	7.8
Manitoba	500	579	15.8	.8	794	931	17.3	2.1
Saskatchewan	710	750	5.6	(8.1)	1,040	1,090	4.8	(8.8)
Alberta	733	719	(1.9)	(14.6)	1,066	1,082	1.5	(11.7)
British Columbia	640	640	0.0	(13.0)	870	870	0.0	(13.0)

	Single, Employable				Single, Disabled			
	1982	1985	Actual Percent Changes 1982-85	Adjusted for Inflation	1982	1985	Actual Percent Changes 1982-85	Adjusted for Inflation
Newfoundland	213	275	29.1	12.4	329	436	32.5	15.3
P.E.I.	434	471	8.5	(5.6)	474	511	7.8	(6.2)
Nova Scotia	NA	366	NA	NA	467	539	15.4	.4
New Brunswick	100	188	88.0	63.6	348	405	16.4	1.3
Quebec	138	160	15.9	.9	376	440	17.0	1.8
Ontario	266	368	38.3	20.4	414	519	25.4	9.1
Manitoba	284	353	24.3	8.2	354	414	16.9	1.7
Saskatchewan	517	345	(33.3)	(41.9)	517	530	2.5	(10.8)
Alberta	556	484	(12.9)	(24.2)	608	695	14.3	(.5)
British Columbia	375	375	0.0	(13.0)	519	548	5.6	(8.1)

Source: Social Planning Council of Metropolitan Toronto, "Welfare Benefits: An
          Interprovincial Comparison," *Social Infopac* vol. 5, no. 1 (March 1986).

Not all of the changes in benefits for the unemployed have been motivated by a simple desire to limit cost increases. Some of the changes also confirm Gough's expectation that the trend in western nations would not be so much the *"dismantling* of the welfare state, but its *restructuring."*[12] In the income security field, this involves attempts to harmonize programs more effectively with the requirements of an efficient labour market through changes encouraging or compelling recipients to work. In Canada, Unemployment Insurance lies at the centre of this particular storm. A labour-market orientation has increasingly come to dominate the management of Unemployment Insurance, and many of the legislative and administrative changes since 1971 have been designed to reinforce work incentives.[13] In addition, the increasing use of the Unemployment Insurance fund to support job creation programs and worksharing, especially during the recession, reflects a similar trend.[14] Proposals for a more radical restructuring of Unemployment Insurance to promote greater labour mobility abound, with the recommendations of the 1986 Commission of Inquiry on Unemployment Insurance (the Forget Commission) being the most sweeping.[15] The political sensitivity of the program may well doom such ideas in perpetuity, as is discussed below. Nevertheless, they had come to constitute the established agenda among policy planners by the mid-1980s.

A similar concern with employment has increasingly shaped social assistance programs. As the economy deteriorated in the late 1970s and 1980s, the number of employables on social assistance grew steadily, especially among young persons who had never been able to establish an attachment to the labour force. While precise figures are not available, federal officials estimate that by the mid-1980s, 30 percent or more of the national caseload were employables.[16] Traditionally, social assistance programs were not well designed for such people. Recipients had little access to training and employment services, and training allowances were deducted fully from their benefits. With the pressure of growing caseloads, however, governments increasingly adopted programs to encourage a return to the workforce. At the federal level, this trend was accentuated by the Task Force on Program Review (the Neilsen Task Force), which was appointed by the new Progressive Conservative government in 1984. The task force produced a report on the Canada Assistance Plan (CAP), which highlighted the increase in welfare costs during the recession and the growing number of employables receiving social assistance. While the report did not consider existing expenditure levels to be excessive, it did argue that "this cost might become unaffordable if present economic trends continue, forcing a change in the open-ended character of funding arrangements. It is both socially and economically important that means to reduce CAP caseloads be found soon."[17]

Shortly after the release of the report, the federal government announced two departures designed to encourage employable social assistance recipients to enter the labour force. First was a decision to increase their participation in the training and employment programs operated by the federal government. Under the terms of a general agreement between both levels of government, targets or informal quotas for participation by social assistance recipients are to be set in each province.[18] According to the subsidiary agreement later negotiated with New Brunswick, for example, a target of 30 percent participation of welfare recipients has been set for a job development program and 25 percent for job entry and re-entry projects. The terms for other provinces vary but the essential direction is the same.[19]

Second, the federal government has altered its approach to the CAP to stimulate the employment of welfare recipients. A number of the regulations have been altered. For example, training allowances are no longer to be deducted fully from welfare benefits, and child care allowances are to be made available to a broader range of social assistance recipients, including part-time trainees, a provision designed to make training programs more accessible to single mothers on social assistance. More importantly, the federal government has agreed to divert funds that would otherwise have been paid under CAP to programs providing training and employment opportunities for social assistance recipients. Thus, in practice, if not in law, CAP funding has been broadened to include a wider range of employment programs for recipients.[20] The full impact of these new initiatives will depend on the response of the provincial governments and the demand for labour in the market place.[21] Nevertheless, the changes clearly reflect the restructuring of welfare programs to encourage participation in the workforce.

The pattern of policy change is thus a mixed one, in part reflecting the uneven political strength and popular support of different beneficiary groups. Pensions have been modestly enriched, despite the recession. Family benefits have been gingerly programmed for a slow, almost surreptitious erosion in the future. On the other hand, unemployment benefits and social assistance payments in some provinces have received sharper reductions, and beneficiaries face more stringent regulations and greater emphasis on retraining and a return to work. This broad pattern shows some similarities to the experience in other western nations, such as the United States and Britain, where programs that benefit the population as a whole have been treated more gently than those reserved for the unemployed and lower-income groups.[22] Although the overall shift in Canada has been more incremental so far, and mitigated by the enrichment of some programs, the general trend is similar.

The Expanding Role of Income Security. While the various restrictions in social programs have captured public attention in recent years the underlying reality remains that the role of income security in the political economy of Canada has expanded. The market continues to be the dominant mechanism for allocating income and other resources, and the state certainly remains a secondary instrument in the general process of societal allocation. Nevertheless, the growth of the elderly population and the erosion of employment opportunities over the last ten years has shifted the balance between the two allocative systems.

The growth of the transfer system can be viewed in several ways. First, the number of Canadians who are dependent on transfer programs has increased steadily since the mid-1970s. As table 41 reveals, only the two major children's benefits, Family Allowances and the Child Tax Credit, have remained static. In comparison, the number of elderly beneficiaries

Table 41 *Number of Recipients of Major Income Security Programs, 1976–85*

Year	Old Age Security	Guaranteed Income	Spouse's Allowance	CPP/QPP	Family[a] Allowances	Child Tax[a] Credit	Unemployment[b] Insurance	Social[c] Assistance
				—thousands—				
1976	1957	1084	59	1067	3525	—	2401	1328
1977	2035	1112	72	1222	3571	—	2479	1322
1978	2098	1127	73	1362	3598	2468	2524	1347
1979	2179	1164	76	1490	3616	2459	2333	1334
1980	2259	1191	81	1629	3632	2478	2274	1418
1981	2326	1232	84	1760	3640	2457	2432	1503
1982	2389	1228	85	1888	3641	2637	3123	1832
1983	2448	1229	86	2024	3639	2579	3396	1895
1984	2511	1246	89	2188	3633	2500	3222	1923
1985	2595	1290	100	2351	3634	—	3181	—
Increase % 1976/85	31	19	69	22	3	1	32	45

a. Number of families receiving benefit

b. Total number of individual beneficiaries during the year

c. Number of persons (including dependents) assisted through Canada Assistance Plan

Data are for fiscal years

Sources: Health and Welfare Canada, "Reference Guide on Income Security Programs" (unpublished); *Social Security Statistics Canada and Provinces, 1958–59 to 1982–83,* plus updates from Health and Welfare Canada; Statistics Canada, *Unemployment Insurance Statistics* (January 1987).

has grown steadily each year, and recipients of Unemployment Insurance and social assistance have increased dramatically in the 1980s. The human consequences of contemporary economic problems are clearly evident in the last two columns of this table. Growing transfer dependency can also be seen in the proportion of personal income that comes from income security programs. Between 1970 and 1984, transfer payments rose from 10.9 to 15.4 percent of total personal income in Canada (well behind wages and salaries, but several percentage points above investment income).[23] Table 42 provides a more detailed view. There has been fairly steady growth in the

Table 42 *Transfer Payments as a Proportion of Total Income, by Quintile*

Quintiles	1971	1973	1975	1977	1979	1981	1982	1983	1984
Families									
Lowest	43.4	41.8	47.0	48.5	45.9	46.9	52.6	54.4	57.6
Second	10.3	11.4	13.6	13.9	12.6	14.0	19.0	20.5	22.1
Middle	4.5	5.8	7.2	6.9	6.3	7.1	9.7	10.1	10.6
Fourth	3.2	4.1	5.0	4.8	4.0	4.3	5.6	6.0	6.3
Highest	1.9	2.4	3.1	3.0	2.5	2.5	3.1	2.8	3.1
Total	6.1	7.0	8.4	8.3	7.5	8.1	10.0	10.3	10.9
Unattached individuals									
Lowest	56.6	59.1	63.8	65.3	66.3	66.7	63.7	67.9	59.5
Second	64.3	67.3	69.4	65.7	61.8	60.3	66.5	71.2	69.9
Middle	14.7	19.6	20.8	20.2	15.4	18.1	22.8	31.0	29.3
Fourth	3.0	5.7	5.9	5.5	5.2	5.2	6.4	9.5	9.5
Highest	1.1	1.7	1.8	1.5	1.5	2.1	2.2	2.4	2.5
Total	10.2	12.9	14.1	13.1	13.0	14.2	15.5	17.9	17.8

Source: Statistics Canada, Income after Tax, Distributions by Size in Canada, 1983.

importance of transfer income for all income classes, but the growth in the first and second quintiles in particular has been significant.

Growing dependency on the state has naturally expanded total expenditures on income security. In comparison with other western nations, Canada remains a modest spender in this sector. Nevertheless, as table 43 indicates, the increase in transfer expenditures as a proportion of GDP in Canada during the first half of the 1980s was significantly larger than in other OECD nations. The reasons behind these striking figures, in comparison to other major industrial nations, would seem to lie in Canada's sharper economic contraction during the recession, the broader coverage of

Table 43   *Income Transfers as a Proportion of GDP in OECD Nations, 1981–84*

	1981	1982	1983	1984	Increase 1981–84
					Percentage
Canada	10.0	11.8	12.5	12.4	24.0
France	22.6	23.6	23.9	24.2	7.1
Germany	15.4	15.8	15.3	14.8	(3.9)
Italy	17.7	18.7	19.9	19.4	9.6
Japan	10.6	11.0	11.3	11.0	3.8
United Kingdom	11.7	12.5	12.4	12.7	8.5
United States	10.2	11.0	10.9	NA	6.9*
Australia	8.6	9.7	10.0	10.1	17.4
Austria	15.5	15.8	16.0	15.7	1.3
Belgium	22.7	22.5	23.0	22.6	(0.4)
Denmark	17.8	18.1	17.8	17.0	(4.5)
Finland	7.0	7.8	8.3	8.3	18.6
Ireland	13.6	15.5	16.2	NA	19.1*
Netherlands	25.9	27.4	28.1	27.0	4.2
Norway	14.5	15.0	15.5	15.2	4.8
Sweden	17.8	17.9	17.9	17.2	(3.4)
Switzerland	12.4	13.2	13.5	13.9	12.1

Source: *OECD National Accounts:* Volume II, Detailed Tables (Paris, 1986), calculations by author.

*Increase from 1981 to 1983.

the labour force by Unemployment Insurance, and to some extent, the less Draconian cuts in benefits.

A final perspective on the underlying role of income transfers comes from an examination of the extent of inequality in Canada during the 1980s. The recession clearly created even greater disparity in the incomes that Canadians derive directly from their roles in the economy. Table 44 bears witness to the decline in the share of pre-transfer income received by the lowest two quintiles of families, and the increased share captured by the richest quintile. However, as the final column of table 44 also shows, income security transfers substantially offset this growth in inequality in market incomes. Personal income taxes worked in the same direction, although to a much smaller degree; and, of course these figures ignore all of the other ways in which the state raises revenue, which tend to neutralize the redistributive consequences of the tax system as a whole. While there appears to have been a marginal movement in an inegalitarian direction even in post-tax income, in fact, the distribution of family income has tended to fluctuate within this same range for at least fifteen years. The overall message is thus one of stability, a stability due in significant part to the redistributive role of the state.[24] Clearly, interpretations of social policy as an instrument of social and political stability in Canada retain considerable force.

Table 44   *Income Distribution for Families, by Quintile, 1981–84*

Quintiles	1981	1982	1983	1984	Change 1981–84
Income Before Transfers					Percentage
Lowest	3.3	2.8	2.6	2.2	–33.3
Second	12.1	11.4	11.0	10.9	–9.9
Middle	18.6	18.2	18.0	18.2	–2.2
Fourth	25.2	25.5	25.5	25.5	1.2
Highest	40.8	42.1	43.0	43.2	5.9
Total income					
Lowest	6.4	6.3	6.2	6.1	–4.7
Second	12.9	12.6	12.3	12.3	–4.7
Middle	18.3	18.0	17.8	18.0	–1.6
Fourth	24.1	24.1	24.1	24.1	0
Highest	38.4	38.9	39.5	39.5	2.9
Income after tax					
Lowest	7.3	7.3	7.2	7.1	–2.7
Second	13.7	13.5	13.3	13.3	–2.9
Middle	18.6	18.4	18.2	18.4	–1.1
Fourth	23.8	23.8	23.9	23.9	0.4
Highest	36.6	37.0	37.4	37.3	1.9

Source: Statistics Canada. Income After Tax, Distributions by Size in Canada (various years).

Federalism and Income Security in the 1980s

The Constitutional Framework. The constitutional debate of the 1960s and 1970s unleashed a flood of proposals for redesigning the basic elements of the Canadian constitution, including both the structure of the central government and the division of powers between the federal and provincial levels of government. The implications for the income security system of a number of the leading elements of this constitutional agenda are investigated in chapter 9. In the end, few of the proposals for sweeping reform of the Canadian political system survived to be incorporated in the Constitution Act of 1982, or in the set of proposals incorporated in the Meech Lake Accord of April 1987. By the standards of the veritable kaleidoscope of options debated in the late 1970s, the Constitution Act was a decidedly modest package. Its primary provisions included an amending formula to govern future changes in the constitution, a Canadian Charter of Rights and Freedoms, a constitutional commitment to the principle of equalization payments to poorer provinces, and a strengthening of provincial control over national resources. The Meech Lake Accord would extend these revisions by recognizing Quebec as a distinct society within Canada, altering the amending formula for a number of items, entrenching a role for provincial governments in immigration policy and in appointments to the Supreme Court and the Senate, and establishing constitutional rules for future shared-cost programs.

The implications for the income security system of these reforms are worth highlighting in two areas: the division of jurisdiction between the two levels of government, and the Charter of Rights and Freedoms.

The general division of jurisdiction between the federal and provincial governments in the field of income security was not changed in the slightest by the 1982 Constitution Act. The Meech Lake Accord, however, does propose one important change. When negotiations to secure the agreement of the government of Quebec to the 1982 constitutional changes began again in 1986, Quebec identified the federal spending power as one of its five key concerns. Quebec has long objected to the use of the federal spending power in areas of provincial jurisdiction, and at the outset of the new discussions, the Quebec minister responsible for constitutional matters restated the historic position: "For all provinces [the federal spending power] has become a type of 'Sword of Damocles' hanging menacingly over all planned policies of social, cultural or economic development."[25] Quebec therefore revived earlier proposals to subject the exercise of the spending power to constitutional limits.

The Meech Lake Accord responded in part to these concerns. The proposed amendment would add the following section to the constitution:

106a. (1) The Government of Canada shall provide reasonable

compensation to the government of a province that chooses not to participate in a national shared-cost program that is established by the Government of Canada after the coming into force of this section in an area of exclusive provincial jurisdiction, if the province carries on a program or initiative that is compatible with the national objectives.

(2) Nothing in this section extends the legislative powers of the Parliament of Canada or of the legislatures of the provinces.

This provision sparked considerable debate on both sides of the Canadian duality: critics in English Canada attacked it as weakening the capacity of the federal government to respond to important social problems in the future; in Quebec, critics insisted that the section would leave too much scope in the hands of the federal government.

In assessing the long-term consequences of such a reform three initial points must be stressed. First, the provision would not apply to other aspects of the federal spending power; the power to make payment to individuals and institutions, such as Family Allowances, the Child Tax Credit, and National Welfare grants, would remain unaltered. Nor would the change have any effect on social insurance programs such as Unemployment Insurance and the Canada Pension Plan, both of which find their constitutional footing elsewhere in the Constitution Act.

Second, in one critical way, the Accord would strengthen the federal spending power. Historically, the constitutional status of the spending power has been highly ambiguous. Critics, especially in Quebec, have argued strongly that the spending power subverted the constitutional division of authority between levels of government, allowing the federal government to invade provincial jurisdiction almost at will; and federal politicians contemplating a new shared-cost initiative have always had to grapple with the political controversy that flowed from this underlying constitutional uncertainty. In addition, serious legal challenges to the use of the spending power were launched by private corporations in the mid-1980s. If upheld, these challenges would undermine a wide range of federal shared-cost programs, including the Canada Assistance Plan.[26] The Meech Lake Accord would eliminate these problems by establishing a clear constitutional basis for the spending power. The constitutional right of the federal government to mount a shared-cost program in any area of exclusive provincial jurisdiction, and to attach conditions relating to national objectives, could no longer be challenged. The fear that this might actually lead to a centralization of the federation prompted Quebec to insist on the addition of the clause affirming that the new section does not extend the legislative powers of either the federal or the provincial governments. Nevertheless, the entrenching of the spending power remains a significant step.

Third, the Accord proposes no restrictions on the right of the federal government to initiate new shared-cost programs. During previous constitutional negotiations, serious consideration had been given to a constitutional requirement that the establishment of a new program would require the prior approval of a majority of provinces. Indeed, in 1969, the federal government itself proposed such a change.[27] During the most recent round of negotiations, however, a similar proposal for prior provincial approval was rejected by several of the poorer provinces, and the agreement would place no limits on the capacity of federal authorities to establish new programs to which provinces would then have to respond. The provisions of the Meech Lake Accord thus represent a less Draconian limitation of the federal spending power than some of those debated in recent years.

The real controversy surrounding the Accord concerns the right of any province to opt out and to receive reasonable compensation if it "carries on a program or initiative that is compatible with the national objectives." Provinces have always had the absolute right to refuse to participate in a shared-cost program. This was a difficult position to sustain indefinitely, however, since the citizens of a province exercising this right still had to pay federal taxes to support the program elsewhere in the country, and recalcitrant provinces tended to come under considerable pressure from their own electorate to join. The provision of reasonable compensation would therefore make it much easier to opt out and mount their own programs.

The key issue is the terms that govern opting out. Quebec opted out of twenty-eight shared-cost programs in 1965, one of which was the Canada Assistance Plan. As chapter 2 noted, however, this proved to be of marginal significance, as Quebec continued to meet CAP program standards. The province's agreement to meet those conditions was initially an interim one, but it has been continuously extended for over twenty years and remains in force. Quebec receives a portion of its CAP resources in the form of tax points instead of a direct cash payment, but it is still subject to the same rules as every other province and still presents an annual audit of its social assistance expenditures to Ottawa. From the perspective of federal-provincial relations, opting out in 1965 proved to be of symbolic importance only.

The great imponderable about the provision in the Meech Lake Accord is whether the requirement that the program of a provincial government opting out must be "compatible with the national objectives" would produce similar constraints. Some have argued that the federal government would be unable to insist on national standards, and that future shared-cost programs would vary more extensively from province to province, reflecting not only regional differences in social needs but also political preferences. Others, however, insist that the national "objectives" might prove to be relatively detailed, and that the courts, if called upon to arbitrate between governments, would be unlikely to challenge the federal authorities' definition of the national objectives being pursued in a shared-cost program.

Given such a wide range of possibilities, predictions are more than usually hazardous. Nevertheless, several observations seem appropriate. The Accord would strengthen the constitutional legitimacy of the spending power, protecting it from both public and private challengers. On the other hand, the Accord would probably lead to greater regional differences in new social service programs. It would do so in two ways. First, federal authorities would likely seek to minimize the number of provinces choosing to opt out of a new program by allowing for considerable regional variation within the program. In effect, the Accord would nudge new initiatives towards the model of the Canada Assistance Plan, with a general umbrella program containing relatively few precise conditions at the national level, and the specific form of each province's program being negotiated separately and set out in a subsidiary bilateral agreement. Second, some provinces would opt out anyway. Quebec would likely do so as a matter of principle, and other provinces might be tempted to follow, although much would depend on the stringency of the national objectives and the formula according to which "reasonable compensation" would be calculated.[28] It is worth noting that if the federal program allowed for substantial flexibility from the outset, the additional degrees of freedom gained by opting out might prove limited. Nonetheless, the cumulative impact of these two dynamics that would be set in motion by the Accord points to a more regionally diverse pattern of social service initiatives in the future.

Finally, the possibility of even greater complexity in negotiating shared-cost agreements with the provinces in the future would incline the federal government to look to its own jurisdiction more closely when deciding how to respond to emerging social needs. The complications of the shared-cost mechanism would bear most heavily on federal initiatives in the social services, and lead to greater emphasis on direct payments to individuals and institutions, thereby enhancing federal reliance on income security programs and the social uses of the tax system. As chapter 9 argued, Canadians would still look to Ottawa for leadership, social reformers among federal politicians would still want to respond, and income security programs would provide the more flexible instrument through which to reach all citizens in all regions directly.

As a result, the proposed constitutional change would, if anything, accentuate the bifurcation of the Canadian welfare state noted in chapter 4, with a relatively centralized system of income security and a relatively decentralized system of social services. Table 45 updates the analysis of the centralization of income security by presenting three different measures of the extent of centralization for the period 1972–84. The first panel measures centralization in terms of which government actually pays the benefit

Table 45 *Centralization of Income Security Expenditure, 1972–84*

	1972	1974	1976	1978	1980	1982	1984
1. Income Security Expenditure							
Federal	78.5	79.2	77.4	77.6	73.8	75.9	73.5
Provincial	21.5	20.7	22.5	22.4	26.2	24.1	26.5
2. Financing of Income Security							
Federal	85.8	85.5	84.6	85.6	82.8	84.7	83.1
Provincial	14.1	14.4	15.3	14.4	17.2	15.3	16.9
3. Authority over Income Security							
Federal	75.5	56.8	57.0	57.2	55.6	59.0	56.3
Shared	19.2	37.3	35.7	34.9	35.3	31.9	32.9
Provincial	5.2	5.7	7.1	7.9	9.1	9.1	10.8

Note: Data on provincial expenditure include municipal relief; federal and provincial tax
credits are not included

Source: Calculated from data in Statistics Canada, *National Income and Expenditure
Accounts, 1970–1984.*

directly to the recipient, and demonstrates the continuing predominance of
the federal government, which pays out approximately three quarters of all
income security dollars. The second panel reveals the roles of the two jurisdictions in financing the income security system; in this case, intergovernmental transfers such as those through the Canada Assistance Plan are
credited to the donor government rather than the recipient government. By
this measure, income security is even more centralized, as 85 percent of the
dollars flowing through the system are federal dollars, and even this figure
ignores the portion of equalization grants that is devoted to provincial
social assistance benefits.

The final panel in table 45 provides the third view of centralization by
examining which levels of government have a legal right to determine, to
some degree at least, the disbursement of funds under income security
programs. The data here confirm the sudden increase in the shared
programs in the early 1970s, reflecting in large part the acceptance of a
provincial right to alter the configuration of payments under the federal
Family Allowance program and the growth of the Canada Pension Plan.
This measure is far from a perfect measure of intergovernmental influences,
as chapter 4 emphasized. Nevertheless, the broad pattern is clear. There has
been remarkably little formal decentralization in the income security
system, but the process of setting national policy is increasingly an inter-

governmental one. This essential pattern emerged during the 1970s, and has not been altered significantly by the economic and constitutional upheavals of the 1980s.

In addition to the proposed changes in the division of powers, the constitutional reform process generated one other innovation that is having an important impact on the income security system: the Canadian Charter of Rights and Freedoms. Several parts of the Charter are directly relevant to social programs. Sections 7–14 entrench a set of legal rights which establish standards of due process for all government activities, including the management of social services. In addition, section 15 establishes a set of equality rights. Section 15(1) states that "every individual is equal before and under the law and has the right to the equal protection and equal benefit of the law without discrimination and, in particular, without discrimination based on race, national or ethnic origin, colour, religion, sex, age or mental or physical disability." Section 15(2) then makes clear that these equality rights do not preclude affirmative action programs designed to assist disadvantaged groups or individuals.

When exploring the potential impact of the Charter, it is important to remember the limitations on the rights and freedoms set forth in it. Section 1 allows for "such reasonable limits prescribed by law as can be demonstrably justified in a free and democratic society." In addition, section 33 enables Parliament or a provincial legislature to exempt legislation from major parts of the Charter, including the legal and equality rights. Such a legislative override must be re-enacted every five years, but it remains an important potential constraint on the role of the Charter.

The Charter is unlikely to be a potent instrument of economic egalitarianism, although some authors have wondered whether the guarantee of "security of the person" in section 7 and of "equal benefit of the law" in section 15 might lead the courts to establish minimum standards of economic security.[29] Most legal authorities, however, suggest that such decisions are unlikely.[30] The primary role of the Charter is to prevent government actions that restrict the rights of citizens, and the courts are unlikely to impose positive obligations on the state to remedy inequalities embedded, not in law, but in the social and economic fabric of the nation.[31] In the words of one court judgment, "the Charter is written in terms of what the state cannot do to the individual, not in terms of what the individual can extract from the state."[32] One legal scholar is much blunter: for the poor, the Charter's effect is "cosmetic . . . The only means of improving the position of the most vulnerable Canadians is through ordinary legislation."[33] As a result, advocates of more sweeping social reform often emphasize the symbolic role of the Charter in legitimizing the values of equality and strengthening their wider political campaigns for legislative action on social problems.

Nevertheless, the more immediate, direct consequences of the Charter for income security programs should not be underestimated. The benefit system is governed by a complex maze of regulations that are often based on the age, sex, or family status of recipients, and a host of Charter issues have been identified by legal advocacy groups,[34] by governments themselves,[35] and by recipients who are increasingly gaining access to the courts.[36] The impact of the Charter on social policy is more pervasive than a simple survey of court decisions rendered so far would suggest. The norms of the Charter are increasingly penetrating the political and bureaucratic cultures of the country and, in some cases, public officials have adapted programs in anticipation of legal challenges, or negotiated agreements with advocacy groups, in order to avoid lengthy and potentially embarrassing court cases.

Most of the issues being raised do not challenge the basic structure of existing income security programs. Rather they focus on the detailed rules governing eligibility and benefits. Pensions, for example, raise a host of issues. In anticipation of challenges to mandatory retirement rules, the Canada and Quebec Pension plans have been amended to allow individuals to receive benefits earlier or later than age sixty-five, according to individual choice, with appropriate actuarial adjustments. In addition, survivor benefits in these plans are being questioned. At the moment, the benefits vary considerably, depending on the surviving spouse's age, physical health, and family responsibilities; at the extreme, survivors younger than thirty-five who have no children and are not disabled receive no benefits at all. In anticipation of Charter challenges, the Parliamentary Committee on Equality Rights recommended in 1985 that the Canada Pension Plan "be amended so that surviving spouses' benefits be awarded without reference to disability, age or family status."[37] Similar issues arise in other pension programs. Does the residency requirement for Old Age Security, which limits payments to many immigrants, constitute discrimination based on "national or ethnic origin?"[38] Is the Guaranteed Income Supplement challengeable because it provides a lower total benefit for a married couple than for two persons who are living together but not in a common law relationship?[39]

The Unemployment Insurance Act also poses issues. The Parliamentary Committee on Equality Rights recommended that the existing system of maternity benefits, which are available only to women, be replaced by a two-tier system. The first tier would be available only to women during late pregnancy and immediately after the birth; but a second tier of benefits would be available to either parent or shared between them.[40] The Committee also recommended that the longer period of employment required to qualify for special benefits, such as the maternity provisions, be reduced to the same period required for regular unemployment benefits.[41]

Provincial social assistance programs are also feeling the weight of the Charter. Traditionally, most provinces have been much more reluctant to support single fathers with dependent children than single mothers. Some provinces eliminated the distinction in anticipation of a challenge, but Nova Scotia did not. When the legislation was challenged under the Charter, the province lost both its original case and a subsequent appeal.[42] In Ontario, attention focused on the controversial "man in the house" rule, according to which the eligibility for benefit of a single mother with dependent children could be jeopardized if welfare authorities concluded that she was living with a man "as husband and wife."[43] Women's groups challenged the regulation, contending that it discriminated on the grounds of sex, by assuming that a male cohabitant should support the woman and her children, while not assuming the same of a female cohabitant. In 1986, the Ontario government settled the case out of court, and agreed to rewrite the rule so as to lessen its intrusive, moralistic character.[44] Other issues continue to emerge. Advocacy groups have argued, for example, that the particularly low level of benefits for young and single recipients in a number of provinces also violates the equality provisions of the Charter, and therefore should be changed.

While none of these issues question the basic structure of income security programs, other cases may result in a more radical restructuring of particular programs. At the federal level, the Spouse's Allowance, which provides income-tested support to a pensioner's spouse who is aged sixty to sixty-four, is under challenge because no allowance is paid to poor individuals of a similar age who are single, separated, or divorced. As one critic argued, "to tie economic relief to marital status rather than to the hardship itself appears arbitrary and therefore discriminatory."[45] This logic led one advocacy group to propose "the elimination of the spousal allowance in order to comply with the Charter."[46] The Parliamentary Committee on Equality Rights, on the other hand, recommended that the program "be replaced with an equivalent benefit that is available without reference to marital status."[47] In effect, this would involve extending eligibility for the OAS-GIS system to everyone sixty years of age, which would be an expensive step with important implications for general policies on the age of retirement. Federal officials have therefore chosen to delay taking action.[48] In the meantime, various cases on the issue are wending their way through the courts.

At the provincial level, workers' compensation programs have also been challenged. In late 1986, the Supreme Court of Newfoundland ruled that the province's act cannot limit the right of a work accident victim to institute civil actions against the employer or other employees to obtain damages in excess of those provided for in the act.[49] Such a decision, if sustained by the Supreme Court of Canada, would strike at the very heart of the political compromise that has underpinned workers' compensation programs since their very beginnings in Ontario in 1914. In effect, employers have agreed to pay for the benefit program, and workers have agreed to surrender their right to sue. If the Charter challenge is sustained, employers will undoubtedly insist that an entirely new approach is needed.

Clearly, the Charter will have a multitude of effects on income security in the coming years. While it may not prove to be a powerful engine of economic egalitarianism, it is likely to be an expansionist element in income security. For the most part, the Charter will be used by individuals who are denied benefits, and the cumulative effect of hundreds of such initiatives will be an incremental expansion in the social commitments of the Canadian state. More fundamental issues also lurk on the horizon. Will the trend of decisions and adjustments undermine the legitimacy of the family unit, as opposed to the individual, as the basis for redistributive policies? Will a growing emphasis on legalistic forms of decision making, with their emphasis on due process, individual rights, and adversarial relations, increasingly displace traditional modes of decision making in the social services, which give much greater weight to professional judgment, discretion, and group needs? Will a growing emphasis on equal benefit of the law undermine the legitimacy of contributory programs, which tie benefit to labour force participation and leave individuals with less than full labour force attachment at a disadvantage? The ripple effects of the entrenchment of the Charter on the income security system extend much further than contemporary observers can hope to see.[50]

Federalism and the Role of the State. The experiences of the 1980s throw further light on a classic controversy about the impact of federalism on the role of the state in western nations. Earlier chapters have argued that federalism has been a conservative force in Canadian welfare politics, one which slowed the development of the income security system in the interwar years and continued to exercise a more modest restraining influence throughout the postwar period. This analysis of the Canadian case is compatible with cross-national studies of the determinants of social expenditures that have demonstrated a relationship between the scope of the social policy sector and political centralization: other things being equal, countries with decentralized systems of government devote a smaller proportion of their GDP to welfare than do those with more centralized governments.

There are, however, two possible versions of the general proposition that federalism is a conservative force, each of which evokes separate meanings of the word "conservative." The first version argues that federalism inhibits the expansion of the state, preserving a larger sphere of economic and social relations in which private action and market forces prevail. Obviously the barriers to expansion of the public sector are not absolute, and can be overcome if political pressures are great enough. On balance, however, this version of the general proposition holds that a federal state is a weaker state. The second version suggests that the bias of federalism is not simply against the expansion of the state, but against change more generally. The fragmentation of power implicit in federal structures creates a set of checks and balances and veto points that increase the probability that any proposal for change—whether involving an expansion or a contraction of the public sector—will be delayed, diluted, or defeated. In effect, the additional opportunities for blocking change raise the level of consensus required before new initiatives can be introduced on a nation-wide basis.

Throughout the postwar period, it was difficult to disentangle the two versions of the general view that federalism is a conservative factor. In a period in which the dominant social, political, and ideological trends favoured the expansion of the public sector, both versions suggested that federal institutions would slow the pace of public-sector growth. The politics of neoconservatism in the 1980s, however, opened up the possibility of distinguishing between the two versions. Has the federal system facil-itated the efforts of neoconservatives during the 1980s, as the first version would suggest? Or have the complexities of fragmented power, which frustrated welfare advocates in earlier generations, now rushed to their aid by inhibiting the advocates of a smaller, less redistributive state?

The broad pattern of income security policy in the 1980s suggests that the second version is more plausible—that federalism constrains both rapid expansion and rapid contraction in the scope of state activity. Federalism is one of the elements of Canadian political life that incline it towards an incremental process of policy change.

At the most general level, the division of power inherent in a federal system complicates the task facing any ideological movement seeking to reshape the role played by the contemporary state. Capturing the federal government alone leaves a formidable phalanx of provincial governments with important areas of jurisdiction and the capacity to offset many federal initiatives. A federal structure does allow for the capture of individual prov-inces and the hope of implementing a radical agenda on a regional basis, with the further hope that the ideas will then prove contagious in other jurisdictions. This has been an important theme in the history of Canadian health insurance, for example. On the other hand, there are also important limits to the local scope for radicalism, as was illustrated by the paralysis of welfare policy during the interwar period, examined in chapter 5.

In addition, the central role of federal-provincial negotiations in designing the programs of both levels of government diversifies the range of interests and ideologies that are brought to bear on major issues. While regional interests are stoutly defended by provincial champions, partisan and ideological differences also flow into federal-provincial channels. The need for consensus among governments representing diverse regional and ideological complexions often constrains boldness and encourages a more gradual process of policy adaptation. In this, as several commentators have observed, the intersection of federalism, regionalism, and ideology generates a pattern of policy change similar to what one might expect from a large coalition government.[51]

The debate over sweeping reforms to the income security system during the Social Security Review of the mid-1970s highlights these dynamics. As chapter 5 notes, the federal-provincial nature of the process increased the access of both reformist and conservative provincial governments to the national debate. This ensured that a wider range of options were actively discussed, but it also maximized the ideological distance among the participants at the bargaining table and decreased the prospects for achieving consensus on comprehensive reform. Yet divided jurisdiction did facilitate incremental progress at both levels of governments in the years following the collapse of the review.

The record of the 1980s continues to provide ample proof that federal-provincial relations inhibit the expansion of the income security system. None is more compelling, however, than the case of the great pension debate. Throughout the late 1970s and early 1980s, the Canadian pension system was subjected to intensive scrutiny. Numerous advisory commissions highlighted its deficiencies; representatives of business, labour, pensioners, and social groups pressed their views on government; and politicians argued about solutions. In contrast to the pervasive retrenchment in virtually every other corner of the welfare state, the entire pensions debate was premised on the need for expansion of the retirement income system; and sweeping proposals for the improvement of both public and private pensions were advanced. For defenders of the welfare state, pensions seemed to offer a unique opportunity for advance in an era otherwise dominated by the need to defend the gains of earlier days.

As the 1980s ground on, however, the momentum for reform receded, and the policies finally adopted represent only the incremental expansion described earlier. The complexity of the conflicts over pensions among business, labour, and various social groups, and the distinctive interests advanced by the governments at the federal-provincial table, have been examined more fully elsewhere.[52] Nevertheless, a central factor in the outcome has been the fragmentation of decision-making authority. The predominant provincial role in the regulation of private pensions militated against proposals for major reforms, such as a requirement for universal coverage of the labour force by private plans or mandatory inflation protection of pension benefits. In addition, the multiple vetoes over changes in the Canada Pension Plan, which are examined in chapter 5, constitute a formidable barrier to the expansionist proposals advocated by organized labour, the women's movement, and other social groups. Political institutions are never the only factor influencing policy outcomes, and in the early 1980s the economic recession proved equally important in tempering the reformist impulses of governments. However, institutional complexity slowed the pace of decision making, and gave the private sector more time to marshall its defences against its challengers. Moreover, the decision rules ensured that reform could only proceed on the basis of a very broad consensus, a system that inevitably benefits those least interested in change.[53]

Evidence that Canadian federalism also limits the capacity of governments to *reduce* their welfare commitments is less decisive, since no other income security program is governed by such an explicit system of vetoes. Nevertheless, the fragmentation of power implicit in federal institutions and the tensions between the two levels of government do create some barriers to sharp reductions in the social role of the state. These barriers are hardly insurmountable, as is witnessed by the lengthy list of benefit reductions discussed earlier. Nor are the complexities of federalism even the most important constraint facing governments intent on reducing the public sector. They do, however, complicate the prospects for radical change.

In the particular case of income security, however, the curbs on neoconservatism implicit in federalism appear to be asymmetrical, constraining the federal government more severely than provincial ones. The reasons for this are rooted in the structure of governmental interests in this sector. Any major reductions in federal social programs are likely to have a negative impact on the programs and budgets of provincial governments, as well as on the economic and social well-being of their regions. As a result, such federal initiatives are quickly met by hostile provincial governments with impressive capacities to mobilize wider public opposition to unwelcome proposals. This general trend is reinforced by the interregional transfers implicit in the income security system and the much greater sensitivity of poorer regions to changes in welfare programs. Provincial governments in poorer parts of the country are especially prone to fight any erosion of the redistributive role of the federal government. While such battles are not always won, the provinces can add considerable weight and often provide strategic leadership to the wider coalitions of forces fighting federal cuts.

Provincial reductions in the income security field are not constrained in a reciprocal manner. During the postwar period of governmental activism, provincial governments determined to expand into new areas regularly confronted angry federal authorities intent on defending their jurisdiction, prerogatives, and prestige. Provincial efforts to reduce their activities do not face comparable resistance. Moreover, given the nature of federal-provincial fiscal arrangements under the Canada Assistance Plan, provincial reductions in social assistance reduce the demands on the federal budget. This stands in sharp contrast to the health and post-secondary education sectors. Under the block-funding provisions of the Established Programs Financing Act, reductions in provincial spending on health and education have no effect on the relevant federal fiscal transfers to the provinces, with the result that the federal government can find itself financing a growing proportion of the costs of the service. In that circumstance, the federal government is financially free to complain about provincial restraint and service reductions and even to act against them, as in the case of the Canada Health Act, which did not raise federal expenditures at all. In the income security sector, however, the federal government can quietly benefit from provincial restraint.

This asymmetry can be seen in the battles over income security initiatives during the last ten years. Provincial scrutiny of federal initiatives has been most vigilant in the case of Unemployment Insurance which, as table 46 demonstrates, is a powerful tool of interregional redistribution. Provincial authorities, especially those from Atlantic Canada and Quebec, fear the general economic impact on their region of reductions in Unemployment Insurance benefits, and remain concerned about any increased social assistance costs that might result, despite federal studies that find relatively little flowthrough onto welfare caseloads. Accordingly, provincial authorities have mobilized repeatedly to defend Unemployment Insurance.

Table 46   *Inter-regional Transfers as a Proportion of UI Expenditures, by Province, 1975-79*

	1975	1976	1977	1978	1979
Newfoundland	+72.8	+72.8	+74.5	+75.7	+75.5
P.E.I.	+66.1	+67.4	+69.7	+70.0	+71.7
Nova Scotia	+31.4	+37.4	+43.0	+41.5	+41.0
New Brunswick	+56.7	+58.9	+62.5	+61.9	+61.9
Quebec	+30.5	+34.1	+35.6	+35.9	+34.9
Ontario	−32.3	−46.4	−57.2	−55.2	−56.8
Manitoba	−108.5	−86.2	−51.5	−28.6	−44.4
Saskatchewan	−92.7	−88.8	−65.3	−46.3	−56.7
Alberta	−268.9	−251.1	−225.5	−208.0	−205.0
British Columbia	+18.1	+6.8	+0.5	+10.0	+0.4

Source: Task Force on Unemployment Insurance, *Unemployment Insurance: Interprovincial Transfers,* Technical Study no. 9 (Ottawa: Employment and Immigration Canada, 1981).

Provincial governments were major opponents of the restrictions on Unemployment Insurance benefits in the second half of the 1970s. To be sure, the provinces did not fight alone. The battle in 1977 against the proposed increase in the qualification period to fourteen weeks of employment was led by Members of Parliament of both major parties from high unemployment regions, and in many ways the final compromise of a variable requirement of from ten to fourteen weeks, depending on the regional unemployment rate, was a triumph for the Atlantic caucus of the governing Liberal party. But provincial support of their campaign was also critical to their success, as the then minister of manpower and immigration, Bud Cullen, later reflected: "We did consult with the provinces and as a result of the news we received from the Atlantic provinces—remember at the time they were Liberal governments—we changed the program from 14 weeks across the board to 10–14. It was also a result of the Atlantic caucus but the Atlantic caucus works hand-in-glove with the provincial governments."[54]

The provinces are not always successful in such campaigns. In 1978, for example, the provinces waged a vigorous campaign for an alternative approach to Unemployment Insurance reform, pressing their case in intergovernmental committees, in the media, and even before a committee of the House of Commons. The campaign failed in its primary goal, however, and only minor gains were won. Nonetheless, in the view of Leslie Pal, the battles of the 1970s ensured that provinces will remain "central actors in UI program evolution and reform."[55]

The provinces also joined the swelling chorus that forced the federal government to abandon its plan for the partial deindexation of Old Age Security payments in 1985. While provincial authorities did not lead the campaign, the existence of another ten political arenas created new opportunities for opponents of the proposal. During the spring and summer of that year, most provincial legislatures adopted motions condemning the change. Moreover, in several instances, the motions were introduced by opposition parties in the legislature, and forced Progressive Conservative provincial governments to abandon their political counterpart in Ottawa rather than support an unpopular cause. Unlike the case of the Canada Pension Plan, the opposition of provincial governments did not create legal impediments to the change. But in the politically charged atmosphere of the controversy, provincial motions did add momentum and credibility to the wider protest.[56]

Provincial governments also stand as potential adversaries of the emerging agenda in the income security fields, as represented by the proposals for a radical restructuring of the system that have been advanced by various commissions in recent years. While these proposals would not always involve a reduction in total social spending, they do reflect a more market-oriented conception of income security, with a greater emphasis on work incentives and labour mobility. These assumptions underpinned the Forget Commission's approach to Unemployment Insurance, but the most comprehensive proposals were those of the Royal Commission on the Economic Union and Development Prospects for Canada (the Macdonald Commission), which recommended a three-part package: first, significant reductions in Unemployment Insurance, including the elimination of regional benefits; second, the transfer of the money saved to a new Transitional Adjustment Assistance Program that would provide enhanced support for retraining, mobility grants, portable wage subsidies, early retirement and other assistance for those displaced by the forces of economic change; and third, the replacement of a number of other tax and transfer programs with a Universal Income Security Program that would provide income supplementation for low-income families and individuals.[57]

Such a radical restructuring of the income security system would be intensely controversial on many counts.[58] One of the major concerns, however, would be its regional implications. The reforms to Unemployment Insurance and the greater emphasis on labour mobility would accelerate the flow of people out of poorer regions. The viability of some communities would thus be undermined, and the population of some provinces would decline, leading inevitably to a comparable reduction in their economic and political importance. The provincial governments in these regions would undoubtedly resist such a prospect with all the political resources at their disposal. Moreover, provinces in general would enter the fray with considerable leverage, since the other parts of such a package, especially the income supplementation proposals, would depend heavily on their agreement. Indeed, the Macdonald Commission itself warned that "a cooperative federal-provincial approach is, in our view, absolutely essential."[59] Federal-provincial conflict was one of the elements that doomed proposals for the restructuring of the income security system during the Social Security Review in the mid-1970s, and that review did not tackle Unemployment Insurance. The addition of significant cuts to Unemployment Insurance to the brew in the 1980s makes for an even more explosive mixture in the intergovernmental world. Provinces are not the only potential opponents of this reform agenda, but they would add considerable weight to the inevitable protests. Small wonder then that the federal government announced in May 1987 that it would not be proceeding with any substantive reforms to Unemployment Insurance.[60]

In comparison, provincial governments determined to reduce welfare benefits have been much less constrained by federal action. As table 40 noted, social assistance benefits have been reduced sharply in real terms in several provinces, and benefits for single employables are often especially low. Yet in public at least, the federal government has, in the words of one analyst, simply turned a "blind eye."[61] Federal officials insist that in the privacy of intergovernmental meetings, federal ministers may urge their provincial counterparts to improve benefit levels, but there have been no public campaigns comparable to those mounted by provincial ministers opposing federal cuts.

This federal silence represents a long tradition, with origins deep in the interwar history of federal support for provincial relief programs.[62] It was certainly a well-established norm by the 1960s when the Canada Assistance Plan was being drafted. In the words of a senior federal official involved, "no serious consideration was given to a universal national standard of adequacy in welfare programs across Canada, for two reasons. First, because it would have been impossible to formulate in specific terms and second, because it would have violated the principle that the terms and conditions of assistance are for the provinces to decide."[63] Federal officials had sought a much milder requirement for an annual review of the administration of the program, province by province, but even this was eliminated at the last moment in response to pressure from the provinces and from senior officials in the central agencies of the federal government.

Moreover, the federal "blind eye" also reflects the fiscal asymmetry of federalism in this sector, noted earlier. Cuts in federal programs normally impose additional burdens on provincial governments; cuts in provincial social assistance reduce the burden on the federal government. Indeed, federal officials accept that this dynamic helps protect the Canada Assistance Plan from any initiative from the federal Department of Finance to "cap CAP" by limiting federal contributions. As one official privately noted, "Finance accepts CAP in part because they know that the brakes are on in the provinces."

The Canada Assistance Plan is not completely without conditions, and some of these do place constraints on provincial proposals. The prohibition of residency requirements remains important. Moreover, federal officials insist that they objected strenuously—in private again—to an Alberta experiment with "work for welfare," insisting that such a program violated the CAP requirement that the province provide assistance to any person in need. Constraints on the provision of welfare services under CAP are more extensive, and the Neilson Task Force noted that the prevailing legal interpretation of the CAP legislation constrained the privatization of social services, frustrating the preferences of several provinces to rely more heavily on commercial firms in the provision of daycare and homemaker services.[64]

Nevertheless, the federal constraints on provincial discretion in income security are limited. This is not a constitutional inevitability. In the health sector, the Canada Health Act imposed significant penalties on provinces that tolerated extra billing for physicians' services. Such federal action provoked strong provincial opposition, however, and could only be sustained because of overwhelming support from the population of the country as a whole. Moreover, the Canada Health Act did not increase federal expenditures. Recipients of social assistance, on the other hand, lack a strong political constituency, and federal efforts to protect their benefits would increase federal spending in an era of fiscal restraint. The federal government is unlikely to ride to their rescue.

The social record of the 1980s is composed of two broad themes, each in tension with the other. One theme encompasses fiscal crisis, neoconservatism, and retrenchment in social benefits. The second involves the continuing expansion of the role of income security in modern economies, and its importance in mitigating the growth of inequality generated by the worst recession in postwar history. These two themes can be traced through the recent experience of many other western nations, but with important variations that reflect the basic political, economic and cultural configuration of each country. In the Canadian case, such variations flow in part from the evolving constitutional framework within which struggles over public policy are conducted.

Retrenchment in the Canadian income security system has been relatively incremental, and the conservatism inherent in the dynamics of federalism helps to explain this pattern. The fragmentation of authority is one factor that constrains radical initiatives, both to expand and reduce the role of the state, and thereby encourages a more incremental process of policy change. In the early postwar decades, federalism did not block the development of a modern welfare state, and in the 1980s, federalism has hardly stopped neoconservatism in its tracks. In both periods, however, institutional complexity slowed the pace of change. Moreover, the logic embedded in federal-provincial relations helps to explain the differential impact of retrenchment in the 1980s. The major income security programs, which operate at the federal level, are defended by stalwart provincial champions. In comparison, intergovernmental relations confer much less protection on social assistance recipients who in several provinces have had to endure retrenchments much more severe than other groups of beneficiaries.

Underlying this pattern of retrenchment has been a major expansion of the role of income security in the economy and society of Canada. When all due credit is given to employment and training projects, it was the income security system that bore the brunt of the worst recession in postwar history and largely neutralized the sharp increase in inequality in market incomes. Stability in perilous times is not to be slighted. Moreover, social and demographic changes point to the continued expansion of the welfare state, and politicians ignore such warnings at their peril. Constitutional change has reinforced this dynamic. While the Charter may disappoint champions of

economic egalitarianism, it will undoubtedly expand the social commitments of the Canadian state, in both its federal and provincial forms.

The language of crisis, which permeated debate about the welfare state
throughout the early 1980s, may be receding both in official documents and
public discourse.[65] Nevertheless, the social policies of western nations will
remain under stress for years to come. The primary forces that generate
such stress lie well outside the particularities of the constitutional
framework of any country, but the complexities of federalism will continue
to condition the ways in which the Canadian state responds to them.

Notes

Notes to Chapter Two

1. Organization for Economic Co-operation and Development, *Public Expenditure on Income Maintenance Programmes* (Paris, 1976), Table 2. For a comparative study of the conditions according to which unemployment benefits are granted, see Economic Council of Canada, *People and Jobs,* Appendix F.

2. D. Guest, *The Emergence of Social Security in Canada,* ch. 4.

3. For more detailed descriptions of provincial administrative patterns, see M. Chandler and W. Chandler, *Public Policy and Provincial Politics,* pp. 188-98; also Canada, Health and Welfare Canada, *Social Security in Canada,* pp. 23-27.

4. Based on correspondence with the Social Service Program Branch of Health and Welfare Canada. There is one procedural difference between Quebec and other provinces. Money is advanced to Quebec on the basis of an annual estimate of eligible expenditures and subsequently verified or adjusted on the basis of an annual claim. In the case of other provinces, adjustments are made on the basis of monthly claims.

5. Claude Morin is also of this opinion. See his *Quebec Versus Ottawa,* 1976.

6. In 1975 the benefit of the Guaranteed Income Supplement was extended to spouses of OAS recipients through the introduction of the Spouses' Allowance.

7. See, for example, the comments of Hon. A. MacEachen, minister of National Health and Welfare, during debate on the second reading of the bill to establish the program. *House of Commons Debates,* First Session, 27th Parliament, vol. 10, especially pp. 10882-84 and 10894.

8. The tradition of provincial supplements to federal pensions is a long-standing one. For a discussion of similar supplements in the 1940s, see K. Bryden, *Old Age Pensions and Policy-Making in Canada,* pp. 92-97.

9. Interprovincial Conference of Ministers Responsible for Social Services, *The Income Security System in Canada,* p. 56.

10. Economic Council of Canada, *Fifth Annual Review,* ch. 6. See also Canada, Senate, Special Committee on Poverty, *Poverty in Canada.*

11. On Britain, see K. Banting, *Poverty, Politics and Policy.* On the United States, see, for example, P. Moynihan, *The Politics of a Guaranteed Annual Income.* For a comparison of Canadian and American concerns in this field, see C. Leman, *The Collapse of Welfare Reform.*

12. For the Quebec studies, see Comité interministériel sur la revision de la sécurité du revenu, *Analyse d'un Programme Québecois de Revenu Familial Garanti* and Ministère du Conseil Exécutif, *Les Diverses Hypothéses d'une Première Etape de Revenu Minimum Garanti.* See also E. Tamagno, "The Quebec Income Supplementation Plan," *Canadian Taxation* 1 (1979): 63-66.

13. For an analysis of this proposal, see D. Hum and H. Stevens, "The Manitoba White Paper on Tax Credit Reform: A Critique," *Canadian Taxation* 2 (1980): 129-34.

14. See G. Riches, "FIP Flops," *Perspectives* (July/August 1978); and Conference on Social Policy, "Saskatchewan Family Income Study," (Mont. Ste-Marie, 1978).

15. Québec, Ministre d'Etat au Développement Social, "Un Bilan Positif Pour Cette Première Année."

16. British Columbia, Department of Human Resources, *Annual Report 1973;* and *Vancouver Sun,* 16 November 1973.

17. A much more elaborate, three-year experiment to test the impact of a guaranteed annual income was commissioned jointly by Manitoba and the federal government, but the now completed program has become something of an administrative embarrassment, and little policy follow-up is expected. For a review of the origins of the project, and an assessment of eleven technical studies that did emerge from it, see R.B. Splane, "Whatever Happened to the GAI?", *Social Work* 48 (1980): 86-87.

18. See E. Todres, "The Dynamics of Canadian Federalism: The Politics of Tax Credits," paper presented to the annual meeting of the American Political Science Association, 1975.

19. On the other hand, the Department of Finance is distinctly unenthusiastic about the prospect of major extensions of the principle. See Canada, Department of Finance, *Integration of Social Program Payments into the Income Tax System.* On the background to the Child Tax Credit, see B. Kitchen, "A Canadian Compromise: The Refundable Child Tax Credit," *Canadian Taxation* 1 (1979): 44-51.

20. Québec, Ministre d'Etat au Développement Social, "Négotiations avec le Fédéral: Une attitude décevante du Fédéral."

21. Economic Council of Canada, *One in Three,* p. 13.

22. On the degree of substitution between public and private welfare in industrial nations generally, see F.L. Pryor, *Public Expenditures in Communist and Capitalist Nations,* pp. 142-45.

23. From the beginning the Canada Pension Plan was designed to provide only minimum levels of income on retirement, and thereby to allow for the continuation and extension of private pension plans and personal savings above these minimal levels. See The Canada Pension Plan Advisory Committee, "Review of the Objectives of the CPP."

24. For a passionate defence of private pensions along these lines, see G.N. Calvert, *Pensions and Survival.* Of course, some critics of occupational pension plans question the concentration of the large pools of capital in private hands. See, for example, R.M. Titmuss, "The Irresponsible Society," in his *Essays on 'The Welfare State'.*

25. For an assessment of these problems, see J.E. Pesando and S.A. Rea, Jr., *Public and Private Pensions in Canada;* and J.E. Pesando, *Private Pensions in an Inflationary Climate.*

26. For a recent examination of the size of tax expenditures, see Canada, Department of Finance, *Tax Expenditure Account.*

27. National Council of Welfare, *The Hidden Welfare System Revisited,* p. 14.

28. *Tax Expenditure Account,* Table 1.

29. For example, an interprovincial taskforce estimated that whereas the average *monthly* caseload of social assistance programs in 1977-78 represented 5.5 percent of the Canadian population, up to 10 percent of the population had received benefits during the entire *year.* Obviously, viewing the caseload over an even longer period, say a decade, would increase the proportion further. See Interprovincial Conference of Ministers Responsible for Social Services, *The Income Security System,* p. 91.

30. Canada, Health and Welfare Canada, *Canada Pension Plan Contributors.*

Notes to Chapter Three

1. The classic statement of this view remains K. Polyani, *The Great Transformation.*

2. P. Cutright, "Political Structure, Economic Development and National Social Security Programs," *American Journal of Sociology* 70 (1965): 537-50. See also his "Income Redistribution: A Cross-National Analysis," *Social Forces* 46 (1967): 180-90.

3. H. Wilensky, *The Welfare State and Equality,* p. 47.

4. Ibid., p. 22; and Frederic Pryor, *Public Expenditure in Communist and Capitalist Nations,* pp. 280-87. There is some disagreement on whether democracy influenced the *speed* of the response. Cutright's evidence suggests that representative governments acted more quickly than less representative ones at similar levels of economic development. ("Political Structure, Economic Development anad National Social Security Programs.") But Rimlinger's historical survey suggests that "the more democratic governments were slower to introduce social protection than authoritarian and totalitarian governments." *Welfare Policy and Industrialization in Europe, America and Russia,* pp. 9, 336-38.

5. Such an assumption can be found in writers representing very different general points of view. See, for example, T. Hockin, *Government in Canada,* pp. 73-78; and L. Panitch, "The Role and Nature of the Canadian State," in L. Panitch, ed., *The Canadian State,* especially pp. 20-22.

6. W.W. Rostow, *The Stages of Economic Growth.*

7. H. Aaron, "Social Security: International Comparisons,' in Otto Eckstein, ed., *Studies in the Economics of Income Maintenance;* Pryor, *Public Expenditures,* pp. 172-73, 473-75; K. Taira and P. Kilby, "Differences in Social Security Development in Selected Countries," *International Social Security Review* 22 (1969): 139-53.

8. Economic Council of Canada, *One in Three,* p. 27.

9. T.R. Marmor, A. Bridges, and W. Hoffman, "Comparative Politics and Health Policies," in D. Ashford, ed., *Comparing Public Policies*, p. 63.

10. Organization for Economic Co-operation and Development, *Public Expenditure on Income Maintenance Programmes*, p. 13. For a general review of program differences, see P.R. Kaim-Caudle, *Comparative Social Policy and Social Security*.

11. See T.H. Marshall, *Class, Citizenship and Social Development*.

12. Rimlinger, *Welfare Policy and Industrialization*, pp. 8-9.

13. A. Shonfield, *Modern Capitalism*; A. King, "Ideas, Institutions and Policies of Government," *British Journal of Political Science* 3 (1973): 291-313, 409-23.

14. D.E. Woodsworth, *Social Security and National Policy*, p. 5.

15. K. Bryden, *Old Age Pensions and Policy-Making in Canada*.

16. J. O'Connor, *The Fiscal Crisis of the State*, p. 138. See also R. Miliband, *The State in Capitalist Society*; F. Piven and R. Cloward, *Regulating the Poor*; V. George, *Social Security and Society*. For analyses of Canadian social policy in this tradition, see A. Finkel, *Business and Social Reform in the Thirties*; L. Panitch, ed., *The Canadian State*; and C.J. Cuneo, "State, Class and Reserve Labour," *Canadian Review of Sociology and Anthropology* 16 (1979): 147-70.

17. On Marxist interpretations that grapple with cross-national differences in welfare policy, see I. Gough, "State Expenditures in Advanced Capitalism," *New Left Review* 92 (1975): 53-92; and *The Political Economy of the Welfare State*. See also R. Mishra, *Society and Social Policy*.

18. See especially Rimlinger, *Welfare Policy and Industrialization*; H. Heclo, *Modern Social Politics in Britain and Sweden*; A. Heidenheimer, H. Heclo, and C. Adams, *Comparative Public Policy*; C. Leman, *The Collapse of Welfare Reform*. For examples of country studies in this tradition, see P. Moynihan, *The Politics of a Guaranteed Income*, and K. Banting, *Poverty, Politics and Policy*.

19. On the relationship between welfare expenditures and the dominance of parties of the right, see F. Castles and R.D. McKinlay, "The Importance of Politics: an analysis of the public welfare commitment in advanced democratic states," in M. Wilson, ed., *Social and Educational Research in Action*, pp. 329-48, and *Democratic Politics and Policy Outcomes*. On the relationships between parties of the left, social expenditures, and income equality see, among others, G. Lenski, *Power and Privilege*; F. Parkin, *Class Inequality and Political Order*; P. Cutright, "Inequality: A Cross-National Analysis," *American Sociological Review* 32 (1967): 562-78; R.W. Jackman, "Political Democracy and Social Equality: A Comparative Analysis," *American Sociological Review* 39 (1974): 29-45; and C. Hewitt, "The Effect of Political Equality and Social Democracy on Equality in Industrial Societies: A Cross-National Comparison," *American Sociological Review* 42 (1977): 450-64. While the findings do not all agree, the most recent and subtle analysis by Hewitt does conclude that "the experience of democratic socialist parties is significantly related to variations in inequality. The stronger the democratic socialist parties, the more egalitarian is the contemporary class system." These findings are paralleled by analyses of the expenditure patterns of state governments in the United States, which have found that party competition assumes much greater importance when attention is directed to redistributive questions. See, for example, C.F. Cnudde and D.J. McCrone, "Party Competition and Welfare Policies in the American States," *American Political Science Review* 63

(1969): 858-66; I. Sharkansky and R. Hofferbert, "Dimensions of State Politics, Economics and Public Policy," ibid., pp. 867-79; and B. Fry and R. Winters, "The Politics of Redistribution," *American Political Science Review* 64 (1970): 508-22.

20. Bryden, *Old Age Pensions*, especially p. 190.

21. P. Williams, "Elite Attitudes Toward Canadian Social Welfare Policy," paper presented to the Annual Meetings of the Canadian Political Science Association, 1980.

22. For an elaboration of this type of argument, see Hockin, *Government in Canada*, ch. 3.

23. For a general statement of this position, see especially R. Simeon, "Regionalism and Canadian Political Institutions," in P. Meekison, ed., *Canadian Federalism*. Also A. Cairns, "The Government and Societies of Canadian Federalism," *Canadian Journal of Political Science* 10 (1977): 695-725, and D.V. Smiley, *Canada in Question*, especially ch. 1.

24. See, for example, E.E. Schattschneider, *The Semi-Sovereign People*; J. MacGregor Burns, *The Deadlock of Democracy*; and Heidenheimer, et al., *Comparative Public Policy*, ch. 9.

25. R. Neustadt, "White House and Whitehall," in R. Rose, ed., *Policy-Making in Britain*, pp. 291-306; A. King, "Ideas, Institutions and Policies of Government."

26. See for example, H.J. Laski, "The Obsolescence of Federalism," in A. Christensen and E.M. Kirkpatrick, eds., *The People, Politics and the Politician*.

27. A.H. Birch, *Federalism, Finance and Social Legislation in Canada, Australia and the United States*.

28. Heidenheimer, et al., *Comparative Public Policy*, and A. Heidenheimer, "The Politics of Public Education, Health and Welfare in the U.S.A. and Western Europe: How Growth and Reform Potentials Have Differed," *British Journal of Political Science* 3 (1973): 315-40. For a similar argument about Canada, see J.R. Mallory, *Social Credit and the Federal Power in Canada*, especially chs. 3 and 4.

29. D.R. Cameron, "The Expansion of the Public Economy: A Comparative Analysis," *American Political Science Review* 72 (1978), pp. 1243-61.

30. Wilensky, *The Welfare State and Equality*, pp. 52-54; Castles and McKinley, "The Importance of Politics," and *Democratic Politics and Policy Outcomes*, ch. 4 and 5.

31. T. Lowi, "American Business, Public Policy, Case Studies and Political Theory," *World Politics* 6 (1964): 677-715.

32. P. Leslie, "Public Policy and Canadian Federalism: What is at Stake in Constitutional Change," in Institute of Intergovernmental Relations, Queen's University, and the Economic Council of Canada, *Workshop on the Political Economy of Confederation* (Ottawa: Minister of Supply and Services, 1979), pp. 252-55.

33. See R.M. Bird, *The Growth of Government Spending in Canada*, p. 125.

34. Schattschneider, *Semi-Sovereign People*, p. 71.

Notes to Chapter Four

1. These grants were repeatedly accompanied by federal government statements that unemployment relief was, and must remain, fundamentally a provincial and municipal responsibility. See A.E. Grauer, *Public Assistance and Social Assistance*, p. 17.

2. These princples were hardly new. The federal Department of Justice had advised a House of Commons committee along similar lines in 1925. See K. Bryden, *Old Age Pensions and Policy-Making in Canada*, p. 68.

3. For a discussion of these decisions, see Canada, *Income Security and Social Services*, pp. 20-30.

4. For the advice of the deputy minister of Justice on this point in 1950, see *Report of the Joint Committee of the Senate and House of Commons on Old Age Security*, p. 93.

5. See P.W. Hogg, *Constitutional Law of Canada*, p. 102.

6. Ibid, ch. 6.

7. On the opposition of the Quebec hospitals, see E. Wallace, "The Changing Canadian State: A Study of the Changing Conception of the State as Revealed in Canadian Social Legislation, 1867-1948," (Ph.D. thesis, Columbia University, 1950), p. 240.

8. In recognition of this reality, the Rowell-Sirois Commission, while admitting that many of its reasons for recommending federal jurisdiction over unemployment insurance applied with equal force to health insurance, accepted provincial jurisdiction over the latter. *Report of the Royal Commission on Dominion-Provincial Relations*, Book II, pp. 42-43. The same logic appears to have underlined the federal approach to the constitutional review in 1969; see *Income Security and Social Services*, p. 96. On the debate over health insurance, see M. Taylor, *Health Insurance and Canadian Public Policy*, p. 182.

9. On the low level of knowledge of, and regard for, constitutional divisions in other areas of policy, see Federal-Provincial Relations Office, *Interim Report on Relations Between the Government of Canada and the Province of Quebec, 1967-1977*.

10. For a slightly different view, which suggests that the 1937 case might not prove binding in the future and that federal social insurance initiatives might be sustained under the peace, order and good government provision, see B. Strayer, "The Flexibility of the BNA Act," in T. Lloyd and J. McLeod, eds., *Agenda 1970: Proposals for a Creative Politics* (Toronto: University of Toronto Press, 1968), pp. 211-12.

11. See Canada, *Federal-Provincial Grants and the Spending Power of Parliament*, especially p. 6 and Appendix One. See also the original defence of the constitutionality of the Family Allowance Act by the then minister of Justice, Louis St. Laurent, *House of Commons Debates*, 1944, p. 5351.

12. For useful surveys of constitutional opinion on the spending power, see D.V. Smiley and R.M. Burns, "Canadian Federalism and the Spending Power: Is Constitutional Restriction Necessary?", *Canadian Tax Journal* 17 (1969): 468-82; and Canada, *Federal-Provincial Grants and the Spending Power of Parliament*.

13. Quoted in ibid., p. 14.

14. Ibid., p. 14.

15. *Report of the Royal Commission of Inquiry on Constitutional Problems*, Volume II, pp. 216-23.

16. *Federal-Provincial Grants*, Appendix.

17. R.M. Bird, *The Growth of Government Spending in Canada*, p. 35.

18. A recent analysis in R. Boadway and H. Kitchen, *Canadian Tax Policy*, suggests that the
     federal share of "transfers to individuals" is much lower than indicated here, and that it
     declined from 68.8 percent to 58.2 percent between 1962 and 1972 (Table 17). However,
     the data used in the calculations, which are taken from Health and Welfare Canada,
     Social Security in Canada, in fact include expenditures on *both* income transfers *and*
     health and social services. As a result, the table is mislabelled and misleading.

19. Different data sources yield marginally different results. A recent sudy by an interprovin-
     cial task force covered a somewhat wider range of programs than does the National
     Accounts data, and on this basis calculated that the proportion of income security
     expenditures financed directly or indirectly by the federal government has declined
     slightly, from 84 percent in 1960 to 76 percent in 1977. However, this data is available for
     a few selected years only, and the National Accounts data has therefore been used in this
     study. See Interprovincial Conference of Ministers Responsible for Social Services,
     Income Security System in Canada, p. 22.

Notes to Chapter Five

1. See, for example, Research Committee of the League for Social Reconstruction, *Social
    Planning for Canada*; B. Claxton, "Social Reform and the Constitution," *Canadian
    Journal of Economics and Political Science* 1 (1935): 407-35; L. Marsh, *Report on Social
    Security in Canada*; H.M. Cassidy, *Social Security and Reconstruction in Canada*; Cana-
    dian Welfare Council, *Welfare Services for the Canadian People*.

2. P.E. Trudeau, "The Practice and Theory of Federalism," in M. Oliver, ed., *Social
    Purpose for Canada*.

3. For a discussion of the forces underlying such a process, see D. Poel, "The Diffusion of
    Legislation among the Canadian Provinces: a statistical analysis," *Canadian Journal of
    Political Science* 9 (1976): 605-26.

4. As quoted in A.H. Birch, *Federalism, Finance and Social Legislation in Canada, Australia
    and the United States*, p. 3.

5. Ibid.; also K.C. Wheare, *Federal Government*, ch. 8.

6. J. Schofield, "Mothers' Allowances" (Unpublished manuscript, University of British
    Columbia).

7. On the inhibiting effects of Mothers' Allowances, see J.W. Willard, "Canadian Welfare
    Programs," in Harry L. Lurie, ed., *Encyclopedia of Social Work*, p. 116.

8. J. Schofield, "Mothers' Allowances," (Unpublished manuscript, University of British
    Columbia).

9. *Report of the Royal Commission on Dominion-Provincial Relations* 1: 133. See also the
    provincial replies to a House of Commons committee on pensions, *Journals of the House
    of Commons*, 1925, pp. 455-58.

10. See K. Bryden, *Old Age Pensions and Policy-Making in Canada*, chs. 4-5; also D. Guest, *The Emergence of Social Security in Canada*, ch. 6.

11. *Report of the Royal Commission on Dominion-Provincial Relations* 2: 163.

12. Ibid., p. 173.

13. *Report of the Royal Commission of Inquiry on Constitutional Problems*, 2: 320.

14. Ibid., pp. 288-94.

15. See, for example, D. Usher, "How Should the Redistributive Power of the State be Divided Between Federal and Provincial Governments?" *Canadian Public Policy* 6 (1980): 16-29; A. Breton and A. Scott, *The Economic Constitution of Federal States*; W. Oates, *Fiscal Federalism*.

16. *Journals of the House of Commons*, 1925, p. 456.

17. Quoted in Schofield, "General Unemployment Relief."

18. *Third Report of the Quebec Social Insurance Commission*, p. 108. The concern was accentuated because the Commission was thinking of family allowances on the French model, with benefits paid as part of wages and financed by a system of employer contributions.

19. *Sixth Report*, p. 203.

20. *Fifth Report*, pp. 155-56.

21. *Report of the Royal Commission on Dominion-Provincial Relations* 2: 36. See also the *Final Report of the National Employment Commission*.

22. *Report of the Royal Commission on Dominion-Provincial Relations* 2: 40-41.

23. These problems were emphasized by the Rowell-Sirois Commission (Ibid., p. 41), and later by the federal government in *Income Security and Social Services*, pp. 86-88.

24. Usher, "How Should the Redistributive Power of the State be Divided?" p. 18.

25. *Report of the Royal Commission of Inquiry on Constitutional Problems* 2: 325.

26. *Report of the Royal Commission on Dominion-Provincial Relations* 2: 43.

27. Usher, "How Should the Redistributive Power of the State be Divided?" pp. 18-19.

28. R. Simeon, *Federal-Provincial Diplomacy*, p. 270.

29. Quebec was the only province to have shown any interest in contributory pensions, but before 1963 such a program was not a provincial priority. The federal initiative dramatically changed that, however, and catapulted the matter to the highest priority. Ibid., pp. 45-46; also Bryden, *Old Age Pensions*, p. 164.

30. This device was well known in Canada in the late 1930s. See, for example, the *Report of the Royal Commission on Dominion-Provincial Relations* 2: 37.

31. Further abroad, in Yugoslavia, a country which spends almost as great a proportion of its GNP on social security as does Canada, federal law requires that each region establish health and income insurance plans, but leaves the design, financing, and administration of programs to the regional level. See S. Pejovich, *Social Security in Yugoslavia*; and D. Woodsworth, *Social Security and National Policy*, Part III.

32. See, for example, the 1921 Liberal party platform; also J. Struthers, "Prelude to Depression: The Federal Government and Unemployment, 1918-1929," *Canadian Historical Review* 58 (1977): 277-93.

33. See M. Taylor, *Health Insurance and Canadian Public Policy.*

34. Bryden, *Old Age Pensions,* ch. 9.

35. As quoted in R. Dyck, "Poverty and Policy-Making in the 1960s: the Canada Assistance Plan" (Ph.D. Thesis, Queen's University, Kingston, 1973), p. 55.

36. R. Dyck, "The Canada Assistance Plan: The Ultimate in Co-operative Federalism," *Canadian Public Administration* 19 (1976): 587-602; and L. Bella, "The Provincial Role in the Canadian Welfare State: the influence of provincial social policy initiatives on the design of the Canada Assistance Plan," *Canadian Public Administration* 22 (1979): 439-52.

37. For an assessment of the differences that have emerged, see Canada Pension Plan Advisory Committee, "Review of the Objectives of CAP."

38. On the influence of the pension industry on Ontario's pension goals during the original negotiations over the establishment of the Canada Pension Plan, see Simeon, *Federal-Provincial Diplomacy,* pp. 281-82.

39. Ibid., ch. 3; also Byrden, *Old Age Pensions,* ch. 8.

40. On the pressures for pay-as-you-go financing in the United States, see M. Derthick, *Policy-Making for Social Security,* ch. 11; and J.D. Brown, *An American Philosophy of Social Security.* For a survey of pension arrangements in a number of countries, see P. Kaim-Caudle, *Comparative Social Policy: A Ten-Country Study,* ch. 6.

41. QPP funds, on the other hand, are invested in both public *and* private securities, with the result that the Quebec plan realizes a better rate of return than the Canada plan. This is not simply an embarrassment to the Canada plan; it is also a potential means of providing different benefit levels from the two plans. See the Canada Pension Plan Advisory Committee, *The Rate of Return on the Investment Fund of the Canada Pension Plan.*

42. Ibid., pp. 7-8 and Appendix IV.

43. In several Ontario budgets, the treasurer proudly announced significant decreases in Ontario's public debt, without at the same time drawing attention to the rapid growth in "non-public" borrowing from the CPP. (Ibid., p. 40).

44. Health and Welfare Canada, *Canada Pension Plan: Report for the Year Ending March 31, 1978,* p. 6.

45. On Ontario's position, see *Financial Post* (Toronto) 27 August 1977 (p. 5), 10 September 1977 (p. 2), 17 June 1978 (p. 38). For the report of the Quebec study group on the issue, see ibid., 8 April 1978 (p. 4).

46. For a discussion of the ways in which government might absorb the costs of indexing private pensions, see J.E. Pesando, *Private Pensions in an Inflationary Climate: Limitations and Policy Alternatives.* See also the policy recommendations (including dissents) in the final chapter of Economic Council of Canada *One in Three.*

47. A. Downs, *Inside Bureaucracy,* and W.A. Niskanen, *Bureaucracy and Representative Government.*

48. See, for example, R.B. Splane, *Social Welfare in Ontario;* D. Roberts, *Victorian Origins of the British Welfare State;* and H. Heclo, *Modern Social Politics in Britain and Sweden.* For a more recent discussion of the role of bureaucratic reformers by one of their numbers, see R.B. Splane, "Social Policy-Making in the Government of Canada;" in S.A. Yelaja, ed., *Canadian Social Policy.*

49. Such studies have discovered that the number of years that a social insurance program has been in operation is the most important variable explaining expenditure levels, more important even than the demographic profile of the population, a finding which has been interpreted by Pryor as, in part, the product of "the bureaucratic extension of social insurance." *Public Expenditures in Communist and Capitalist Nations,* p. 150. See also H. Aaron, "Social Security: International Comparisons," in O. Eckstein, ed., *Studies in the Economics of Income Maintenance;* H. Wilensky, *The Welfare State and Equality;* and P. Cutright, "Income Redistribution: A Cross-National Analysis," *Social Forces* 46 (1967): 180-90.

50. See, for example, A. Cairns, "The Governments and Societies of Canadian Federalism," *Canadian Journal of Political Science* 10 (1977): 695-725; and "The Other Crisis of Canadian Federalism," *Canadian Public Administration* 22 (1979): especially pp. 188-192.

51. Cairns, "The Other Crisis of Canadian Federalism," p. 189.

52. C. Leman, "Patterns of Policy Development: Social Security in the United States and Canada," *Public Policy* 25 (1977): 287. Leman predicted that the need to prove the federal system viable would rescue the Social Security Review from the deadlock that seemed to be developing at the time. In fact, as he later conceded, it did not. See his *The Collapse of Welfare Reform,* p. 144.

53. See Simeon, *Federal-Provincial Diplomacy,* pp. 54-60; and Bryden, *Old Age Pensions,* pp. 162-75.

54. Quebec, Commission of Inquiry on Health and Social Welfare, *Report,* vols. 1-4.

55. The impact of Quebec's Commission is emphasized in both R.J. Van Loon, "Reforming Welfare in Canada: The Case of the Social Security Review," *Public Policy* 27 (1979): 469-504, and Leman, *The Collapse of Welfare Reform,* pp. 67-70, 77.

56. On the design options, see Federal-Provincial Social Security Review, *Background Paper on Income Support and Supplementation.*

57. See notes 28 and 29 to chapter three. Cameron's study is particularly relevant since it specifically tests the bureaucratic-expansion proposition that "nations with a federal structure of government experience larger increases in the scope of the public economy than those with a unitary structure." But the finding was that, contrary to the prediction, federalism dampened expansion. D.R. Cameron, "The Expansion of the Public Economy: A Comparative Analysis," *American Politican Science Review* 72 (1978): 1243-61.

58. L. March, *Report on Social Security in Canada,* p. 251.

59. Ibid., pp. 52-55, 93, 217-22.

60. Ibid., p. 251.

61. Ibid., p. xxii.

62. Canada, *Working Paper on Social Security in Canada,* p. 15.

63. *Report of the Commission of Inquiry on Health and Social Welfare,* especially vol. 5, tomes I-III.

64. For an account of this battle, see S. McInness, "Federal-Provincial Negotiation: Family Allowances, 1970-1976" (Ph.D. Thesis, Ottawa, 1978), chs. 3-4.

65. Government of New Brunswick, "Persons Awaiting Unemployment Insurance Benefits: Problems and Proposals," document prepared for the 1978 Interprovincial Conference of Ministers of Social Services.

66. *Globe and Mail* (Toronto), 8 April 1977 and 27 April 1978.

67. Ibid., 2 September 1978.

68. "Estimated Change in Social Assistance Expenditures," figures tabled by the deputy minister of National Health and Welfare, Federal-Provincial Meeting of Deputy Ministers of Manpower, October 1978. In 1980 the report of an interprovincial task force admitted that actual size of the flow of beneficiaries between Unemployment Insurance and social assistance was still unknown. Interprovincial Conference of Ministers Responsible for Social Services, *The Income Security System in Canada,* p. 98.

69. See Province of British Columbia, "An Alternative Approach to a Revised Unemployment Insurance Program," (November 1978); statement by the minister of Social Services, New Brunswick, for the Federal/Provincial Meeting of Ministers of Social Services (November 1978); statement by the minister of Social Services, New Brunswick, to the Standing Committee on Labour, Manpower and Immigration, House of Commons, November 1978. For the attitude of some Liberal MPs, see the *Globe and Mail* (Toronto) 2 October 1978.

70. See the conclusion of the statement by Hon. L. Hull, minister of Social Services to the Standing Committee on Labour, Manpower and Immigration, House of Commons, 30 November, 1978.

71. Interprovincial Conference of Ministers Responsible for Social Services, *The Income Security System in Canada,* p. 53. Chapter 4 of this study is an excellent analysis of the administrative tensions among income security programs.

72. Ibid., p. 113.

73. *Working Paper on Social Security in Canada,* p. 14.

74. The minister of National Health and Welfare, Marc Lalonde, sought cabinet approval to incorporate Unemployment Insurance into the Review, but was turned down. Leman, *The Collapse of Welfare,* p. 116.

75. K. Banting, *Poverty, Politics and Policy: Britain in the 1960s,* p. 151. For a comparable problem in Ontario, see M. Kelly and M. Poynter, "Stacking: new villain in public assistance," *Social Work* (1978): 475-79.

Notes to Chapter Six

1. For recent cross-national analyses of income distributions, see D.P. Ross, *The Canadian Fact Book on Income Distribution,* pp. 40-41; A.B. Atkinson, *The Economics of Inequality,* pp. 25-28; P. Cutright, "Inequality: A Cross-National Analysis," *American Sociological Review* 32 (1967): 562-78; F. Paukert, "Income Distribution at Different Levels of Development: A Survey of Evidence," *International Labour Review* 108 (1973): 97-125; F.L. Pryor, *Economic System and the Size Distribution of Income and Wealth;* and M. Schnitzer, *Income Distribution.*

2. For a review of studies on income distribution in Canada, see G. Reuber, "The Impact of Government Policies on the Distribution of Income in Canada: A Review," *Canadian Public Policy* 4 (1978): 505-29.

3. See Atkinson, *The Economics of Inequality;* also S.M. Miller and M. Rein, "Can Income Redistribution Work?", *Social Policy* 6 (1975): 3-18.

4. For a stimulating discussion of the origins of alternative conceptions of inequality, see F. Parkin, *Class Inequality and Political Order,* ch. 3.

5. As quoted in W.I. Gillespie and R. Kerr, *The Impact of Federal Regional Economic Expansion Policies on the Distribution of Income in Canada.*

6. A. Cairns, "The Governments and Societies of Canadian Federalism," *Canadian Journal of Political Science* 10 (1977): 718. See also E.R. Black, *Divided Loyalties,* p. 3.

7. Gillespie and Kerr, *Impact of Federal Regional Expansion Policies,* p. 97. Emphasis added.

8. A. Cairns, "The Electoral System and the Party System in Canada, 1921-1965," *Canadian Journal of Political Science* 1 (1968): 74.

9. "Regionalism and Canadian Political Institutions," in J.P. Meekison, ed., *Canadian Federalism: Myth or Reality,* p. 302.

10. A.M. Moore, "Income Security and Federal Finance," *Canadian Public Policy* 1 (1975): 473-80.

11. D. Smiley, "An Outsider's Observations of Federal-Provincial Relations Between Consenting Adults," in R. Simeon, ed., *Confrontation and Collaboration,* p. 108.

12. See Hardin's discussion of "The Canadian Redistribution Culture," which focuses exclusively on inter-regional redistribution. H. Hardin, *A Nation Unaware,* part V. Also A. Careless, *Initiative and Response,* especially p. 6.

13. Economic Council of Canada, *Living Together,* Table 9-17. For surveys of regional policy in other countries, see Organisation for Economic Co-operation and Development, *Reappraisal of Regional Policies in OECD Countries; Regional Problems and Policies in OECD Countries,* vols. 1 and 2; and *Regional Policies: The Current Outlook.*

14. For a discussion of such transfers in the United Kingdom, See A.H. Birch, *Political Integration and Disintegration in the British Isles,* pp. 41-48; also Great Britain, Commission on the Constitution, *Financial and Economic Aspects of Regionalism and Separatism.*

15. The figure for health includes an amount, approximately one-half of the previous federal obligation, provided by way of income tax vacated under recent agreements. See Canadian Tax Foundation, *The National Finances 1977-78.*

16. See J.E. Cloutier, *The Distribution of Benefits and Costs of Social Security in Canada, 1971-75; D.P. Ross, The Canadian Fact Book on Income Distribution,* ch. 4; and Economic Council of Canada, *Reflections on Canadian Incomes.* For studies which examine the redistributive impact of government taxes and expenditures generally, see W.I. Gillespie, "On the Redistribution of Income In Canada," *Canadian Tax Journal* 24 (1976): 417-50; and D. Dodge, "Impact of Tax, Transfer, and Expenditure Policies of Government on the Distribution of Personal Income in Canada," *Review of Income and Wealth* 21 (1975): 1-52.

17. A.E. Grauer, *Public Assistance and Social Insurance,* pp. 23-25; L. Marsh, *Report on Social Security for Canada,* ch. 2; and Canadian Council on Child and Family Welfare, *Problems in the Social Administration of General and Unemployment Relief.*

18. *Report of the Royal Commission on Dominion-Provincial Relations* 2: 18.

19. Ibid., 1: 163-64.

20. In 1977, $48 million was spent on fishing benefits. Employment and Immigration Commission, *Annual Report 1977-78,* Appendix 16.

21. E. Minville, *Labour Legislation and Social Services in the Province of Quebec,* p. 86.

22. Grauer, *Public Assistance and Social Insurance,* p. 51.

23. E. Wallace, "The Changing Canadian State" (Ph.D. thesis, Columbia University, 1950), p. 298.

24. Ibid., p. 209.

25. The parliamentary committee that preceded the new policy did not even raise the question. See *Report of the Joint Committee of the Senate and House of Commons on Old Age Security.*

26. *Report of the Royal Commission of Inquiry on Constitutional Problems* 2: 321.

27. One former minister of National Health and Welfare recounted the reaction to a suggestion of a consultant that regionalized pension benefits be instituted progressively. As soon as word leaked out to his caucus, MPs from Atlantic Canada raised "an almighty row," with the result that the suggestion was dismissed and the consultant was sent back to his university.

28. R. Simeon and R. Miller, "Regional Variations in Public Policy," in D. Elkins and R. Simeon, *Small Worlds,* pp. 242-84.

29. For a brief survey of these patterns, see M.A. Chandler and W.M. Chandler, *Public Policy and Provincial Politics,* pp. 190-94. See also B.L. Vigod, "Ideology and Institutions in Quebec: The Public Charities Controversy, 1921-1926," *Social History* 11 (1978): 167-82.

30. On the impact of the Unemployment Assistance Act, see Interprovincial Conference of Ministers Responsible for Social Services, *The Income Security System in Canada,* p. 20. For the impact in Quebec, see Quebec, Study Committee on Public Assistance, *Report.* See also R. Dyck, "Poverty and Policy-Making in the 1960s," (Ph.D. thesis, Queen's University, Kingston, 1973).

31. See especially L. Bella, "The Provincial Role in the Canadian Welfare State," *Canadian Public Administration* 22 (1979): 439-52.

32. Advisory Commission on Intergovernmental Relations, *In Search of Balance—Canada's Intergovernmental Experience* (Washington, D.C.: U.S. Government Printing Office, 1971), p. 7. Also C. Leman, *The Collapse of Welfare Reform*, pp. 12-13.

33. Dyck, "Poverty and Policy-Making," pp. 278, 313.

34. *Report of the Royal Commission on Dominion-Provincial Relations* 2: 21. Deportation as a "public charge" was also used. See Canadian Council on Child and Family Welfare, *Problems in the Social Administration of General and Unemployment Relief*, pp. 31-32.

35. British Columbia, *The Problem of Overlapping Services in Health and Welfare as Between the Dominion and the Province.* Submission to the Royal Commission on Dominion-Provincial Relations, 1938, pp. 17-18.

36. E. Govan, *Residence and Responsibility in Social Welfare.*

37. E.K. Grant and J. Vanderkamp, *The Economic Causes and Effects of Migration*, p. 29.

38. Dyck, "Poverty and Policy-Making," pp. 260, 279.

39. The Social Services Financing Act, which the federal government proposed in 1977, would have prohibited many such restrictions, a fact that raised provincial opposition, notably again from British Columbia. And in response to similar provincial objections, the mobility rights section of the federal government's 1981 Charter of Rights and Freedoms also made explicit provision for the continuance of "reasonable residence requirements as a qualification for publicly provided social services."

40. For a study of the importance of these and other transfers in one province, see Economic Council of Canada, *Newfoundland: From Dependency to Self-Reliance.*

41. For another analysis that adopts a different method of measuring the inter-regional transfers inherent in such programs but comes to broadly similar conclusions, see G. Young, "Federal-Provincial Grants and Equalization," in Ontario Economic Council, *Intergovernmental Relations: Issues and Alternatives*, pp. 39-53.

42. N. Swan, P. MacRae, and C. Steinberg, *Income Maintenance Programs*, ch. 4.

43. Wallace, "The Changing Canadian State," pp. 316-17.

44. J.W. Pickersgill and D.F. Foster, *The Mackenzie King Record*, vol. 2, 1944-45, pp. 34-36; and S. McInnes, "Federal-Provincial Negotiation," (Ph.D. thesis, Carleton University, Ottawa, 1978), pp. 88-90.

45. One sign of the greater legitimacy of interpersonal redistribution through income security is the attitude of the Social Credit governments of British Columbia, which have frequently advocated the replacement of equalization grants to provincial governments with income transfers to individuals, perhaps in the form of a guaranteed annual income. See R. Simeon, *Federal-Provincial Diplomacy*, p. 166.

46. Economic Council of Canada, *Living Together*, pp. 188-89.

47. R.M. Titmuss, *The Gift Relationship.*

Notes to Chapter Seven

1. D.V. Smiley, *Canada in Question,* p. 202; J. Meisel, "Citizen Demands and Government Response," *Canadian Public Policy* 2 (1976): 564-72. See also Smiley's "An Outsider's Observations on Federal-Provincial Relations among Consenting Adults," in R. Simeon, ed., *Confrontation and Collaboration.*

2. E. Wallace, "The Changing Canadian State" (Ph.D. thesis, Columbia University, 1950), pp. 325-26.

3. Ibid., p. 308.

4. Canadian Institute of Public Opinion (CIPO) release, 27 March 1971.

5. See S. McInnes, "Federal-Provincial Negotiations" (Ph.D. thesis, Carleton University, 1978), ch. 3.

6. Transcript of CBC interview with the minister of National Health and Welfare, 26 April 1973. For another discussion of the electoral reasons for the reversal, see *Globe and Mail* (Toronto) 21 December, 1972.

7. A. Johnson, "Cabinet Ministers and Policy-Making: The Case of Unemployment Insurance," paper presented to the annual meetings of the Canadian Political Science Association, 1979.

8. See Table 31, below.

9. R. Dyck, "Poverty and Policy-Making in the 1960s" (Ph.D. thesis, Queen's University, 1973), pp. 205-6.

10. C. Leman, *The Collapse of Welfare Reform;* and "Problems of Centralizing Data in Federal Systems," paper presented to the 1978 annual meeting of the American Political Science Association.

11. Leman builds his case on the assumption that Canadians and Americans are equally critical of welfare in general, yet he presents remarkably little data on attitudes towards welfare, especially in the Canadian case. In addition, his data do not distinguish between attitudes towards Unemployment Insurance on one hand and social assistance on the other. For a comprehensive examination of available data on attitudes towards welfare in the two countries, which highlights important differences in the level of popular support welfare in the two, see R.M. Coughlin, "Ideology and Social Policy" (Ph.D. thesis, University of California, Berkeley, 1977).

12. Leman does note these provincial restrictions. *Collapse of Welfare Reform,* pp. 126, 209.

13. Government of Canada, *Income Security and Social Services,* Appendix C.

14. Ibid., p. 74.

15. *Report of the Royal Commission on Dominion-Provincial Relations: Book 2,* p. 27.

16. T.J. Courchene, "Avenues of Adjustment," in the Fraser Institute, *Canadian Confederation at the Crossroads;* A.E. Safarian, *Canadian Federalism and Economic Integration,* pp. 88-91; M.J. Trebilock, et al., "Interprovincial Restrictions on the Mobility of Resources," in Ontario Economic Council, *Inter-governmental Relations.*

17. Courchene, "Avenues of Adjustment." Also Economic Council of Canada, *Newfoundland: From Dependency to Self-Reliance,* especially p. 58. The most recent study of

migration patterns concludes that, whatever the impact of such transfer mechanisms, they have not offset other factors encouraging such behaviour and that "the migration process contributes to the elimination of regional disparities." E.K. Grant and J.K. Vanderkamp, *The Economic Causes and Effects of Migration,* p. 89.

18. G. Rimlinger, *Welfare Policy and Industrialization in Europe, America and Russia,* ch. 4. Lidtke, however, suggests that the strategy was not particularly effective and that any resulting check on the growth of the Social Democrats was only transitory. V. Lidtke, *The Outlawed Party,* pp. 158-64.

19. A.E. Grauer, *Public Assistance and Social Insurance,* p. 34.

20. *Income Security and Social Services,* p. 68. See also D.V. Smiley, *Canada in Question,* pp. 217-20; and G. Stevenson, *Unfulfilled Union,* p. 100.

21. *Report of the Royal Commission of Inquiry on Constitutional Problems* 3, Book 1, pp. 129-30.

22. D. Usher, "How Should the Redistributive Power of the State be Divided Between Federal and Provincial Governments?" *Canadian Public Policy* 6 (1980), pp. 16-29. See E.G. West and S.L. Winer, "Will Federal Centralization Help the Poor?", with a subsequent reply by D. Usher, *Canadian Public Policy* 6 (1980), pp. 662-69.

23. Usher, "How Should the Redistributive Power of the State be Divided?", p. 26.

24. For a brief discussion of the Victoria Charter, see D. Smiley, *Canada in Question,* pp. 69-79. For a more detailed report, see Canadian Intergovernmental Conference Secretariat, *The Constitutional Review 1968-1971.*

25. For a discussion of the administrative savings, as well as the administrative constraints, see Intergovernmental Conference of Ministers Responsible for the Social Services. *The Income Security System in Canada,* pp. 108-10.

26. Part of British Columbia's complaint was that the federal government introduced major tax expenditures, which the provinces helped fund, "without consultation with the provinces and without the provinces receiving recognition for their contributions." *Budget* (Victoria, 1981), p. 31. See also *Background Papers to the 1981 Budget* (Victoria, 1981) section C.

Notes to Chapter Eight

1. E. Wallace, "The Changing Canadian State" (Ph.D. thesis, Columbia University, 1950), pp. 128-32, 252. Also, J. Schofield, "General Unemployment Relief" (unpublished manuscript, University of British Columbia).

2. A.E. Grauer, *Public Assistance and Social Insurance,* p. 67.

3. Statistics Canada, *Statistical Report on the Operation of the Unemployment Insurance Act, October-December 1979 and Annual Supplement,* Table 31.

4. R. Simeon and D. Elkins, "Regional Political Cultures in Canada," *Canadian Journal of Political Science* 7 (1974): 397-437; J. Wilson, "The Canadian Political Cultures: Towards a Redefinition of the Canadian Political System," *Canadian Journal of Political Science* 7 (1974): 438-83; M. Ornstein, M. Stevenson, and P. Williams, "Regions, Class and Political Culture in Canada," *Canadian Journal of Political Science* 13 (1980): 227-71; D. Bell and L. Tepperman, *The Roots of Disunity.*

5. It is interesting to note in passing that when Elton and Gibbins examined the jurisdictional preferences of the Alberta electorate, Unemployment Insurance was the only federal program that a plurality of Albertans would like to be operated by the provincial government. D. Elton and R. Gibbins, "Western Alienation and Political Culture," in R. Schultz, O.M. Kruhlak, and J.C. Terry, eds., *The Canadian Political Process*, pp. 82-97.

6. Ornstein, et al., "Regions, Class and Political Culture in Canada," p. 259.

7. Ibid., pp. 257, 263.

8. D. Blake and R. Simeon, "Regional Preferences: Citizens' Views of Public Policy," in D. Elkins and R. Simeon, *Small Worlds*.

9. Ibid., p. 100.

10. Canadian Institute of Public Opinion (CIPO) 250 (Question 20A); 326 (Question 10); 339 (Question 5B); and 360 (Question 10A).

11. CIPO 292 (Question 13B); 298 (Question 7); 321 (Question 9); 339 (Questions 5D, E, F); 350 (Question 1A); and 356 (Question 8).

12. CIPO 212 (Question 2); 320 (Question 11); 337 (Question 4); 345 (Question 7); and 356 (Question 9).

13. A.E. Grauer, *Public Assistance and Social Insurance;* L. Marsh, *Report on Social Security for Canada;* Research Committee of the League for Social Reconstruction, *Social Planning for Canada;* H.M. Cassidy, *Social Security and Reconstruction in Canada.*

14. See B.L. Vigod, "Ideology and Institutions: The Public Charities Controversy: 1921-1926," *Social History* 11 (1978): 167-82.

15. E. Minville, *Labour Legislation and Social Services in the Province of Quebec*, pp. 45-46.

16. Ibid., p. 97.

17. Quebec, *Report of the Royal Commission of Inquiry on Constitutional Problems* 3: 131-32.

18. Quebec, *Report of the Study Committee on Public Assistance*, pp. 110, 117. See generally ch. 4, "The Role of the State." In light of subsequent developments, it is interesting to note that one member of the committee was Claude Morin.

19. Quebec, *Report of the Commission of Inquiry on Health and Social Welfare* 3, Tome I, p. 227.

20. On the impact of the Boucher Report, see R. Dyck, "Poverty and Policy-Making in the 1960s" (Ph.D. thesis, Queen's University, 1973), ch. 3; and S. Mongeau, *Evolution de l'Assistance au Québec.* On the impact of the Castonguay-Nepveu Report, see C. Leman, *The Collapse of Welfare Reform.*

21. *Report of the Commission of Inquiry on Health and Social Welfare*, especially vol. III, Tome II, pp. 165-67 and vol. V, Tome III, pp. 35-36.

22. R. Simeon, *Federal-Provincial Diplomacy*, p. 169.

23. Document prepared by officials of Quebec, Manitoba, Saskatchewan, and British Columbia (Victoria, 6 and 7 March 1975). Ontario's position was that income supplementation should be carried out through the tax system, preferably by a refundable tax credit.

24. These arguments are often inconclusive since, as one federal official pointed out, there is no way of knowing by how much provincial social assistance rates would have been raised if federal benefits had remained unchanged.

25. R. Dyck, "The Canada Assistance Plan," *Canadian Public Administration* 19: 597-98. Atlantic provinces pressed again for differential sharing under CAP in 1969-70, but again without success. They did seem to be making some progress during the ill-fated Social Security Review, however. See "Nova Scotia's Concerns With the Federal Proposal for a New Cost Sharing Formula for a Reformed Income Support and Supplementation System," (30 April 1975), and the accompanying "Financing of a Reformed Income Support and Supplementation."

26. Quebec, *Report of the Royal Commission on Constitutional Problems* 1, fourth part.

27. See K. Bryden, *Old Age pensions and Policy-Making in Canada*, pp. 87-92.

28. *Le Devoir* (Montreal) 17 February 1945. This fascinating debate, which took place six months *after* the federal legislation had been passed but just before the benefits were first paid, can be followed in *Le Devoir*, 5, 7, 16, 17 February 1945.

29. Bryden, *Old Age Pensions*, p. 203.

30. See note 20 above; also statement of Mr. Claude Forget, minister of Social Affairs for the Province of Quebec to the Federal-Provincial Conference on Social Security, 30 April 1975.

31. Quebec, *Quebec's Traditional Stands on the Division of Powers 1900-1976* (Quebec, 1978), pp. 50-51.

32. Quebec, statement to the Federal-Provincial Constitutional Conference, third meeting, December 1969.

33. Quebec, opening statement of the premier of Quebec, Federal-Provincial Constitutional Conference, June 1971.

34. Quebec, statement of premier of Quebec to the Federal-Provincial Conference, July 1965, p. 52.

35. Quebec, "Outline of Quebec's Constitutional Proposals on Income Security," June 1971, p. 7.

36. For a comparison of spending patterns in Quebec and Ontario, which points to similar conclusions, see J. Maxwell, G. Belanger, with P. Basset, *Taxes and Expenditures in Quebec and Ontario*.

37. E. Wallace, "The Changing Canadian State," ch. 13.

38. Debate in French Canada originally focused on *industrial* family allowances modelled on the French system, with benefits paid as part of wages and financed by employer contributions. Elements in the hierarchy of the Catholic Church were much less enthusiastic about family allowances paid by the state to the mother, as such a system might undermine the role of the father in family life.

39. The critical documents are Quebec, Minister of Family and Social Welfare, *Guidelines for a New Quebec Family Allowance Policy*, and *Report of the Commission of Inquiry*, vol. 5, Tome II, ch. 6. See also the speech of the minister of Social Services, during debate over the bill to configurate Family Allowances in Quebec, *Journal des Debats* le session, 30e Legislature 14, 8 (1973), especially pp. 261-62.

40. *Report of the Commission of Inquiry,* vol. 3, Tome I, p. 62.

41. See also CIPO 337 (Question 4), 1969; and 345 (Question 7), 1971.

42. A final sign of this is perhaps the growing reliance on the logic of *planification* rather than the logic of cultural distinctiveness in statements by the Quebec government. The 1979 White Paper on Sovereignty-Association, for example, summarized the case thus: "The Quebec Government, whatever party has been in power, has always maintained that an integrated social security system administered entirely in Quebec—if it repatriated the fiscal resources required—would be more logical, less costly, better adapted and consequently more advantageous to Quebecers than the present system." Quebec, *Quebec-Canada: A New Deal.*

Notes to Chapter Nine

1. For useful reviews of recent constitutional proposals, see A. Cairns, "Recent Federalist Constitutional Proposals: A Review Essay," *Canadian Public Policy* 5 (1979): 348-65, and "From Interstate to Intrastate Federalism in Canada?" *Bulletin of Canadian Studies* (December 1978); R. Simeon, ed., *Must Canada Fail?;* E. McWhinney, *Quebec and the Constitution 1960-1978.*

2. W. Irvine, *Does Canada Need a New Electoral System?;* The Task Force on Canadian Unity, *A Future Together: Observations and Recommendations;* R. Simeon, "Regionalism and Canadian Political Institutions," in J.P. Meekison, ed., *Canadian Federalism;* A. Cairns, "The Strong Case for Modest Electoral Reform in Canada," paper delivered to the Harvard University Seminar on Canadian-American Relations, September 1979. For statements of interest among leading politicians, see F. Macdonald, "Towards a Revitalized Confederation," in E. Feldman and N. Nevitte, *The Future of North America;* E. Broadbent, Testimony, *Minutes of Proceedings and Evidence of the Special Joint Committee of the Senate and of the House of Commons on the Constitution of Canada;* P.E. Trudeau, speech at the University of Montreal, *Vancouver Province,* 25 November 1979. Trudeau argued that "the concept of proportional representation is an excellent idea that could save Canada." For a useful critique of the assumptions underlying these proposals, see J. Courtney, "Reflections on Reforming the Canadian Electoral System," *Canadian Public Administration* 23 (1980): 427-57.

3. Irvine, *Does Canada Need a New Electoral System?,* p. 79.

4. Ibid., p. 49.

5. For a similar argument, see Cairns, "From Interstate to Intrastate Federalism in Canada?"

6. S. McInnes, "Federal-Provincial Negotiation" (Ph.D. thesis, Carleton University, 1978).

7. For an exception, see E. McWhinney, "If We Keep a Senate, It Should Be Elected," *Options* 1 (1980): 32-35.

8. Canada, *The Constitutional Amendment Bill: Text and Explanatory Notes* (June 1978), and *Constitutional Reform: House of the Federation.*

9. For advocates of such an approach, see The Task Force on Canadian Unity, *A Future Together;* The Constitutional Committee of the Quebec Liberal Party, *A New Canadian Federation;* Ontario, Advisory Committee on Confederation, *First Report;* British

Columbia, *British Columbia's Constitutional Proposals, Paper No. 3, Reform of the Canadian Senate;* D. Elton, et al., *Alternatives;* Progressive Conservative Party, discussion paper no. 3, *The Constitution and National Unity* (Ottawa: n.d.).

10. R. Simeon, *Federal-Provincial Diplomacy,* p. 55.

11. Canada, *Income Security and Social Services,* p. 90.

12. Special Joint Committee of the Senate and of the House of Commons on the Constitution of Canada, *Final Report,* p. 71.

13. Canada, *Working Paper on Social Security in Canada,* pp. 36-39.

14. Committee on the Constitution, The Canadian Bar Association, *Towards a New Canada.*

15. For a discussion of the political problems surrounding configuration, see McInnes, "Federal-Provincial Negotiations."

16. *Working Paper on Social Security in Canada,* p. 38.

17. Canada, *Federal-Provincial Grants and the Spending Power of Parliament,* pp. 34-50.

18. The complex formula was based on the four divisions in Senate appointments, but the essential requirement was as follows: a new program would require the approval of three of the following: 1) Ontario; 2) Quebec; 3) two Atlantic provinces having at least sixteen of the thirty Senate seats of that region; and 4) two western provinces having twelve of the twenty-four seats of that region. Ibid., pp. 40-42.

19. For the debate during the constitutional review, see Canadian Intergovernmental Conference Secretariat, *The Constitutional Review 1968-1971,* (Ottawa) pp. 172-77.

20. For a discussion of this battle, see Canadian Tax Foundation, *The National Finances 1978-79,* pp. 164-65.

21. For a brief exception, see P.C. Findlay, "The Implications of 'Sovereignty-Association' for Social Welfare Policy in Canada," pp. 141-48; plus the responses by D. Woodsworth and D. Guest, in *Canadian Journal of Social Work Education* 6 (1980): 141-55.

22. Quebec Liberal Party, *A New Canadian Federation,* pp. 90-93.

23. For an account of the discussion at the party convention, see *Le Devoir* (Montreal), 3 March 1980 and the *Financial Post* (Toronto), 8 March 1980.

24. See, for example, C. Morin, *Quebec Versus Ottawa,* especially pp. 62-64. Morin refers to income security as "a Trojan horse. Once it was inside the conference room, the debate on division of powers could not be side-stepped." (p. 63). He also refers to it as "an experiment" to test Ottawa's resolve on the distribution of powers (p. 64).

25. See also, Quebec Liberal Party, *A New Canadian Federation,* p. 90.

26. The experience of other nations with decentralized income security systems is not particularly encouraging. For example, the Yugoslavian constitution requires inter-regional redistribution through "solidarity funds" designed to help equalize the revenues of local organizations that operate social security programs. The funds certainly are partially successful, as differences in benefit levels in the various regions are less than differences in average regional wages. But the funds are certainly not large enough to counter the full effects of regional economic disparity, and benefit levels are still significantly higher in more affluent parts of the country. See D.E. Woodsworth, *Social Security and National Policy,* p. 88.

for example, Charter of Rights Educational Fund, *Report on the Statute Audit* ...ect (Toronto: 1985) pp. 6.8–6.9.

..., p. 6.11; H. Brun, "The Canadian Charter of Rights and Freedoms as an Instrument ...ocial Development," and M. Eberts, "The Equality Provisions of the Canadian ...rter of Rights and Freedoms and Government Institutions," in C. Beckton and A.W. ...kay, eds., *The Courts and the Charter* (Toronto: University of Toronto Press, 1986).

...example, one authority argues that "it is conceivable, of course, that a judge might ...sider it within his or her powers to order legislation as remedial action in a successful ...lication under section 24, but such actions depend in the first instance on there having ...n a violation of a Charter right, presumably because of some shortcoming of existing ...slation." Eberts, "The Equality Provisions" p. 170.

... Justice Pennell of the Ontario High Court in *Baxter v. Baxter* (1983), 36 R.F.L. (2d) ...6 at p. 189, as quoted in Eberts, p. 169.

...un, "The Canadian Charter of Rights and Freedoms," pp. 6–7.

...e most thorough public study is the *Report on the Statute Audit Project*, conducted by ...e Charter of Rights Educational Fund.

...ee, for example, Department of Justice, *Equality Issues in Federal Law: a Discussion ...aper*; Report of the Parliamentary Committee on Equality Rights, *Equality for All ...Minutes of Proceedings and Evidence of the Sub-Committee on Equality Rights of the ...tanding Committee on Justice and Legal Affairs, First Session of the Thirty-Third Parlia...nent, 1984–85)*; and *Toward Equality: The Response to the Report of the Parliamentary ...Committee on Equality Rights*. For an example of a provincial audit, see Department of ...ustice of Saskatchewan, *Compliance of Saskatchewan Laws with the Canadian Charter ...f Rights and Freedoms* (Regina: 1984).

...An interesting decision of the Supreme Court of Canada in favour of the legal standing of ...a social assistance recipient in a challenge to the Canada Assistance Plan is *Finlay v. ...Canada (Minister of Finance)*, [1986] 2 S.C.R. 607 (S.C.C.).

...*Equality for All*, pp. 40–42. For a similar critique of survivor benefits, see *Report of the ...Statute Audit Project*, pp. 8.10–8.13. The government's response to the parliamentary ...committee's recommendation was that "there is no widespread agreement on the best way ...to deal with the present aged-based structure of pre-retirement survivor benefits." ...*Towards Equality*, p. 19.

...*Report of the Statute Audit Project*, p. 8.2.

...*Equality Issues in Federal Law*, pp. 55–56.

...*Equality for All*, pp. 9–13.

...Ibid., pp. 13–14. The Committee also recommended that the aggregate limit on both ...sickness and maternity benefits be removed, so that a parent could benefit from both. ...*Attorney-General of Nova Scotia v. Phillips* (1987), 76 N.S.R. (2d) 240 (N.S.S.C., App. ...Div.).

... In the previous decade, more than a half dozen cases involving the rule had worked their ...way into the courts, and in most of them the courts effectively restored welfare benefits. ...Canadian Civil Liberties Association, "Social Assistance and the 'Man in the House' Rule" ...submission to the Minister of Community and Social Services of Ontario (Toronto: ...March 1986).

27. D. Guest, *The Emergence of Social Security in Canada*, p. 203.

28. See, for example, Quebec Liberal Party, *A New Canadian Federation*, p. 92.

29. D.V. Smiley, *Conditional Grants and Canadian Federalism*, p. 64.

30. Probably the strongest proponent of this argument has been Prime Minister Trudeau. See, for example, the foreword to his *Federalism and the French Canadians*.

31. Interviews with officials of National Health and Welfare confirm that the issue was never considered within the government, and a careful reading of parliamentary debates on the amendments confirms that it was never raised there. *House of Commons Debates*, 1st Session, 29th Parliament, vol. 1, pp. 7313-37, 7354-83, 7402-17; 2nd Session, 29th Parliament, vol. II, pp. 1291-98. Also *Debates of the Senate*, 1st Session, 29th Parliament, vol. II, pp. 1292, 1311-13, 1317; 1st Session, 30th Parliament, vol. I, pp. 242-52, 277-79, 300, 307.

32. It is interesting to note in this context that the White Paper on Sovereignty-Association, published by the Parti Québécois government, pledged to maintain "acquired rights" to "family allowances" and "old age pensions and supplements," but that no similar commitment was made to maintain existing standards under Unemployment Insurance. Québec, *Québec-Canada: A New Deal*, p. 81.

33. See especially the minister's speech in the House of Commons. *House of Commons Debates* 1st Session, 32nd Parliament, vol. 124, pp. 107-12.

34. For the reply of the Quebec minister of Social Affairs, M. Denis Lazure, to the assertions made by the federal minister, see *Le Devoir* (Montreal), 23 April 1980, p. 8. Lazure did not deny that Quebec benefits from some net transfers implicit in federal income security, but contended that this was offset by deprivations in other areas of federal policy.

Note to Chapter Ten

1. P. Goldman, "A Critique of the Dependency Model of Canadian Political Science," (Unpublished paper, Queen's University, 1973), p. 9.

Notes to Chapter Eleven

1. For a fuller development of the analysis in this section, see Keith Banting, "The Welfare State and Inequality in the 1980s," *Canadian Review of Sociology and Anthropology*, 24, 3 (1987): 309–38.

2. Open economies such as that of Canada are particularly vulnerable to shifts in the international economy. Throughout the postwar period, governments in countries with open economies appear to have been readier to protect their societies from the full force of economic change in a variety of ways, including the provision of greater social support to individuals. See D. Cameron, "The Growth of Government Spending: The Canadian Experience in Comparative Perspective," in K. Banting, ed., *State and Society: Canada in Comparative Perspective*, pp. 21–51.

3. For a survey of demographic projections, see D. Green, J. Gold, and J. Sargent, "A Note on Demographic Projections for Canada: Review and Implementations," in J. Sargent, ed., *Economic Growth: Prospects and Determinants*, pp. 193–228.

4. The full financial burden of this aging of the population will not be felt until well into the next century, however. Indeed, a recent study by the International Monetary Fund projected that if existing benefit and service levels are maintained and a reasonably steady rate of economic growth is attained, total social spending as a proportion of GDP will actually decline somewhat in Canada over the next decade, and not rise again until after 2010. See P.S. Heller, R. Hemming, and P. Kohnert, *Aging and Social Expenditure in the Major Industrial Countries 1980–2025.*

5. B. Fortin, "Income Security in Canada," in F. Vaillancourt, ed., *Income Distribution and Economic Security in Canada*, p. 181. For a more theoretical discussion on the tension between social programs and international economic trends, see A. Martin, "The Politics of Employment and Welfare: National Policies and International Interdependence," in K. Banting, Ed., *The State and Economic Interests*, pp. 157–241.

6. See, for example, "Labour Market Flexibility: A Controversial Issue," *OECD Observer* (July 1986). For a Canadian emphasis on the importance of labour market flexibility in the design of social programs, see the *Report of the Royal Commission on the Economic Union and Development Prospects for Canada*, (Macdonald Report) Volume II, Part 5; and T.J. Courchene, *Social Policy in the 1990s: Agenda for Reform.*

7. For an excellent discussion of these trends in an international perspective, see R. Mishra, *The Welfare State in Crisis.*

8. For a fuller discussion, see K. Banting, "The Welfare State and Inequality in the 1980s;" and R. Johnston, *Public Opinion and Public Policy.*

9. See D. Bercuson, J.L. Granatstein, and W.R. Young, *Sacred Trust? Brian Mulroney and the Conservative Party in Power*, ch. 6.

10. National Council of Welfare, *Progress Against Poverty* (October 1985) p. 1.

11. See G. Riches, *Food Banks and the Welfare Crisis.*

12. I. Gough, *The Political Economy of the Welfare State*, p. 138 (emphasis in the original).

13. L. Pal, *State, Class and Bureaucracy: Canadian Unemployment Insurance and Public Policy* (Kingston and Montreal: McGill-Queen's University Press, 1987); also A. Johnson, "Political Leadership and the Process of Policy-making: The Case of Unemployment Insurance in the 1970s" (Ph.D. dissertation, McGill University, 1983).

14. L. Pal, "The Fall and Rise of Developmental Uses of UI Funds," *Canadian Public Policy* (IX) 1983, pp. 81–93.

15. Commission of Inquiry on Unemployment Insurance, *Report* (November 1986); Royal Commission on the Economic Union and Development Prospects for Canada, *Report*, Volume II, Part 5.

16. The Nielsen Task Force Report suggested that employables represented 48 percent of the assistance caseload on a national basis, but this figure reflects considerable variations among provinces in the definition of unemployables. Health and Welfare Canada officials estimate that employing a consistent definition across all provinces would produce an estimate of 30 to 35 percent. See Study Team Report to the Task Force on Program Review, *Canada Assistance Plan*, p. 48.

17. Ibid., p. 14.

18. Federal-Provincial-Territorial Conference of Ministers *Regarding Enhancing the Employment Opportunities* (Ottawa: 17–18 September 1985).

19. "Federal-Provincial Agreement on Enhancing the Emp Recipients: Canada and New Brunswick" (January 1987)

20. Agreement Regarding Enhancing the Employment Oppo Recipients, section 5.

21. As of February 1987, agreements had been concluded Columbia, Saskatchewan, Newfoundland, Manitoba, and

22. See J.L. Palmer and I.V. Sawhill, eds., *The Reagan Record,* Government.

23. Statistics Canada, *National Income and Expenditure Acc* Minister of Supply and Services, 1985) table IV.

24. This broad conclusion is supported by the recent analysis 1965–83 by Michael Wolfson, who also concludes that the s total money income has not changed appreciably in the last tw transfers have been critical to this outcome. Wolfson goes furth out the impact of different economic and social trends on in results are at times intriguingly counterintuitive. In partic increasing unemployment, high interest rates, and stagnant ecc had a serious adverse impact on income inequality; quite the c 'safety nets' put in place in the late 1960s and their automatic res economy, and the substantial concentration of private savings have below average incomes, higher nominal interest rates and ec been apparently equalizing." These trends have offset other c disequalizing, particularly demographic changes and higher fem pation. M. Wolfson, "Statis Amid Change—Income Inequality i *Canadian Statistical Review* (February 1986): vi-xxvii.

25. The Honourable Gil Rémillard, speech to the conference on "Rebuil Quebec and its Confederation Partners," Mont Gabriel, Quebec, 9 in P.M. Leslie, ed., *Canada: The State of the Federation 1986*, pp.

26. The most important case is *Winterhaven Stables*, initiated in N Winterhaven Stables Limited, an Alberta company, filed a state contended that the federal Income Tax Act is *ultra vires*, as it involv order to raise revenues for purposes that fall within the exclusive legis the provinces under section 92(2) of the Constitution Act. The cons spending power was upheld in the judgment of the Alberta Court of the decision is being appealed. *Winterhaven Stables Ltd.* v. *Attorney* (1986), 29 D.L.R. (4th) 394 (Alta. Q.B.).

27. Canada, *Federal-Provincial Grants and the Spending Power of Parliam*

28. For example, if the calculation of "reasonable compensation" is to be b average costs of a new program, provinces with above average salaries have an incentive to remain in the shared-cost system, whereas province would have the opposite incentive.

29. See, Pro

30. Ibid of Cha Ma

31. For cor ap be leg

32. M 18

33. Br

34. T th

35. S

36.

37.

38.

39.

40.

41.

42.

43.

44. The rule was replaced with a temporary regulation which placed the emphasis on actual economic support being provided by the man. The issue was also referred to an existing Social Assistance Review Committee for a more permanent resolution of the issue. Ministry of Communication and Social Services, News Release, 18 September 1986.

45. *Report of the Statute Audit Project,* p. 8.4.

46. Ibid.

47. *Equality for All,* pp. 44–45.

48. See, for example, the debate in 1985 on legislation to extend the Spouses' Allowance to widows and widowers aged 60 to 64. The Minister of National Health and Welfare acknowledged the possible Charter challenge, but argued financial constraints precluded going further in extending the benefit. House of Commons Debates, 4 February 1985, pp. 1941–44.

49. *Piercey* v. *General Bakeries Ltd., Newfoundland, and Workers' Compensation Commission (Nfld.),* (1987), 61 Nfld. and P.E.I.R., 147 (Nfld. S.C.).

50. On these more general issues, see P. Russell, "The First Three Years in Charterland," *Canadian Public Administration* 28 (1985): 367–96; and R. Barnhorst, "The Charter, Legalization and Social Policy," paper presented to the Third National Conference on Provincial Social Welfare Policy, Banff, April 1987.

51. C. Tuohy, "Federalism and Canadian Health Policy," paper presented to the Conference on the Challenges to Federalism in Canada and in the Federal Republic of Germany: Policy-making in the 1980s (n.d.). For a similar argument concerning the West German case, see P. Katzenstein, "Policy and Politics in West Germany: A Semi-Sovereign State" (unpublished manuscript).

52. Keith Banting, "Institutional Conservatism: Federalism and Pension Reform," in J.S. Ismael, ed., *Canadian Social Welfare Policy: Federal and Provincial Dimensions,* pp. 48–74, and "The Decision Rules: Federalism and Pension Reform," in D.W. Conklin, J.H. Bennett, and T. Courchene, eds., *Pensions Today and Tomorrow: Background Studies,* pp. 189–209.

53. Ibid.

54. As quoted in A. Johnson, "Political Leadership and the Process of Policy-Making: The Case of Unemployment Insurance in the 1970s," pp. 320–21.

55. L. Pal, "Revision and Retreat: Canadian Unemployment Insurance, 1971–1981," in J.S. Ismael, ed., *Candian Social Welfare Policy,* p. 98.

56. For a discussion of the other forces at work in the struggle over Old Age Security, see D. Bercuson, J.L. Granatstein, and W.R. Young, *Sacred Trust?* ch. 6.

57. Report of the Royal Commission on the Economic Union and Development Prospects for Canada, Volume II, Part 5.

58. For critical assessments of the proposals, see D. Hum, "UISP and the Macdonald Commission: Reform and Restraint," and J. Kesselman, "The Royal Commission's Proposals for Income Security Reform," in *Canadian Public Policy* XII Supplement (1986) pp. 92–100, 101–12.

59. Report of the Royal Commission on the Economic Union, Vol. II, p. 801.

60. *Globe and Mail,* 20 May 1987.

61. G. Riches, *Food Banks and the Welfare Crisis,* p. 93.

62. For an excellent study of the interwar period, see J. Struthers, *No Fault of their Own: Unemployment and the Canadian Welfare State 1914-1941.*

63. R.B. Splane, "Social Welfare Development in Alberta: the Federal-Provincial Interplay," in J.S. Ismael, ed., *Canadian Social Welfare Policy,* p. 180.

64. Study Team Report to the Task Force on Program Review, *Canada Assistance Plan.* See also Health and Welfare Canada, *Notes on Welfare Services Under the Canada Assistance Plan,* especially pp. 10-11.

65. One sign of this trend can be seen in the orientation in OECD documents. The 1981 report, *The Welfare State in Crisis,* gave way by 1985 to another report which concluded that in most western nations existing social programs can "survive more or less unamended." *Social Policies, 1960-1990,* p. 62. See also the findings of a recent analysis by the International Monetary Fund discussed in note 4 above.

Bibliography

I. Government Documents

Alberta. *Harmony in Diversity: A New Federalism for Canada*. Edmonton, 1978.

British Columbia. *British Columbia's Constitutional Proposals, Paper No. 3, Reform of the Canadian Senate*. Victoria, 1978.

_____. Department of Human Resources, *Annual Report, 1973*. Victoria, 1974.

_____. Ministry of Finance. *Budget* and *Background Papers to the 1981 Budget*. Victoria, 1981.

Canada. *The Constitutional Amendment Bill: Text and Explanatory Notes*. June 1978.

_____. *Constitutional Reform: House of the Federation*. Ottawa: Canadian Unity Information Office, 1978.

_____. *Federal-Provincial Grants and the Spending Power of Parliament: Working Paper on the Constitution*. Ottawa: Queen's Printer, 1970.

_____. *Income Security and Social Services: Working Paper on the Constitution*. Ottawa: Queen's Printer, 1969.

_____. Commission of Inquiry on Unemployment Insurance. *Report*. Ottawa: Minister of Supply and Services, 1986.

_____. Department of Finance. *Integration of Social Program Payments into the Income Tax System: A Discussion Paper*, Ottawa: Budget Papers, 1978.

_____. Department of Finance. *Tax Expenditure Account*. Ottawa: Budget Papers, 1979.

_____. Department of Justice. *Equality Issues in Federal Law: A Discussion Paper*. Ottawa: Minister of Supply and Services, 1985.

_____. Department of Justice. *Towards Equality: The Response to the Report of the Parliamentary Committee on Equality Rights.* Ottawa: Minister of Supply and Services, 1986.

_____. Department of National Health and Welfare. *Working Paper on Social Security in Canada.* Ottawa: Information Canada, 1973.

_____. Economic Council of Canada. *Fifth Annual Review.* Ottawa: Queen's Printer, 1968.

_____. Economic Council of Canada. *Living Together: A Study of Regional Disparities.* Ottawa: Minister of Supply and Services, 1977.

_____. Economic Council of Canada. *Newfoundland: From Dependency to Self-Reliance.* Ottawa: Minister of Supply and Services, 1980.

_____. Economic Council of Canada. *One in Three: Pensions for Canadians to 2030.* Ottawa: Minister of Supply and Services, 1979.

_____. Economic Council of Canada. *People and Jobs: A Study of the Canadian Labour Market.* Ottawa: Information Canada, 1976.

_____. Economic Council of Canada. *Reflections on Canadian Incomes.* Ottawa: Minister of Supply and Services, 1980.

_____. Employment and Immigration Canada. *Fourth Marketing Research Study on Unemployment Insurance.* Ottawa, 1978.

_____. Employment and Immigration Canada. *Studies on Advertising For Unemployment Insurance: Reports of Three Studies.* Ottawa, 1978.

_____. Employment and Immigration Canada. *Annual Report, 1977-78.* Ottawa: Minister of Supply and Services, 1978.

_____. Employment and Immigration Canada. Task Force on Unemployment Insurance. *Unemployment Insurance: Interprovincial Transfers.* Ottawa, 1981.

_____. Federal-Provincial Relations Office. *Interim Report on Relations Between the Government of Canada and the Province of Quebec, 1967-1977.* Ottawa, no date.

_____. Federal-Provincial Social Security Review. *Background Paper on Income Support and Supplementation.* Ottawa: Information Canada, 1975.

_____. Health and Welfare Canada. *Canada Pension Plan Contributors.* Ottawa, 1979.

_____. Health and Welfare Canada. *Canada Pension Plan: Report for the Year Ending March 31, 1978.* Ottawa, 1978.

_____. Health and Welfare Canada. *Social Security in Canada.* Ottawa: Information Canada, 1974.

_____. Health and Welfare Canada. *Social Security Statistics: Canada and the Provinces 1950-51—1977-78.* Ottawa, 1979.

_____. Health and Welfare Canada, Canada Pension Plan Advisory Committee. *The Rate of Return on the Investment Fund of the Canada Pension Plan.* Ottawa, 1975.

_____. Health and Welfare Canada, Canada Pension Plan Advisory Committee. *Review of the Objectives of the Canada Pension Plan.* Ottawa, 1978.

_____. Health and Welfare Canada. *Social Security Statistics, Canada and Provinces, 1958–59 to 1982–83.* Ottawa, 1985.

_____. Health and Welfare Canada. *Notes on Welfare Services under the Canada Assistance Plan.* Ottawa, 1985.

_____. National Employment Commission. *Final Report.* Ottawa: King's Printer, 1938.

_____. Parliament, Joint Committee of the Senate and House of Commons on Old Age Security. *Minutes of Evidence* and *Report.* Ottawa: King's Printer, 1950.

_____. Parliament, Senate, Special Committee on Poverty. *Poverty in Canada.* Ottawa: Information Canada, 1971.

_____. Parliament, Special Joint Committee of the Senate and of the House of Commons on the Constitution of Canada. *Final Report.* Ottawa: Information Canada, 1972.

_____. Parliament, House of Commons, Sub-Committee on Equality Rights of the Standing Committee on Justice and Legal Affairs, *Equality for All.* Ottawa: Minister of Supply and Services, 1985.

_____. Royal Commission on Dominion-Provincial Relations. *Report.* Ottawa: King's Printer, 1940.

_____. Royal Commission on the Economic Union and Development Prospects for Canada. *Report* Vols. 1–3. Ottawa: Minister of Supply and Services, 1985.

_____. Statistics Canada. *Income Distribution by Size in Canada.* Ottawa: Minister of Supply and Services, 1980.

_____. Statistics Canada. *National Income and Expenditure Accounts, 1964-1978.* Ottawa: Minister of Supply and Services, 1979.

_____. Statistics Canada. *Pension Plans in Canada, 1976.* Ottawa: Minister of Supply and Services, 1978.

_____. Statistics Canada. *Pension Plans in Canada, 1978.* Ottawa: Minister of Supply and Services, 1979.

_____. Statistics Canada. *Social Security: National Programs, 1976.* Ottawa: Minister of Supply and Services, 1976.

_____. Statistics Canada. *Social Security: National Programs, 1978.* Ottawa: Minister of Supply and Services, 1978.

_____. Statistics Canada. *Statistical Report on the Operation of the Unemployment Insurance Act: October-December 1979 and Annual Supplement.* Ottawa: Minister of Supply and Services, 1980.

_____. Statistics Canada. *Trusted Pension Plans: Financial Statistics, 1978.* Ottawa: Minister of Supply and Services, 1980.

_____. Statistics Canada. *National Income and Expenditures Accounts, 1970–1984*. Ottawa: Minister of Supply and Services, 1985.

_____. Statistics Canada. *Income after Tax, Distribution by Size in Canada, 1984*. Ottawa: Minister of Supply and Services, 1986.

_____. Statistics Canada. *Unemployment Insurance Statistics, January 1987*. Ottawa: Minister of Supply and Services, 1987.

_____. Study Team Report to the Task Force on Program Review. *Canada Assistance Plan*. Ottawa: Minister of Supply and Services, 1986.

_____. Task Force on Canadian Unity. *A Future Together: Observations and Recommendations*. Ottawa: Minister of Supply and Services, 1979.

Canadian Intergovernmental Conference Secretariat. *The Constitutional Review 1968-1971: Secretary's Report*. Ottawa: Information Canada, 1974.

Federal-Provincial-Territorial Conference of Ministers of Social Services. *Agreement Regarding Enhancing the Employment Opportunities for Social Assistance Recipients*. Ottawa: September 1985.

Great Britain, Commission on the Constitution, research paper (10) *Financial and Economic Aspects of Regionalism and Separation*. London: HMSO, 1973.

Interprovincial Conference of Ministers Responsible for Social Services. *The Income Security System in Canada*. Ottawa: Canadian Intergovernmental Conference Secretariat, 1980.

National Council of Welfare. *The Hidden Welfare System*. Ottawa, 1976.

_____. *The Hidden Welfare System Revisited*. Ottawa, 1979.

_____. *Progress Against Poverty*. Ottawa: 1985.

Nova Scotia. "Nova Scotia's concerns with the federal proposal for a new cost sharing formula for a reformed income support and supplementation system," Federal-Provincial Conference of Welfare Ministers. April 1975.

Ontario, Advisory Committee on Confederation. *First Report*. Toronto, 1978.

_____. Advisory Committee on Confederation. *Second Report: The Federal-Provincial Distribution of Powers*. Toronto, 1979.

_____. Ontario Economic Council. *Intergovernmental Relations: Issues and Alternatives*. Toronto, 1977.

Organisation for Economic Co-operation and Development. *Public Expenditure on Income Maintenance Programmes*. Paris, 1976.

_____. *Reappraisal of Regional Policies in OECD Countries*. Paris, 1974.

_____. *Regional Problems and Policies in OECD Countries*. Paris, 1974.

_____. *Regional Policies: The Current Outlook*. Paris, 1977.

_____. *The Welfare State in Crisis.* Paris, 1981.

_____. *Social Policies, 1960–1990.* Paris, 1985.

_____. "Labour Market Flexibility: A Controversial Issue," *OECD Observer* (July 1986).

_____. *National Accounts: Volume II, Detailed Tables.* Paris, 1986.

Quebec. "Opening statement of the Premier of Quebec," Federal-Provincial Constitutional Conference. June 1971.

_____. "Outline of Quebec's constitutional proposals on income security," Paper presented to the Federal-Provincial Constitutional Conference. June 1971.

_____. *Quebec-Canada: A New Deal.* Québec: Editeur officiel, 1979.

_____. *Quebec's Traditional Stands on the Division of Powers 1900-1976.* Québec: Editeur officiel, 1978.

_____. "Statement of the Premier of Quebec to the Federal-Provincial Conference." July 1965.

_____. "Statement to the Federal-Provincial Constitutional Conference," Third Meeting. December 1969.

_____. Comitée Interministériel sur la Revision de la Sécurité du Revenu. *Analyse d'un Progamme Québécois de Revenue Familial Garanti.* Québec: Editeur officiel, 1976.

_____. Commission of Inquiry on Health and Social Welfare. *Report.* Québec: Editeur officiel, 1971.

_____. Minister of Family and Social Welfare. *Guidelines for a New Quebec Family Allowance Policy.* Quebec, 1969.

_____. Ministère du Conseil Exécutif. *Les Diverses Hypothèses d'une Première Etape de Revenu Minimum Garanti.* Québec: Editeur officiel, 1978.

_____. Ministre d'Etat au Développement Social. "Un bilan positif pour cette première année." Communiqué de Presse, 16 janvier 1980.

_____. Ministre d'Etat au Développement Social. "Négotiations avec le Féderal: une attitude décevante du Fédéral." Communiqué de Presse, 16 janvier 1980.

_____. Royal Commission of Inquiry on Constitutional Problems. *Report.* Quebec, 1956.

_____. Social Insurance Commission. *Report.* Quebec, 1933.

_____. Study Committee on Public Assistance. *Report.* Quebec, 1963.

Saskatchewan. Department of Justice. *Compliance of Saskatchewan Laws with the Canadian Charter of Rights and Freedoms.* Regina, 1984.

United States of America. Advisory Commission on Intergovernmental Relations. *In Search of Balance—Canada's Intergovernmental Experience.* Washington, D.C.: U.S. Government Printing Office, 1971.

II. Books, Theses, and Reports

Armitage, A. *Social Welfare in Canada: Ideals and Realities.* Toronto: McClelland and Stewart, 1975.

Ashford, D., ed., *Comparing Public Policies: New Concepts and Methods.* Beverly Hills, Calif.: Sage, 1978.

Atkinson, A.B. *The Economics of Inequality.* Oxford: Clarendon Press, 1975.

Banting, K. *Poverty, Politics and Policy: Britain in the 1960s.* London: Macmillan, 1979.

————. ed., *State and Society: Canada in Comparative Perspective.* Toronto: University of Toronto Press, 1986.

————. ed., *The State and Economic Interests.* Toronto: University of Toronto Press, 1986.

Bell, D., and L. Tepperman, *The Roots of Disunity: A Look at Canadian Political Culture.* Toronto: McClelland and Stewart, 1979.

Bercuson, D., J.L. Granatstein, and W.R. Young, *Sacred Trust? Brian Mulroney and the Conservative Party in Power.* Toronto: Doubleday, 1986.

Birch, A.H. *Federalism, Finance and Social Legislation in Canada, Australia and the United States.* Oxford: Clarendon Press, 1955.

————. *Political Integration and Disintegration in the British Isles.* London: Allen and Unwin, 1977.

Bird, R.M. *The Growth of Government Spending in Canada.* Toronto: Canadian Tax Foundation, 1970.

Black, E.R. *Divided Loyalties: Canadian Concepts of Federalism.* Montreal: McGill-Queen's University Press, 1975.

Boadway, R., and H. Kitchen, *Canadian Tax Policy.* Toronto: Canadian Tax Foundation, 1980.

Breton, A., and A. Scott, *The Economic Constitution of Federal States.* Toronto: University of Toronto Press, 1978.

Brown, J.D. *An American Philosophy of Social Security.* Princeton, N.J.: Princeton University Press, 1972.

Bryden, K. *Old Age Pensions and Policy-Making in Canada.* Montreal: McGill-Queen's University Press, 1974.

Burns, J. MacGregor. *The Deadlock of Democracy.* Englewood Cliffs, N.J.: Prentice-Hall, 1963.

Calvert, G.N. *Pensions and Survival: The Coming Crisis of Money and Retirement.* Toronto: Maclean-Hunter Ltd., 1977.

Canadian Bar Association, Committee on the Constitution. *Towards a New Canada.* Montreal: Canadian Bar Association, 1978.

Canadian Civil Liberties Association, "Social Assistance and the 'Man in the House' Rule," submission to the Minister of Community and Social Services of Ontario. Toronto, 1986.

Canadian Council on Child and Family Welfare. *Problems in the Social Administration of General and Unemployment Relief.* Ottawa, 1933.

Canadian Tax Foundation. *The National Finances, 1979-80.* Toronto, 1980.

Canadian Welfare Council. *Welfare Services for the Canadian People.* Ottawa: Council House, 1938.

Careless, A. *Initiative and Response: The Adaptation of Canadian Federalism to Regional Economic Development.* Montreal: McGill-Queen's University Press, 1977.

Cassidy, H.M. *Social Security and Reconstruction in Canada.* Toronto: Ryerson Press, 1943.

Castles, F., and R.D. McKinlay, *Democratic Politics and Policy Outcomes.* Milton Keynes: Open University, 1979.

Chandler, M., and W. Chandler, *Public Policy and Provincial Politics.* Toronto: McGraw-Hill Ryerson, 1979.

Charter of Rights Educational Fund. *Report of the Statute Audit Project.* Toronto, 1985.

Christensen, A., and E.M. Kirkpatrick, eds., *The People, Politics and the Politician.* New York: Holt, 1941.

Cloutier, J.E. *The Distribution of Benefits and Costs of Social Security in Canada, 1971-75.* Ottawa: Economic Council of Canada, Discussion Paper no. 108, 1978.

Conklin, D.W., J.H. Bennett, and T. Courchene, eds., *Pensions Today and Tomorrow: Background Studies.* Toronto: Ontario Economic Council, 1984.

Coughlin, R.M. "Ideology and Social Policy: A Comparative Study of the Structure of Public Opinion in Eight Rich Nations." Ph.D. thesis, University of California, Berkeley, 1977.

Courchene, T.J. *Refinancing the Canadian Federation: A Survey of the 1977 Fiscal Arrangements Act.* Montreal: C.D. Howe Research Institute, 1979.

————. *Economic Management and the Division of Powers.* Toronto: University of Toronto Press, 1986.

————. *Social Policy in the 1990s: Agenda for Reform.* Toronto: C.D. Howe Institute, 1987.

Denton, F.T., M.L. Kliman and B.G. Spencer, *Pensions and the Economic Security of the Elderly.* Montreal: C.D. Howe Institute, 1981.

Derthick, M. *Policy-Making for Social Security.* Washington, D.C.: Brookings Institution, 1979.

Downs, A. *Inside Bureaucracy.* Boston: Little Brown, 1964.

Dyck, R. "Poverty and Policy-Making in the 1960s: the Canada Assistance Plan." Ph.D. thesis, Queen's University, Kingston, 1973.

Eckstein, O., ed. *Studies in the Economics of Income Maintenance.* Washington, D.C.: Brookings Institution, 1967.

Elkins, D., and R. Simeon, *Small Worlds: Provinces and Parties in Canadian Political Life.* Toronto: Methuen, 1980.

Elton, D., et al. *Alternatives: Towards the Development of an Effective Federal System for Canada: Amended Report.* Calgary: Canada West Foundation, 1978.

Feldman, E., and N. Nevitte, *The Future of North America: Canada, the United States and Quebec Nationalism.* Cambridge, Mass.: Centre for International Affairs, Harvard University, 1979.

Finkel, A. *Business and Social Reform in the Thirties.* Toronto: James Lorimer, 1979.

Fraser Institute. *Canadian Confederation at the Crossroads: The Search for a Federal-Provincial Balance.* Vancouver: 1978.

George, V. *Social Security and Society.* London: Routledge and Kegan Paul, 1973.

Gillespie, W.I., *In Search of Robin Hood: The Effect of Budgetary Policies During the 1970s on the Distribution of Income in Canada.* Montreal: C.D. Howe Institute, 1978.

Gillespie, W.I., and R. Kerr, *The Impact of Federal Regional Economic Expansion Policies on the Distribution of Income in Canada.* Ottawa: Economic Council of Canada, 1977.

Gough, I. *The Political Economy of the Welfare State.* London: Macmillan, 1979.

Govan, E. *Residence and Responsibility in Social Welfare.* Ottawa: Canadian Welfare Council, 1952.

Grant, E.K., and J. Vanderkamp, *The Economic Causes and Effects of Migration: Canada, 1965-71.* Ottawa: Economic Council of Canada, 1976.

Grauer, A.E. *Public Assistance and Social Assistance: A Study Prepared for the Royal Commission on Dominion Provincial Relations.* Ottawa: King's Printer, 1939.

Guest, D. *The Emergence of Social Security in Canada.* Vancouver: University of British Columbia Press, 1980.

Hardin, H. *A Nation Unaware: The Canadian Economic Culture.* Vancouver: J.J. Douglas, 1974.

Heclo, H. *Modern Social Policies in Britain and Sweden.* New Haven: Yale University Press, 1974.

Heidenheimer, A., H. Heclo, and C. Adams, *Comparative Public Policy: The Politics of Social Choice in Europe and America.* New York: St. Martin's Press, 1975.

Heller, P.S., R. Hemming, and P. Kohnert. *Aging and Social Expenditure in the Major Industrial Countries 1980–2025.* Washington, D.C.: International Monetary Fund, 1986.

Hockin, T. *Government in Canada.* Toronto: McGraw-Hill Ryerson, 1976.

Hogg, P.W. *Constitutional Law of Canada.* Toronto: Carswell, 1977.

Institute of Intergovernmental Relations, Queen's University, and the Economic Council of Canada. *Workshop on the Political Economy of Confederation.* Ottawa: Minister of Supply and Services, 1979.

Irvine, W. *Does Canada Need a New Electoral System?* Kingston: Institute of Intergovernmental Relations, Queen's University, 1979.

Ismael, J.S., ed., *Canadian Social Welfare Policy: Federal and Provincial Dimension.* Kingston and Montreal: McGill-Queen's University Press, 1985.

Johnson, A. "Political Leadership and the Process of Policy-Making: The Case of Unemployment Insurance in the 1970s." Ph.D. thesis, McGill University, 1983.

Johnston, R. *Public Opinion and Public Policy.* Toronto: University of Toronto Press, 1986.

Kaim-Caudle, P.R. *Comparative Social Policy and Social Security: A Ten-Country Study.* London: Martin Robertson, 1973.

Katzenstein, P. *Policy and Politics in West Germany: A Semi-Sovereign State* (forthcoming).

Laframboise, J. *A Question of Needs.* Ottawa: Canadian Council on Social Development, 1975.

Leman, C. *The Collapse of Welfare Reform: Political Institutions, Policy and the Poor in Canada and the United States.* Cambridge, Mass.: The MIT Press, 1980.

Lenski, G. *Power and Privilege.* New York: McGraw-Hill, 1966.

Leslie, P.M., ed., *Canada: The State of the Federation 1986.* Kingston: Institute of Intergovernmental Relations, Queen's University, 1987.

Liberal Party of Quebec, Constitutional Committee. *A New Canadian Federation.* Montreal, 1980.

Lidtke, V. *The Outlawed Party: Social Democracy in Germany, 1878-1890.* Princeton, N.J.: Princeton University Press, 1966.

Lower, A.R.M., and F.R. Scott, et al., *Evolving Canadian Federalism.* Durham, N.C.: Duke University Press, 1958.

Lurie, H.L., ed. *Encyclopedia of Social Work.* New York: National Association of Social Workers, 1965.

McInnes, S. "Federal-Provincial Negotiation: Family Allowances, 1970-1976." Ph.D. thesis, Carleton University, Ottawa, 1978.

McWhinney, E. *Quebec and the Constitution, 1960-1978.* Toronto: University of Toronto Press, 1979.

Mallory, J.R. *Social Credit and the Federal Power in Canada.* Toronto: University of Toronto Press, 1954.

Marsh, L. *Report on Social Security in Canada.* Toronto: University of Toronto Press, reprint version, 1975.

Marshall, T.H. *Class, Citizenship and Social Development.* New York: Doubleday, 1965.

Maxwell, J., G. Bélanger, with P. Basset, *Taxes and Expenditures in Quebec and Ontario: A Comparison.* Montreal: C.D. Howe Institute, 1978.

Meekison, P., ed. *Canadian Federalism: Myth or Reality?* Toronto: Methuen, third edition, 1977.

Miliband, R. *The State in Capitalist Society.* London: Weidenfeld and Nicolson, 1969.

Minville, E. *Labour Legislation and Social Services in the Province of Quebec: A Study Prepared for the Royal Commission on Dominion-Provincial Relations.* Ottawa: King's Printer, 1939.

Mishra, R. *Society and Social Policy: Theoretical Perspectives on Welfare.* London: Macmillan, 1977.

————. *The Welfare State in Crisis.* Brighton: Wheatsheaf Books, 1984.

Mongeau, S. *Evolution de l'Assistance au Québec.* Montréal: Editions du Jour, 1967.

Morin, C. *Quebec Versus Ottawa: The Struggle for Self-Government, 1960-1972.* Toronto: University of Toronto Press, 1976.

Moynihan, P. *The Politics of a Guaranteed Annual Income.* New York: Random House, 1973.

Niskanen, W.A. *Bureaucracy and Representative Government.* Chicago: Aldine, 1971.

Norrie, K., R. Simeon, and M. Krasnick, *Federalism and the Economic Union in Canada.* Toronto: University of Toronto Press, 1986.

Oates, W. *Fiscal Federalism.* New York: Harcourt Brace Jovanovich, 1978.

O'Connor, J. *The Fiscal Crisis of the State.* New York: St. Martin's Press, 1973.

Oliver, M., ed. *Social Purpose for Canada.* Toronto: University of Toronto Press, 1961.

Pal, L., *State, Class and Bureaucracy: Canadian Unemployment Insurance and Public Policy.* Kingston and Montreal: McGill-Queen's University Press, 1987.

Palmer, J.L. and I.V. Sawhill, eds., *The Reagan Record.* Cambridge, Mass.: Ballinger Publishing, 1984.

Panitch, L., ed. *The Canadian State: Political Economy and Political Power.* Toronto: University of Toronto Press, 1977.

Parkin, F. *Class Inequality and Political Order: Social Stratification in Capitalist and Communist Societies.* London: MacGibbon and Kee, 1971.

Pejovich, S. *Social Security in Yugoslavia.* Washington, D.C.: American Enterprise Institute, 1979.

Pesando, J.E. *Private Pensions in an Inflationary Climate: Limitations and Policy Alternatives.* Ottawa: Economic Council of Canada, Discussion Paper no. 114, 1979.

Pesando, J.E., and S.A. Rea Jr., *Public and Private Pensions in Canada: An Economic Analysis.* Toronto: Ontario Economic Council and the University of Toronto Press, 1977.

Pickersgill, J.W., and D.F. Foster, *The Mackenzie King Record, 1944-45.* Toronto: University of Toronto Press, 1968.

Piven, F., and R. Cloward, *Regulating the Poor: The Functions of Public Welfare.* New York: Ramdom House, 1971.

Polyani, K. *The Great Transformation: The Political and Economic Origins of Our Time.* New York: Rinehart, 1944.

Progressive Conservative Party. *The Constitution and National Unity.* Ottawa: Discussion Paper no. 3, n.d.

Pryor, F.L. *Economic System and the Size Distribution of Income and Wealth.* Bloomington, Indiana: International Development Research Centre, Indiana University, 1971.

_____. *Public Expenditures in Communist and Capitalist Nations.* London: Allen and Unwin, 1968.

Research Committee of the League for Social Reconstruction. *Social Planning for Canada.* Toronto: Nelson and Sons Ltd., 1935.

Riches, G. *Food Banks and the Welfare Crisis.* Ottawa: Canadian Council on Social Development, 1986.

Riddell, P. *The Thatcher Government.* Updated edition. Oxford: Blackwell, 1985.

Rimlinger, G. *Welfare Policy and Industrialization in Europe, America and Russia.* New York: John Wiley and Sons, 1971.

Roberts, D. *Victorian Origins of the British Welfare State.* New Haven, Yale University Press, 1960.

Rose, R., ed. *Policy-Making in Britain.* London: Macmillan, 1969.

Ross, D.P., *The Canadian Fact Book on Income Distribution.* Ottawa: Canadian Council on Social Development, 1980.

Rostow, W.W. *The Stages of Economic Growth.* London: Cambridge University Press, second edition, 1971.

Safarian, A.E. *Canadian Federalism and Economic Integration.* Ottawa: Information Canada, 1974.

Schattschneider, E.E. *The Semi-Sovereign People.* New York: Holt, Rinehart and Winston, 1960.

Schnitzer, M. *Income Distribution: A Comparative Study of the United States, Sweden, West Germany, East Germany, The United Kingdom and Japan.* New York: Praeger, 1974.

Schultz, R., O.M. Kruhlak, and J.C. Terry, eds., *The Canadian Political Process.* Toronto: Hold, Rinehart and Winston of Canada, third edition, 1979.

Shonfield, A. *Modern Capitalism: The Changing Balance of Public and Private Power.* London: Oxford University Press, 1969.

Simeon, R., ed. *Confrontation and Collaboration—Intergovernmental Relations in Canada Today.* Toronto: Institute of Public Administration of Canada, 1979.

_____. *Federal-Provincial Diplomacy: The Making of Recent Policy in Canada.* Toronto: University of Toronto Press, 1972.

_____. ed. *Must Canada Fail?* Montreal: McGill-Queen's University Press, 1977.

_____. ed., *Division of Powers and Public Policy.* Toronto: University of Toronto Press, 1985.

Smiley, D.V. *Canada in Question: Federalism in the Eighties.* Toronto: Methuen, 1980.

_____. *Constitutional Grants and Canadian Federalism.* Toronto: Canadian Tax Foundation, 1963.

Splane, R.B. *Social Welfare in Ontario.* Toronto: University of Toronto Press, 1965.

Strayer, B., and J. McLeod, eds., *Agenda 1970: Proposals for a Creative Politics.* Toronto: University of Toronto Press, 1968.

Struthers, J. *No Fault of their Own: Unemployment and the Canadian Welfare State, 1914–1941.* Toronto: University of Toronto Press, 1983.

Swan, N., P. MacRae, and C. Steinberg, *Income Maintenance Programs: Their Effect on Labour Supply and Aggregate Demand in the Maritimes.* Ottawa: Economic Council of Canada, 1976.

Taylor, M. *Health Insurance and Canadian Public Policy.* Montreal: McGill-Queen's University Press, 1978.

Titmuss, R.M. *The Gift Relationship.* Harmondsworth, Middx.: Penguin, 1973.

Trudeau, P.E. *Federalism and the French Canadians.* Toronto: Macmillan, 1968.

Vaillancourt, F., ed., *Income Distribution and Economic Security in Canada.* Toronto: University of Toronto Press, 1985.

Wallace, E. "The Changing Canadian State: A Study of the Changing Conception of the State as Revealed in Canadian Social Legislation, 1867-1948." Ph.D. thesis, Columbia University, 1950.

Wheare, K.C. *Federal Government.* London: Oxford University Press, fourth edition, 1963.

Wilensky, H. *The Welfare State and Equality.* Berkeley, Calif.: University of California Press, 1975.

Wilson, M., ed. *Social and Educational Research in Action.* London: Longmans, 1978.

Woodsworth, D.E. *Social Security and National Policy: Sweden, Yugoslavia, Japan.* Montreal: McGill-Queen's University Press, 1977.

Yelaja, S.A., ed. *Canadian Social Policy.* Waterloo, Ontario: Wilfred Laurier University Press, 1978.

III. Articles

Banting, K. "The Decision Rules: Federalism and Pension Reform," in D.W. Conklin, J.H. Bennett and T. Courchene, eds., *Pensions Today and Tomorrow: Background Studies.* Toronto: Ontario Economic Council, 1984, pp. 189–209.

_____. "Institutional Conservatism: Federalism and Pension Reform," in J.S. Ismael, ed., *Canadian Social Welfare Policy: Federal and Provincial Dimensions.* Kingston and Montreal: McGill-Queen's University Press, 1985, pp. 48–74.

_____. "Federalism and Income Security: Themes and Variations," in T. Courchene, D.W. Conklin and G. Cook, eds., *Ottawa and the Provinces: The Distribution of Money and Power,* Volume 1. Toronto: Ontario Economic Council, 1985, pp. 253–76.

_____. "The Welfare State and Inequality in the 1980s," *Canadian Review of Sociology and Anthropology* 24 (1987): in press.

Barnhorst, R.F. "The Charter, Legalization and Social Policy," paper presented to the 3rd National Conference on Provincial Social Welfare Policy, Banff, Alberta, April 1987.

Bella, L. "The Provincial Role in the Canadian Welfare State: The Influence of Provincial Social Policy Initiatives on the Design of the Canada Assistance Plan," *Canadian Public Administration* 22 (1979): 439–52.

Broadbent, E., Testimony. *Minutes of Proceedings and Evidence of the Special Joint Committee of the Senate and of the House of Commons on the Constitution of Canada* no. 1 (15 August 1978).

Brun, H. "The Canadian Charter of Rights and Freedoms as an Instrument of Social Development," in C. Beckton and A.W. Mackay, eds., *The Courts and the Charter.* Toronto: University of Toronto Press, 1985, pp. 1–36.

Cairns, A. "The Electoral System and the Party System in Canada, 1921-1965," *Canadian Journal of Political Science* 1 (1968): 55-80.

_____. "From Interstate to Intrastate Federalism in Canada?" *Bulletin of Canadian Studies* (December 1978).

_____. "The Governments and Societies of Canadian Federalism," *Canadian Journal of Political Science* 10 (1977): 695-725.

_____. "The Other Crisis of Canadian Federalism," *Canadian Public Administration* 22 (1979): 188-92.

_____. "Recent Federalist Constitutional Proposals: A Review Essay," *Canadian Public Policy* 5 (1979): 348-65.

_____. "The Strong Case for Modest Electoral Reform in Canada," paper presented to the Harvard University seminar on Canadian-American Relations, September 1979.

Cameron, D.R. "The Expansion of the Public Economy: A Comparative Analysis," *American Political Science Review* 72 (1978): 1243-61.

_____. "The Growth of Government Spending: The Canadian Experience in Comparative Perspective," in K. Banting, ed., *State and Society: Canada in Comparative Perspective*. Toronto: University of Toronto Press, 1986, pp. 21-51.

Claxton, B. "Social Reform and the Constitution," *Canadian Journal of Economics and Political Science* 1 (1935): 407-35.

Cnudde, C., and D.J. McCrone, "Party Competition and Welfare Policies in the American States," *American Political Science Review* 63 (1969): 858-68.

Courtney, J. "Reflections on Reforming the Canadian Electoral System," *Canadian Public Administration* 23 (1980): 427-57.

Cuneo, C.J. "State, Class and Reserve Labour: The Case of the 1941 Canadian Unemployment Insurance Act," *Canadian Review of Sociology and Anthropology* 16 (1979): 147-70.

Cutright, P., "Inequality: A Cross-National Analysis," *American Sociological Review* 32 (1967): 562-78.

_____. "Income Redistribution: A Cross-National Analysis," *Social Forces* 46 (1967): 180-90.

_____. "Political Structure, Economic Development and National Social Security Programs," *American Journal of Sociology* 70 (1965): 537-50.

Dodge, D. "Impact of Tax, Transfer and Expenditure Policies of Government on the Distribution of Personal Income in Canada," *The Review of Income and Wealth* 21 (1975): 1-52.

Dyck, R. "The Canada Assistance Plan: The Ultimate in Co-operative Federalism," *Canadian Public Administration* 19 (1976): 587-602.

Eberts, M. "The Equality Provisions of the Canadian Charter of Rights and Freedoms and Government Institutions," in C. Beckton and A.W. Mackay, eds., *The Courts and the Charter*. Toronto: University of Toronto Press, 1985, pp. 133-222.

Findlay, P.C. "The Implications of 'Sovereignty-Association' for Social Welfare in Canada: An Anglophone Perspective" *Canadian Journal of Social Work Education* 6 (1980): 141-48.

Fortin, B. "Income Security in Canada," in F. Vaillancourt, ed., *Income Distribution and Economic Security in Canada.* Toronto: University of Toronto Press, 1985, 153–86.

Fry, B., and R. Winters, "The Politics of Redistribution," *American Political Science Review* 64 (1970): 508-22.

Gillespie, W.I. "On the Redistribution of Income in Canada," *Canadian Tax Journal* 24 (1976): 417-50.

_____. "Towards a Test of Government Redistributive Activity During the Postwar Period in Canada," Carleton Economic Papers, Carleton University, Ottawa, 1979.

Gough, I. "State Expenditure in Advanced Capitalism," *New Left Review* 91 (1975): 53-92.

Green, D., J. Gold and J. Sargent. "A Note on Demographic Projections for Canada," in J. Sargent, ed., *Economic Growth: Prospects and Determinants.* Toronto: University of Toronto Press, 1986, pp. 193–228.

Heidenheimer, A. "The Politics of Public Education, Health and Welfare in the U.S.A. and Western Europe: How Growth and Reform Potentials Have Differed," *British Journal of Political Science* 3 (1973): 315-40.

Hewitt, C. "The Effect of Political Equality and Social Democracy on Equality in Industrial Societies: A Cross-National Comparison," *American Sociological Review* 42 (1977): 450-64.

Hum, D. "USIP and the Macdonald Commission: Reform and Restraint," *Canadian Public Policy* XII (1986): 92–100.

Hum, D., and H. Stevens, "The Manitoba White Paper on Tax Credit Reform: A Critique," *Canadian Taxation* 2 (1980): 129-34.

Jackman, R.W. "Political Democracy and Social Equality: A Comparative Analysis," *American Sociological Review* 39 (1974): 29-45.

Johnson, A. "Cabinet Ministers and Policy-Making: The Case of Unemployment Insurance," paper presented to the 1979 annual meeting of the Canadian Political Science Association.

Kaliski, S.F. "The 1978-79 Unemployment Insurance Act Amendments," *Canadian Taxation* 2 (1980): 55-59.

Kelly, M., and M. Poynter, "Stacking: New Villain in Public Assistance," *Social Work* (1978): 475-79.

Kesselman, J. "The Royal Commission's Proposals for Income Security Reform," *Canadian Public Policy* XII (1986): 101–12.

King, A. "Ideas, Institutions and Policies of Government," *British Journal of Political Science* 3 (1973): 291-313, 409-23.

Kitchen, B. "A Canadian Compromise: The Refundable Child Tax Credit," *Canadian Taxation* 1 (1979): 44-51.

Leman, C. "Patterns of Policy Development: Social Security in the United States and Canada," *Public Policy* 25 (1977): 261-91.

————. "Problems of Centralizing Data in Federal Systems: Welfare Programs in Canada and the United States," paper presented to the 1978 annual meeting of the American Political Science Association.

Lowi, T. "American Business, Public Policy, Case Studies and Political Theory," *World Politics* 6 (1964): 677-715.

Martin, A. "The Politics of Employment and Welfare: National Policies and International Interdependence," in K. Banting, ed., *The State and Economic Interests*. Toronto: University of Toronto Press, 1986, pp. 157-241.

McWhinney, E. "If We Keep a Senate, It Should Be Elected," *Options* 1 (1980): 32-35.

Meisel, J. "Citizen Demands and Government Response," *Canadian Public Policy* 2 (1976): 564-72.

Miller, S.M., and M. Rein, "Can Income Redistribution Work?" *Social Policy* 6 (1975): 3-18.

Moore, A.M. "Income Security and Federal Finance," *Canadian Public Policy* 1 (1975): 473-80.

Ornstein, M., M. Stevenson, and P. Williams, "Regions, Class and Political Culture in Canada," *Candian Journal of Political Science* 13 (1980): 227-71.

Pal, L. "The Fall and Rise of Developmental Uses of UI Funds," *Canadian Public Policy* IX (1983): 81-93.

————. "Revision and Retreat: Canadian Unemployment Insurance, 1971-1981," in J.S. Ismael, ed., *Canadian Social Welfare Policy: Federal and Provincial Dimensions*. Kingston and Montreal: McGill-Queen's University Press, 1985, pp. 75-104.

Paukert, F. "Income Distribution at Different Levels of Development: A Survey of Evidence," *International Labour Review* 109 (1973): 97-125.

Peters, B.G. "Income Redistribution: A Longitudinal Analysis of France, Sweden and the United Kingdom," *Political Studies* 22 (1974): 311-23.

Poel, D. "The Diffusion of Legislation among the Canadian Provinces: A Statistical Analysis," *Canadian Journal of Political Science* 9 (1976): 605-26.

Reuber, G. "The Impact of Government Policies on the Distribution of Income in Canada: A Review," *Canadian Public Policy* 4 (1978): 505-29.

Riches, G. "FIP Flops," *Perspectives*, July/August 1978.

Russell, P. "The First Three Years in Charterland," *Canadian Public Administration* 28 (1985): 367-96.

Sharkansky, I., and R. Hofferbert, "Dimensions of State Politics, Economics and Public Policy," *American Political Science Review* 63 (1969): 867-79.

Simeon, R., and D. Elkins, "Regional Political Cultures in Canada," *Canadian Journal of Political Science* 7 (1974): 397-437.

Smiley, D.V., and R.M. Burns, "Canadian Federalism and the Spending Power: Is Constitutional Restriction Necessary?" *Canadian Tax Journal* 17 (1969): 468-82.

Social Planning Council of Metropolitan Toronto. "Welfare Benefits: An Interprovincial Comparison," *Social Infopac* 5:1 (1986): 1-9.

Splane, R.B. "Whatever Happened to the GAI?" *Social Work* 48 (1980): 86-87.

_____. "Social Welfare Development in Alberta: the Federal-Provincial Interplay," in J.S. Ismael, ed., *Canadian Social Welfare Policy: Federal and Provincial Dimensions*. Kingston and Montreal: McGill-Queen's University Press, 1985, pp. 173-87.

Struthers, J. "Prelude to Depression: The Federal Government and Unemployment, 1918-29," *Canadian Historical Review* 58 (1977): 277-93.

Taira, K., and P. Kilby, "Differences in Social Security Development in Selected Countries," *International Social Security Review* 22 (1969): 139-53.

Tamagno, E. "The Quebec Income Supplementation Plan," *Canadian Taxation* 1 (1979): 63-66.

Todres, E. "The Dynamics of Canadian Federalism: The Politics of Tax Credits," paper presented to the 1975 annual meeting of the American Political Science Association.

Tuohy, C. "Federalism and Canadian Health Policy," paper presented to the Conference on the Challenges to Federalism in Canada and in the Federal Republic of Germany. (n.d.)

Usher, D. "How Should the Redistributive Power of the State be Divided Between Federal and Provincial Governments?" *Canadian Public Policy* 6 (1980): 16-29.

Van Loon, R.J. "Reforming Welfare in Canada: The Case of the Social Security Review," *Public Policy* 27 (1979): 469-504.

Vigod, B.L. "Ideology and Institutions in Quebec. The Public Charities Controversy, 1921-1926," *Social History* 11 (1978): 167-82.

Williams, P. "Elite Attitudes Towards Canadian Social Welfare Policy," paper presented to the 1980 annual meeting of the Canadian Political Science Association.

Wolfson, M. "Stasis Amid Change—Income Inequality in Canada, 1965-1983," *Canadian Statistical Review* (1986): vi-xxvii.

Index